GREAT THINGS HAPPEN

GREAT THINGS HAPPEN

A personal memoir

Remigius F. McCoy, M.Afr.

with
Rene Dionne, M.Afr.

Field Research by Joan Cameron Dewart

The Society of Missionaries of Africa
Montreal

The Society of Missionaries of Africa was founded in Algiers in 1868 by Charles Cardinal Lavigerie. Known popularly as the "White Fathers" (because of the traditional white religious habit, of Arab North African origin, worn by its members), it is an international society of priests and brothers living a common life in dedication to the service of the Church in Africa.

ISBN 0-9693146-1-2

We are grateful to North American Liturgy Resources for permission to use the title GREAT THINGS HAPPEN by Carey Landry, from the song collection HI GOD published by NALR. This and other liturgical collections are available from NALR at 10802 N. 23rd Ave. Phoenix, Arizona 85029.

To the Christian community of northwest Ghana

Great things happen when God mixes with us.
Great things happen when God mixes with us.
Great and beautiful, wonderful things;
Great things happen when God mixes with us.

Some find life, some find peace;
   some people even find joy.
Some see things as they never could before,
   and some people find that they can now begin to trust.

Some find health, some find hope;
   some people even find joy.
Some see themselves as they never could before,
   and some people find that they can now begin to live.

Some find peace, some are disturbed;
   some people even find joy.
Some see their lives as they never could before,
   and some people find that they can now begin to change.

Rev. Carey Landry

Contents

Maps

Foreword

On a recent visit to Ghana, I was asked by young people everywhere to tell them about the "old days" when the Christian faith first began to be preached among their grandparents. They wanted to know what northwest Ghana had been like then, and how it had felt to be the first Christian missionaries in a region as yet untouched by Christianity. How had their ancestors regarded us (queerlooking strangers that we undoubtedly were in beards, white robes, sun helmets, and large-beaded rosaries hanging from our necks)? Were they hostile, friendly, afraid, bemused? How had we approached them in the beginning to gain their confidence? What obstacles had we to overcome before we could present our message (undreamed of by them until then) of a God who cared for them as a Father and whose only Son had not hesitated to give His very life to save them from the consequences of their own sin?

I was thrilled to see this awakening of interest in the subject among young Ghanaians, which comes as part of a new-found interest in African history as a whole. It is a healthy sign, I believe, that the Christians of today value their religious history as much as their political or ethnic history and want to preserve it.

In the present volume, my good friend and fellow missionary Remigius McCoy answers all these questions and more from his own first-hand experience of those exciting times. As one of the original founders of the first mission in northwest Ghana, he was present at the birth of Christianity among the Dagaabas and

Sissalas and has been a constant witness to its progress among them for the last sixty years. No one could be better qualified to tell the story.

I had the privilege and joy to be part of that story and to witness to much of what he writes in this book. My first assignment after ordination to the priesthood in 1933 was to a newly-opened mission station at Nandom, twenty-five miles northwest of the original mission founded at Jirapa some four years earlier. Those were absorbing and fulfilling times for us, when the Spirit of God seemed very close indeed. We threw ourselves into the work with enthusiasm, which was perhaps the main reason we felt so fulfilled in what we were doing. The task before us called for bold measures sometimes and for frequent innovations. Obstacles were always plentiful, but we were young and eager for challenges.

When I returned to northern Ghana last December and January, I found the fruit of our labours in a firmly-established and thriving Church. Where once there had been nothing, I now visited parish after parish, schools of higher learning, hospitals, clinics, a nursing school, trade schools, and agricultural projects, all aimed at improving the quality of Ghanaian life. One thing in particular brought joy to my heart: to find the major and minor seminaries of the North well-staffed and filled with promising young seminarians. At every turn I found Ghanaian-born bishops, priests, sisters, brothers, catechists, and lay-workers engaged in building up the Kingdom of God in the hearts of their compatriots. The Church of Ghana has certainly come of age and the harvest is abundant.

In early December I was invited to attend the ordination to the diaconate of sixteen young seminarians. The ceremony was to take place at Saint Victor's Seminary in Tamale, an institution especially dear to me for the simple reason that I had served as its first rector in the 1940s. Archbishop Peter Dery, one of my early students there, was the ordaining prelate. Afterwards we reminisced about the years spent together in Nandom when he was still a boy and going to school in Navrongo. He went on to talk about his major seminary training in Wiagha (where Saint Victor's began before finally moving to Tamale). Then the seminary had consisted of one large room in the missionaries' house.

It served as dormitory, dining room, and classroom for our first group of seminarians. That was in 1945. Today Saint Victor's is a fully-organized and competently-staffed major seminary with a respectable enrollment of 112 seminarians.

A week later, on 17 December, I attended the ordination of two priests of the Wa diocese. This time Bishop Gregory Kpiebaya was the ordaining prelate. He replaced Archbishop Dery in 1974 when the latter went to Tamale. Bishop Gregory is also one of the seeds planted in the mid-1930s. Like all the other Dagaabas in those early days, he was illiterate; just another mischievous little "pagan" boy, though admittedly a very bright one. One day I caught his attention and asked him if he would like to go to school and learn to read and write.

"Read and write?" he said with a puzzled look on his small face. "What's all that?"

I laughed and said, "Just come and see for yourself."

He came and saw, got an education, went on to study for the priesthood, and is now the bishop of Wa.

At the end of the ordination ceremony, just before he was to give the final blessing, Bishop Gregory surprised me by telling the huge crowd of priests, religious, and laity in attendance that he had someone he wanted to introduce to them.

"This person is responsible for my being here today as your bishop," he explained.

Then he went on to relate the story of how his life had been radically changed many years ago when I challenged him to come to school and learn to read and write. He ended by inviting me to say a few words to the people. I was a little hesitant at first to speak to them in their own language, which I had not had the occasion to use in quite a long time. But as I looked out over that really impressive gathering of the faithful, many of whom I knew personally, many of whose parents and grandparents I had instructed, baptized, married, and buried, the shyness fell away and I began to address them simply from a heart filled with joy and gratitude to the Father of us all for giving me one more opportunity to be among my children and grandchildren in the faith. It was a homecoming I shall never forget.

That is why I am so grateful to Father McCoy for producing this book. With an abundance of love and a wealth of anecdote culled in great part from his own long personal experience in northern Ghana, he tells the fascinating story of how the tiny seed of Christian faith was brought to the Northwest and planted there, and of how it grew to be the great tree it is today, sinking its roots ever deeper into the Ghanaian soil and stretching out its leafy branches to give shelter and sustenance to all creatures great and small.

It is a wonderful story that deserves to be known beyond the limits of the area in which it took place. I am especially happy that in telling it he pays due tribute to some of the many outstanding Ghanaian Christians of those early times (which were not, after all, so long ago) who are its real heroes and worthy sources of inspiration for the young Christians of today. They were genuine apostles of Jesus Christ to their people. Now their grandsons and granddaughters are becoming the first generation of the Church in northwest Ghana to carry the seed of the faith in their turn to other lands.

May God continue to bless the Church in Ghana and increase its capacity to serve Him by serving the real needs of His people.

J. Alfred Richard, M.Afr.
St. Petersburg, Florida (USA)
22 March 1988

Father Richard (West Warwick, Rhode Island) served in Ghana from 1933 until 1947. In 1948 he became the first provincial superior of the newly constituted United States province of the Missionaries of Africa, a post he held until 1960 when he was appointed the society's regional superior for Ghana and Nigeria. He returned to the United States in 1965 and, until his retirement in 1982, coordinated efforts of the Missionaries of Africa to raise awareness among West Coast Catholics of the plight of the Third World, especially Africa.

Preface

This book was "conceived" on 30 November 1929. That was the day Father Arthur Paquet and I arrived in Jirapa to open the first mission in northwest Gold Coast (now Ghana). As every such venture needs a faithful chronicler, he became that day our recording secretary and keeper of the Jirapa mission diary, which has been a great source of information in compiling the present volume.

Every mission in those days kept a record of all the important and many of the ordinary events that happened locally. With the passing years, these diaries would become precious historical documents. But in their day they were already useful, not only in charting the progress of the mission or for settling arguments on dates and events, but as the main source of information when composing the yearly personal letter each Missionary of Africa was obliged to write to the superior general of the society in Algiers. Called the "Letter of the Rule", it was meant as much for the one writing it as it was for the superior general. In composing it, the missionary was forced to reflect on his faithfulness to the rule of the institute as well as on the quality of his participation in community life, his spiritual exercises, and the work assigned to him. It was an excellent way to put order in one's life at least once a year.

One of the things the early diaries reflected was the initial difficulty of penetrating the wall of fear Satan had thrown up about the people as a defense against the Gospel. The Dagaabas and the Sissalas were religious by nature. They believed in God as the most powerful of beings. But they conceived of Him as being very remote from them. They dared not address Him directly but always through intermediaries, lesser spirits who were often harmful to the well-being of the people. Fear of these spirits made their religion a servile one which caused them considerable, if not continual, anxiety.

Enter the missionaries. We were marked immediately as being persons distinct from other "Europeans" they had known until then, mainly colonial officials, by the efforts we made from the start to identify ourselves with them (the people). We began by eating the same food they did and drinking *pito* (a mild millet beer), visiting their sick and learning their language. They were impressed, and a little of the wall around them began to crumble.

The area in which they lived was part of the Sahel and consequently subject to frequent droughts that threatened their crops and made survival problematical for all but the very strong. When the spirits to whom they sacrificed could give them no satisfaction, they began to come to the mission, asking us to pray to God to send them rain. Anything was worth a try in dire necessity. We used such occasions to persuade the people to approach God directly themselves with their needs. The answers to their prayers were often dramatic in form and extraordinarily swift in coming. More of the wall fell away.

Then at last, on a Sunday afternoon in mid-August 1930, the first two Dagaabas walked bravely through the breach into the arms of Jesus. They were Kyefondeme and his brother Yelesigra, sons of Gala, a respectable member of Jirapa society. For all practical purposes, from that moment the wall ceased to exist. Thousands of Dagaabas and Sissalas would soon begin to cast aside fear and commit themselves to the *Ngwinsore* (Way of God).

From the early thirties, it was like a new Pentecost in the northwest Gold Coast. The Spirit of God roamed the land breathing life into the hearts of the people. The early catechumens seemed animated with new concern for one another. Returning from Sunday worship and instruction at the mission, they would patiently relate everything they had learned of God to all who cared to listen, encouraging their listeners to accompany them to

Jirapa the following weekend. A surprising number did so, even though it frequently entailed a ten to twenty-five mile walk one-way.

As the number of people displacing themselves to Jirapa increased with each passing week, the authorities saw, or thought they saw, a threat of revolution in this great human movement. The British had imposed chiefs on the people in 1913, mainly to simplify their task of administering the territory. These chiefs were not hereditary, therefore, and both they and their colonial sponsors grew nervous as the wave of Christianity grew higher and catechists began to be installed in the villages to help attend to the needs of the catechumens and the newly-baptized Christians. The catechists were seen as being a direct threat to the authority of the chiefs and an indirect one to that of the colonial government. It was nothing more than the proverbial tempest in a teapot, however. Once it began to be evident that there was nothing political in the aims of the Christians, so long as they were treated fairly and permitted to practise their religion freely, fears of revolution evaporated. There were still some misunderstandings to clear up between the chiefs and the village catechists, but they were never more than that. With time the chiefs came to see that the Christians, far from being a threat, were among their best and most loyal subjects. That is not to say that the Ngwinsore suddenly found itself without enemies or obstacles to its progress in the Northwest. Problems continued for many years, but the main source of difficulty had been defused in the early thirties.

Meanwhile, the people came to believe that God truly did love them as He said He did. They had never even suspected the possibility of such a thing. The early catechists composed a song called "Nangmwin nono Dagaaba" (God loves the Dagaabas) which expressed the feeling that their massive conversion to Christ was proof of God's special grace in their regard.

This, then, is the story of how God, at a certain moment in history, chose to show His love in a special way to the people of northwest Gold Coast and of how they responded to it. It is also the story of what I have been blessed to witness during the greater part of my life, ever since arriving in Jirapa in November 1929.

This is not a book of fiction, therefore. It is the true story of men and women who heard God's call to leave home and country and seek Him in Africa among the Dagaabas and the Sissalas. They found Him there and they helped the Dagaabas and the Sissalas to rediscover Him themselves in a totally new way. I thank God with all my heart for having granted me a share in that work.

The writing of this book has been a rewarding experience for me. Though fifty-nine years in gestation, its immediate preparation began in earnest only last year (see Acknowledgements). As the actual writing got underway, I found myself reliving those great days of the past when the world (at least my world) seemed fresh and new and just a bit larger and more mysterious than it does now. I had expected some excitement, of course, otherwise I would never have become a missionary to Africa. But God surprised me by the power of His love and the dramatic way He chose to manifest it in the Northwest. It is a consolation for me to know that though my treking days in Ghana on His behalf may be over, this book will continue to make known to His people there His love for them.

And so, as I have said before but can never say often enough, I am eternally grateful to God for having included me in His plan to reach out to the Dagaabas and the Sissalas and, through them, to so many others. It has been a joy and a privilege to share the best years of my life with them.

If I could say a final word to them, it would be this: To whom much is given, much will be required. If God has brought you to maturity in your faith, it is to shoulder responsibility in His Church and in your country. Do not disappoint Him. Without the input that each of you is capable of, according to your individual gifts, God's plan for Ghana and her people will not advance as it should. Many will be prevented from coming to know Him and love Him as you do. And if that happens, we shall all be poorer for it. So do not be afraid. Just as God was with your ancestors in the faith, so He is with you today. Open your hearts to Him still more and let your faith in Him change your lives. Do not be discouraged by setbacks or the slowness of the transformation — either of yourselves or of the world. Be willing to make the effort required and leave the results to Him. Conversion is a gradual and continuing process that we must keep working at calmly and hopefully all the days of our lives, until at last we reach our true home in God.

May all our paths coincide one day in Him.

Remigius F. McCoy, M.Afr.
St. Petersburg, Florida (USA)
10 April 1988

A Note on Usage

For the sake of clarity, especially for those readers unfamiliar with the inflected forms of nouns and adjectives found in Ghanaian languages, the plural form adopted in this book for all names of ethnic groups is the simple addition of an "s" to the collective noun. Thus:

Dagaaba, Dagaabas
Sissala, Sissalas
Kassena, Kassenas, etc.

Technically speaking, this is equivalent to writing English, Englishes; French, Frenches; or even Canadian, Canadianses, since one is really attempting to pluralize an already plural form. But it is a practice that has become acceptable in English when treating foreign words that form their plurals irregularly, at least by English language standards.

Nevertheless, the singular form *(Dagao)* and the preferred form of the adjective *(Dagati)* will be used throughout. These should present no problem so long as one remembers that they all pertain to the same ethnic group. In cases of doubt, a quick glance in the glossary at the back of the book will find all such terms explained.

R.F.M.

Acknowledgements

The writing of this book has been a project of mine for many years, though the closest I ever got to accomplishing it was to collect material and prepare short articles for magazines or talks for schools, communion breakfasts, or mission funding appeals. The material was filed away but I never got around to putting it in order and sitting down to write. There always seemed to be something more urgent to be done.

Then, in 1986, a young cousin of mine, Joan Cameron (now Mrs. Colin Dewart), decided to leave her job as occupational therapist at the Hospital for Sick Children in Toronto, Ontario (Canada), and accompany me back to Ghana. She wanted to meet the people and see for herself the places about which I had told her so much over the years. At the same time, she would make herself useful by working with the handicapped children at Jirapa Hospital and use her spare time to sort out and compile the material for the oft-proposed book. This she did with admirable industry despite the unaccustomed heat. She had access to the early mission diaries and was able to check and verify dates, names, and events. It is thanks to her determination that this book finally got underway.

One day in June 1987, as Joan and I were making preparations to return to Canada (my health had been poor since the previous February), Father Guido Krämer, the regional superior of the Missionaries of Africa in Ghana, came to visit me. He asked me about the progress of the book and I told him we had more or less completed the research stage and were ready for the next step. We now needed someone to take the raw material and shape it into readable form. As I was telling him this, a name suddenly popped into my mind. "Why not ask Rene Dionne to handle it?" I said. "He has had a lot of editorial experience." (Besides, we had been friends since 1961 when he was assigned briefly to our Chicago community, of which I was then in charge.) I remembered that he was now assigned to the Spanish province of the society. Father Krämer offered to contact him and his superiors for me and ask his help on the project. Fortunately, Rene was willing to cooperate and his provincial superior, Father Javier Larraya, graciously agreed to release him from his duties in the province for the time necessary to complete the book. This was another big gift from God who loves the Dagaabas.

I take this opportunity to thank Joan and Father Rene in a special way. Without their help, I doubt very much that this memoir would ever have seen the light of day. May God reward them as only He can for their patience, hard work, and devotion to the project from start to finish.

Thanks also to all those who urged me to this task over the years, some of whom were involved in the earlier stages of its evolution — like Sister Carrol Regina Thomas of the Daughters of Mary and Joseph (DMJ) and Sister Helen Scullion of the Missionary Sisters of Our Lady of Africa (MSOLA) — or whose contributions served as documentation or as inspiration for parts of the final draft — like those of Sister Marie Therese Chambers of the Franciscan Missionaries of Mary (FMM). If I hesitate to mention more names in this connection, it is for fear of inadvertently overlooking someone. But those in question know who they are. To them and to all who have ever helped me in my apostolate in any way, spiritually or materially, I offer my humble gratitude.

Various persons were helpful in providing or checking items of needed information during the book's final stages of preparation. Among these, Father Dionne and I would like to thank Archbishop Peter P. Dery of Tamale; Father Martin S. Ninnang, chancellor of Wa diocese and secretary to the bishop; Father René Lamey, head archivist at our Generalate in Rome; Sister Monique LeBrun, FMM, director of the *Centre Missionnaire des Soeurs*

Franciscaines de Marie in Montreal; Sister Hermine Audet, FMM; Father Roland Frenette, director of our *Centre d'Information Africaine* in Montreal; Father Michel Fortin, editor of *Mission*, magazine of the Missionaries of Africa in Canada; Sister Arlene Gates, provincial superior of the MSOLA in the United States; Father John Maguire of our British province; Father Benjamin Maatuo Kuu of Wa diocese; Mr. Michael Wood of Cumbria, England; and Dick Gordon who contributed the cover art, maps, and photo layout, among other things.

In the search for a printer who would maintain a high standard of quality throughout the book while respecting the limits of our budget, we owe special thanks to the staff at Novalis in Ottawa, Ontario. Michael O'Hearn and Bede Hubbard were particularly helpful to us. Their good advice saved us much time and effort. We appreciate their generosity.

Our gratitude also extends to various communities of our religious family in Canada and the United States: in particular to the St. Petersburg, Florida, community where I was graciously received and sheltered all last winter and early spring as I recuperated from two attacks of pneumonia in six months; to the Washington, D.C., community whose members and secretarial staff cheerfully cooperated with Father Dionne in every possible way to facilitate his work on the text during the several months he was among them; and to the Argyle avenue community in Ottawa and that of the boulevard de l'Acadie in Montreal, both of which extended to us at different times the kind of warm and fraternal hospitality for which our Canadian confreres have always been known.

Thanks must also go to our major superiors at the Generalate of the Missionaries of Africa in Rome, as well as to the provincial and regional superiors in Canada, the United States, and Ghana. Their encouragement and support have meant a great deal to all of us who have been involved in this project in the last year.

And finally, deep thanks to a truly wonderful family in Waterloo, Ontario — Doctor Donald J. Cameron, his lovely wife Mary, and their children — who not only welcomed me into their home and cared for me when I returned from Ghana last summer desperately ill, but also opened their arms and their hearts to

Father Rene when he joined me there in early October to begin shaping and editing the book. I know I speak for him too when I say that we shall never forget them. In the warmth and naturalness of their hospitality and the generosity of their love, they recalled for me the finest qualities of the people of northwest Ghana. And that is the highest compliment I could pay either of them.

Abbreviations

ACOSCA	Africa Cooperative Savings and Credit Association
CUSO	Canadian University Students Overseas
DC	District Commissioner
D.C.	District of Columbia
E.N.T.	Ear, Nose, Throat (doctor)
FIC	*Fratres Immaculatae Conceptionis* (Brothers of the Immaculate Conception)
FMM	Franciscan Missionary of Mary
G.P.	General Practicioner
M.Afr.	Missionary of Africa ("White Father")
Msgr.	Monsignor
MSOLA	Missionary Sister(s) of Our Lady of Africa ("White Sisters")
Ob-Gyn	Obstetrics-Gynecology
QRN	Qualified Registered Nurse
Res.Int.Med.	Resident in Internal Medicine
RN	Registered Nurse
Rt. Rev.	Right Reverend
SEN	State Enrolled Nurse
SMI	Sister(s) of Mary Immaculate
SRN	State Registered Nurse
U.S.	United States (of America). Also USA
V.R.	Volta Region

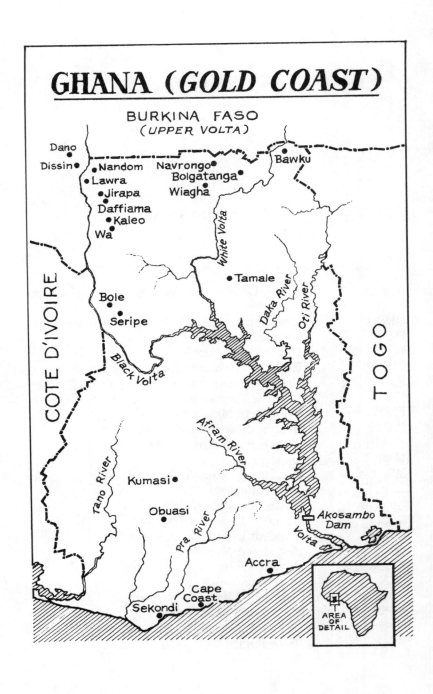

GHANA (*GOLD COAST*)

BURKINA FASO
(*UPPER VOLTA*)

Dano
Dissin
Nandom
Navrongo
Bawku
Lawra
Bolgatanga
Jirapa
Wiagha
Daffiama
Kaleo
Wa

White Volta

Tamale

COTE D'IVOIRE

Bole
Seripe

Daka River

Oti River

TOGO

Black Volta

Afram River

Tano River

Kumasi

Obuasi

Pra River

Akosambo Dam

Volta

Accra

Cape Coast

Sekondi

AREA OF DETAIL

1

Gold Coast Mission

To tell the story of the Church in northwest Ghana, one must go back at least to the arrival of the first Missionaries of Africa in northern Gold Coast, as Ghana was then called.[1] It was a time when dioceses as such did not exist in subsaharan Africa. For administrative purposes, the Church's mission headquarters in Rome (Propaganda Fide) divided various parts of the continent into prefectures or vicariates. These were huge territories, each administered by a bishop or priest whose official title was that of vicar apostolic or prefect apostolic.

One of these vicariates, the Sudan, covering the entire area of French colonial influence then called the French Sudan, had begun to spill over into the northern Gold Coast, an English protectorate. There was a special reason for this, besides a natural concern to extend the boundaries of the Church. The French government had embarked upon a policy of violent anticlericalism in the home country, and Bishop Bazin, then vicar apostolic of the Sudan, feared that one day this policy might be extended to its colonies. In such a case, the missionaries in French Sudan would be faced with expulsion.

Bishop Bazin looked with longing toward the Gold Coast as a potential haven for his apostolic workers should that possibility become fact. He was not the only one to have this thought. The British consul at Dakar, who at that time represented the Gold

Coast as well, had suggested that the missionaries open a station there, for the same reason.

The task of exploring the area to find a suitable site for the first mission station fell to Father Oscar Morin. Mounted on horseback, he spent five weeks surveying the entire northern part of the country before deciding to settle in the vicinity of Wa. The British officer in charge there was not favourable to the opening of a Catholic mission in that area because, as in the case of northern Nigeria, the colonial authorities wanted to leave Wa to the Muslims. The pretext was the unsettled state of affairs after "the wars".[2] The military forces were still in charge in Wa and they did not want to add to their troubles by admitting the provocative presence of a Christian band of missionaries into a Muslim stronghold. The White Father was advised to try Navrongo, to the northeast.

At Navrongo, the British proved hospitable to the idea, provided the new mission be located in Navrongo town itself, for security reasons, and that its superior be a British subject. The first condition was easily agreed to, while the appointment of Canadian Father Morin to head the new foundation satisfied the second. The door to the evangelization of the Northern Territories was at least ajar.

In March of 1906, the first Catholic mission station in northern Gold Coast was officially inaugurated at Navrongo. It was staffed by Fathers Morin and Léonide Barsalou, both Canadians; Father Jean-Marie Chollet, a Frenchman from Brittany; and Brother Eugène, an Alsatian from Dambach in the diocese of Strasbourg.

If the missionaries expected to be welcomed by the people whom they had come to serve, they were soon disappointed. The first two years in Navrongo saw little fruit from their efforts to approach the Kassena and Nankanna populations. They studied and learned to master Kassem, and in the process compiled the first dictionary and grammar of that language. Soon they were preaching the Good News of Jesus Christ to all who would listen to them. But aside from the children, with their natural curiosity and inability to resist any kindness shown them, the missionaries found few listeners and little response. Even the children remained aloof in the beginning, warned no doubt by their elders to beware of the suspicious-looking foreigners. The people feared them and avoided them if at all possible. Slowly, however, the persistence of the missionaries began to make inroads into this fear and they were able to gain the confidence of a small but promising nucleus of Kassenas. In June of 1908, there were seven serious catechumens among them. Three months later, the number had grown to eighty. Because of the White Fathers' lengthy and progressive method of preparation for baptism, however, it was not until 1913 that the first six adults were baptized.

The danger of a mass expulsion of Catholic missionaries from French territory passed; and in the midst of the First World War, the French prime minister even asked the vicar apostolic of the Sudan, Bishop Lemaître, to personally oversee the morale of the troops from West Africa. Bishop Lemaître accepted the challenge. Before leaving to do so, he appointed two temporary administrators for his vicariate: one of these, Father Morin, was to be responsible for the eastern part of the vicariate.

Oscar Morin's zeal, prudence, and piety fully justified the vicar apostolic's confidence in him. Moreover, his good humour and native simplicity were disarming. In his hands difficult problems, which might merely have become more complicated in those of another, often found satisfactory solutions.

He took his appointment as administrator seriously without ever falling into the error of taking himself the same way. Always progressive in outlook, he began almost immediately to work toward bringing the missionary and the motor together in fruitful alliance. The vicariate was immense; and distances, in an age when missionaries had normally to travel on foot or bicycle, were prohibitive. Some 120 miles separated the new mission at Navrongo from the vicar apostolic's headquarters at Wagadugu. To his mind, there was a clear need for some sort of motorized transport and he determined to put the vicariate on wheels.

The first motorcycle to arrive in the region was his. Its infernal racket and the truly traumatic experience of seeing him hurtle through the bush at the incredible speed of twenty-five miles per hour struck terror in the hearts of many at first. But they, and Father Morin, soon discovered that this "demon" was not invulnerable. There was (and is) in that part of Africa a triple-pointed thorn called locally *pogh'kyeghse* (the old woman) because, as the people say, "There is no safe way to pick it up!" One of its points is always facing upward. Motorcycle tires, however, picked them up easily. But Father Morin was not a man to allow the inconvenience of punctures, even though frequent, to discourage his pursuit of progress. Little by little, the motorization of the mission proceeded and the radius of its activity increased as well.

In 1921, rumours began to reach him that the general council of the White Fathers was considering his appointment as the society's superior in the Wagadugu region of the vicariate. He immediately sought out a member of the council to protest that he was not suitable for the job.

"I have always been the first one to show a take-it-or-leave-it attitude toward the rule," he confessed, "and it would be difficult for me to impose it on others. It would remind me of my past misdeeds. In my sane moments I tell myself that the major superiors are too intelligent to think of me for that position."

But the general council was not moved by such arguments. Besides, unknown to him, the councillor he had singled out for his confession of ineptitude was the man most convinced of his superior capabilities for the post. Worthy or not, when Father Morin returned to West Africa that year, it was as superior of the White Fathers working in the Wagadugu region.

For some time the vicar apostolic of the Sudan and the British authorities had been convinced, though for different reasons, of the desireability of removing the Navrongo mission from the jurisdiction of Wagadugu. It was not proper, in the opinion of His Majesty's chief commissioner in the Gold Coast, that missionaries in a British-administered territory should depend on a vicar apostolic in a foreign territory. In anticipation of the separation, Bishop Thévenoud (who had succeeded Bishop Lemaître as vicar apostolic of the Sudan) gave Father Morin all the ecclesiastical faculties necessary for him to administer the two mission stations in the gold Coast.[3] The following year, on 14 April 1926, the apostolic prefecture of Navrongo was erected with Father (now Monsignor) Morin appointed its first superior.

As ordinary of the Northern Territories of the Gold Coast, Monsignor Morin was now responsible for bringing the Good News to the people of an area roughly the size of Portugal or the state of Ohio. He decided it was time to make a second attempt to evangelize the Northwest. Negotiations were begun with the colonial government in 1927 to obtain authorization. While there was no problem in the Northeast, where a new mission station was established that same year among the Builsa people at Wiagha, south of Navrongo, the Northwest still seemed out of reach. The reason for this was no longer the same as it had been some twenty years earlier. Then it had been the Muslims; now it was the Anglicans.

When Monsignor Morin wrote to the British colonial governor at Accra, Sir Gordon Guggisberg, to request authorization, the latter replied that he had no objection to the White Fathers opening missions anywhere in the Northern Territories *except* in the Northwest. He had promised Anglican Church officials, he explained, that the Northwest would be reserved exclusively for their missionary endeavours at least until 1932, and that no other religious denomination would be allowed to establish a mission there in the meantime. If the Anglicans failed to take advantage of this before the stated deadline, the field would then be open to anyone, including the Catholics.

Monsignor Morin's reply was cordial but firm. This restriction was unacceptable, he told the governor, and if he persisted in closing the Northwest to Catholic missionary activity, the matter would have to be referred to Rome. He followed this with a letter to Archbishop (later Cardinal) Hinsley, the Holy See's first apostolic delegate to Africa, briefing him on the matter. After studying it carefully, the archbishop left for Accra to discuss the question with Governor Guggisberg personally.

Sometime later, Monsignor Morin received a letter from the governor in which he withdrew his objections to the opening of a Catholic mission in the Northwest. For that matter, he wrote, as far as His Majesty's government in the Gold Coast was concerned, Monsignor Morin was free to open missions anywhere and whenever he chose. Furthermore, there would be no restrictions regarding the nationalities of staff members assigned to these missions.

It now remained only to decide where the first outpost of Christianity in the Northwest should be located. Earlier, when the first negotiations with the colonial government had begun at district level, the district commissioner of Lawra, Mr. Ayersmith (a Catholic), had praised the character of the Dagaabas. They were good, hard-working people, known for their solid family traditions. They had a good reputation among other ethnic groups and, in his estimation, would make good Christians one day. He and Mr. Cardinal, a former district commissioner at Lawra, as well as Colonel Whittal, the provincial commissioner at Navrongo, proved to be very helpful in advising Monsignor Morin about the best location for the first mission in the Northwest. The site finally chosen, because it was the most central of the Dagati villages, was Jirapa.

2

The Dagaabas

The area destined for the new mission was part of the Sahel, an arid region stretching across the breadth of North Africa, where drought and famine are as frequent and persistent today as they were then. Situated a few hundred miles south of the Sahara Desert, northwest Ghana is open, level country. Grass grows tall (six to eight feet) in the red laterite soil; and trees, stunted by the annual seven-month dry season and recurrent brush fires, sprout singly or in spare clusters at widely-spaced intervals, as if they were on individual display in a vast open-air museum. Though the Black Volta River borders it on the west, there are few other rivers of any importance in the region. In 1929 it was a completely rural area of subsistence farmers, with much of the land between Jirapa and Navrongo, and south of Jirapa as well, lying open and uncultivated due in part to the wars at the beginning of the century which had driven the people away.[1]

Two ethnic groups dominated the region: the Dagaabas and the Sissalas. Then as now, the Dagaabas were by far the more numerous, accounting for some seventy per cent of the total population of the Northwest to the Sissalas' twenty per cent. The remainder, in the southern part of the region, was made up of many smaller ethnic groups.[2]

The Dagaabas had come originally from eastern Ghana, from among the Manprussi (Mamprusi) and the Dagomba tribes. They had migrated westward some three or four centuries earlier out of discontent with the oppression and exactions of the Manprussi and Dagomba chiefs. So strong had been their discontent that when they reached their new home they vowed not to have any chiefs ever again. Disputes among them would be settled by the elders, who were also responsible for drawing up the rites and regulations governing the group's traditional customs and way of life. It was only when the white men came, in the form of British colonial officers, to set up their administration in the Northwest in 1913 that chiefs were introduced for the first time among the Dagaabas and Sissalas there.

As the story is told, prior to the coming of the white men, the Gbare people kidnapped a Dagati woman from Jirapa. An expedition of warriors, led by one Ganaa, was sent out in pursuit and succeeded in rescuing her and restoring her to her family. When the British arrived, intent on dealing with someone in authority, they inquired: "Who is chief here?" At first there was no response. Then Ganaa stepped forward. "I am," he said, and no one moved to dispute it.

Ganaa, still reigning at the time of the missionaries' arrival in 1929, was the first chief of Jirapa. His example broke the ice, and soon other chiefs began to appear throughout the Northwest.

As Mr. Ayersmith had observed to Monsignor Morin, the Dagaabas were a gracious, hardworking people with a reputation for honesty. They not only worked hard at tilling their land, but contractors in the South considered them to be excellent labourers and set high value on their services (though not always high pay). Strong, hardy individuals, there was a marked sense of unity among them. When young men went south to work in the gold and manganese mines around Obuasi, they brought back what they earned to be shared among the "family" (a term which for the Dagaabas meant three generations living and farming together). Theirs was a traditional patriarchal system of life: communal living, communal farming, communal granary.

This rural population lived on the produce of its land, dependent on a rainy season that extended, in normal times, from May to October with little, if any, rain the rest of the year. The main crops included millet, guinea corn, groundnuts (peanuts), yams, rice, beans, and maize. All tilling of the soil was done by hand, using a short-handled, curved hoe which obliged the user to bend down toward the ground. For most of their crops, the people made mounds to retain the moisture in the soil and thus assure a better yield. The men did the hoeing, while the women did the planting and helped with the harvesting. There were organized "farming bees" in which a farmer would recruit his friends and neighbours to come and help him at certain key moments of the agricultural season. In return, the volunteers would be fed and given the local beer *(pito)* to drink. The women usually brought the meal and refreshments to the men in the fields where they were working.

It was also a custom at that time for a young man to cultivate his father-in-law's farm. At this stage in Dagati social history, there was no remunerative labour among them as there was in the South.

The mines deep in the Ashanti territory of the southern Gold Coast provided one of the few means for the Dagaabas to acquire a little hard cash. In the time before our arrival in Jirapa, I was told later, the mining companies had experienced difficulty in recruiting labourers and had appealed to the chiefs and elders of the Northwest to help them. The chiefs had done so by simply requisitioning young men from the different compounds and sending them down to the mine agents in Kumasi. As there was no transport at that time, they travelled the three hundred miles on foot, taking ten or twelve days to do so. Later, the companies began to send up lorries fitted with two-by-six mahogany boards for seats, enabling forty-five passengers per lorry to ride down to Kumasi in unaccustomed, if relative, comfort. They took food with them, mostly groundnuts, and carried a goat skin for a suitcase. Their clothing consisted of a cover cloth made of hand-spun cotton and a supply of loincloths. Shoes or sandals did not yet form part of their wardrobe. A straw mat was taken along to sleep on. Money, if they had any, was carried in a cotton belt.

Once in Kumasi, the agents brought the men to their mines which were located anywhere from 20 to 120 miles from the town. There they were lodged and fed by the mining company and paid a monthly wage as unskilled labourers. The usual agreement made with the chiefs was that the men would work at the mines during the dry season and be free to return home to farm during the rainy season.

On arrival back in their villages, the migrant labourers' first visit was to the chief. They told him what they had received in payment for their work and handed the money over to him. In some cases the chief would keep a good part of it for himself and return the rest. Each man would then present the remainder to the elder or head of his compound. If the latter were generous, he might allow him some pocket money, but it was never very much. No wonder the Dagaabas were reluctant to return to Kumasi under such arrangements.

Sometime around 1935, the managers of one mine wrote to the Catholic mission at Jirapa to inform the missionaries that they intended to recruit labourers in the area, and that on a particular day they would send lorries to pick them up and transport them down to Kumasi. By now the chiefs had ceased their practice of forcible recruiting on behalf of the mines, obliging owners to resort to enticements if they hoped to attract the Dagaabas southwards. After stating what they were willing to pay, and even promising one month's salary in advance, the managers ended their letter with the request that its contents be made known to the people.

Though the terms were more generous than they had been in the past, they were obviously not generous enough to suit the majority of the Dagaabas. Their response to the offer, when we brought it to their attention, was anything but enthusiastic. Experience had made them wary. They preferred to go down to Kumasi without any previous contract so as to be free to bargain and work on their own terms, rather than bind themselves ahead of time as virtual slaves.

When the lorries finally came to Jirapa, their drivers were surprised to find so few waiting to accept the offer of free transportation, advance pay, and guaranteed seasonal employment.

3

Pathfinders

With the colonial government and the local authorities in agreement about the proposed mission at Jirapa, Monsignor Morin and his advisers proceeded to select the staff to pioneer the new venture. Brother Basilide Koot, from the Netherlands, and two Canadians — Father Arthur Paquet, from Levis, and myself, from Mayo (both in the province of Quebec) — were chosen and notified of our new assignment.

Brother Basilide had arrived at Navrongo a few months earlier, after completing a two-year training program in carpentry and construction at Thibar, Tunisia. Father Paquet, ordained a priest in June of that year (1929), was due to arrive in November. As the "veteran" of the group, with four years of experience in Navrongo, I was appointed superior of the nascent community.

I had come to the Gold Coast from Canada a few months after my ordination to the priesthood (in Carthage, Tunisia, on 28 June 1925). Travelling in a group of half a dozen newly-ordained Canadians, all heading for our first mission assignments in different parts of Africa, it had taken us nearly seven weeks to make the trip since we had had to go by way of Marseilles, France, to pick up supplies and bring them with us. These included, among other things, camp beds and bedding, deck chairs, mosquito nets, quinine for the ever-present malaria, and bicycles. We even had to bring flour to make altar breads. Flour for table bread was a luxury our slender budget could not afford, so we did without bread in those years. At that time there were no stores in the northern Gold Coast where such things could be bought.

Upon arrival at Navrongo, my first assignment was to start a school there to educate the future leaders of the country. The British had begun to prepare the people for a gradual move toward "indirect rule", and they wanted the sons of the chiefs to be educated so that they could eventually participate in the administration. That was as far as the colonial authorities were prepared to go at the time in granting concessions to the democratic ideal in their colony-protectorate. If they envisaged its eventual independence, it was only as the dimmest of prospects in a far, far distant and improbable future.[1]

With a grant of eighty pounds from the government, I had to build, equip, and run a plant consisting of three classrooms and an office. The grant had also to cover the costs of translating text books and mimeographing them. As a young greenhorn missionary, I was fortunate to have the help of Fathers Jean-Baptiste Dagenais and Lucien Melançon both in supervising the construction work and in translating and producing the texts.

It is rule of the White Fathers that every missionary assigned to an area for the first time must devote the first six months to learning the language and studying the customs of the local people. While Father Melançon was busy preparing the catechumens for baptism, I took over his job as foreman of works. This included training ten labourers to become masons. With time and application, my on-the-job practice, together with some expert coaching from the fathers, gave me sufficient familiarity with Kassem (the language of the Kassenas) to be able to open the school in April 1926.

This Navrongo school was the first of those opened in the northern part of the Gold Coast to be officially recognized by the government. Father Dagenais had started a similar school a few years before, but it had not received government approval and he had had to close it down.

The time for educating women in northern Gold Coast was not yet ripe, it seemed. We were told to take only boys, with Colonel Whittal himself seeing to the recruitment. He presented me with eighty-five beginners between the ages of seven and thirteen. These were divided into three groups. As the only teacher, I enlisted the help of three of the more intelligent boys to act as monitors while I rotated from classroom to classroom the whole day.

It was a day school and charged no fee. A midday meal was provided by the mission, for which the boys paid a token sum. To earn enough to pay it, they worked on a groundnut farm or found other odd jobs. Because of a severe shortage of food, most of the students could not expect more than a light meal at home. They arrived at school without their breakfast and, had we not moved heaven and earth to provide them with something at midday, they would have had to go without lunch as well.

The walls of the school were three feet thick. Desks were made of mud and dried in the sun. Blackboards were of mud as well, with a coating of manganese and crushed rock. Crayons were fashioned from slivers of talc, while sand on the floor served the students as slates for working out sums or practising their writing skills. Except in the office, doors and windows were covered by mats.

A very popular sports program included soccer, field hockey, and baseball, with used tennis balls supplied to us by a European club at Tamale.

The boys were so eager to learn that they would return to the school on Saturdays — some of them coming great distances on foot — and plead with me to give them additional help with their studies. But on weekends I was assistant priest in the parish and had to shoulder my share of the pastoral duties. Any spare time I might have was spent in making text books in Kassem and supervising their binding.

This first school at Navrongo produced several priests, one cabinet minister, two members of parliament, one police commissioner (Special Branch, Central Intelligence Department), and many others who went on to hold important posts in the country.

*
**

As soon as word reached us of our assignment to northwest Gold Coast, Brother Basilide and I began the none-too-easy task

of assembling the essential provisions that would enable the new
foundation to survive until the annual supplies arrived from
Marseilles at the end of the year. Our inventory read as follows:

1 table
3 iron beds with kapok mattresses & pillows
towels and linen
a few cooking utensils
plates, cups, saucers, glasses
wash basins
sugar for one year (2 cubes/person/day)
flour for hosts
coffee beans & coffee grinder
3 kerosene lanterns
4 gallon tins kerosene
4 tins petrol
Mass box & essentials for Mass & Benediction
crucifixes
personal effects
a few crates in which to store things
a few empty kerosene crates to be used as chairs

By the time Father Paquet arrived from Canada in November,
eager to begin his first assignment, all was in readiness. We had
only to await the reopening of the Navrongo-Lawra road which
was being repaired after the rainy season.

On 29 November 1929, at 7:15 in the morning, the little caravan
set off from Navrongo, not on foot, as had the early White Fathers
on their way from the Tanzanian coast to the interior in 1878-79;
or on horseback, as had a young Father Morin on his first explor-
atory trip to Wa in 1905; but by car and lorry. None of us, as we
rolled out out of the mission yard, waving good-bye to the familiar
faces of those gathered to see us off, could have had the slightest
idea what the future held in store for us in the Northwest. We
only knew that we were determined to get there and find out.
That was why we had become missionaries in the first place, to
push back the frontiers of ignorance and bring the Good News of
God's love to places where it had never been proclaimed before.
At the same time, I think we felt we were actually bringing God
to the Dagaabas, whereas we were really going out to meet Him
in them. We would need a little more experience to discover that

there was nowhere God hadn't already been and no heart that hadn't already discovered Him, even though in an imperfect and sometimes confused manner. He had been at work among the Dagaabas for a very long time, preparing the soil of their hearts for the sowing of the seed of His Word, and He would be waiting to greet us in them when we finally bounced into Jirapa.

Monsignor Morin, with me sitting beside him as his only passenger, had taken the lead in his little car. Behind us came Brother Aidan (John Ryan from England) driving the one-and-a-half ton lorry belonging to Navrongo mission. He carried Father Paquet and Ludger, our newly-hired cook, and whatever essential baggage he had been able to fit into the small vehicle. Brother Basilide, who had suffered an attack of malaria at the last moment, had had to postpone his departure. He would arrive a month later with Anna, Ludger's wife, and Hector Awia, our steward and handyman, and his wife Odilla.

Progress was slow as the lorry was not functioning properly. Outside Nakon, a village some twenty-five miles into our journey, which one day would mark the boundary between the diocese of Wa and that of Navrongo, we suddenly spied a large herd of animals gathered beneath a clump of scrawny trees. They were too far away to identify, but Monsignor Morin slowed down immediately and proceeded with utmost caution.

"If they are bush cows," he said, "I want nothing to do with them."

He spoke from long experience with the fauna of the region. Bush cows were daring and dangerous animals when they got it into their heads to charge at something or someone, and they could inflict a lot of damage to a small car like ours. As we drew closer, there was an abrupt movement in the herd and one of the animals suddenly leapt into a tree and climbed to the top. There was a sigh of relief from my companion.

"They're baboons!" he said.

Indeed they were; the biggest herd I had seen until then or would ever see again; some thirty or forty of them, perhaps more. They began moving out as soon as their scout had sighted us and alerted them to the daring and dangerous animals *we* might well prove to be.

After a stop for lunch at Tumu, we continued on our way and arrived at Lawra around five o'clock in the afternoon. We were welcomed there by Captain Armstrong, the DC (district commissioner), and Colonel Whittal, the provincial commissioner. The latter had made it his business to be on hand for the occasion. Food and lodging were graciously offered by the DC and gladly accepted by all.

Early the next morning, on the feast of Saint Andrew the Apostle, Mass was celebrated for the first time in Dagati territory. After breakfast, the caravan, now complete with the addition of the DC's car, started on the last lap of its journey to Jirapa. From there the Son of God would begin to make Himself known to the Dagaabas and Sissalas of the Northwest, and to transmit His life and love to them.

Accompanied by the two commissioners, Monsignor Morin and I took the shorter road through Duori. The Duori road had not been repaired since the end of the rainy season, but it would present no problem for our smaller, lighter cars. The lorry, meanwhile, had been sent by way of Babile. It was a longer route, but we felt it would be a safer one for the heavier vehicle. However, at a village with the intriguing name of Konyukoan (Won't drink water), Brother Aidan was forced to make a detour and promptly got stuck. It was some time before he was able to join us at the rendezvous spot.

The old Jirapa *naa* (chief), Ganaa, had been alerted by the DC and was at the foot of the hill near the rest house with his headmen and elders when Colonel Whittal and Captain Armstrong arrived, followed by Monsignor Morin and his missionaries. It was a memorable reception, made all the more unforgettable by the simultaneous arrival of a swarm of locusts. Gunshots rang out; whether to welcome us or to try to scare off the locusts, I could not be sure. The DC, with the help of Mr. Karbo, his interpreter (later to become the Lawra naa), introduced us to Chief Ganaa and his people, and explained the purpose of our coming.

It was God's idea to send these men to live and work in their midst, he told them, so that they could come to know Him better. But He was also sending them to the Dagaabas today to help them to improve their health with medical care and to improve their knowledge and capabilities for a better quality of life through education.

Colonel Whittal then added a few words to make it absolutely clear that the missionaries were not government officials or civil servants but volunteers whose only reason for coming to Jirapa was to help the people. He had seen the good work they were doing at Navrongo, he said, and because of that they were his friends. He hoped the chief and his people would receive them well and give them full cooperation in their work. They would need some land, he told the chief, and he asked him to allow them to recruit labourers to help them build themselves a house.

The Jirapa naa then spoke. He was very diplomatic. He expressed his joy that Jirapa had been chosen by the "men of God" as their destination. He promised the district and provincial commissioners that he would take good care of the missionaries, see to it that they had a good place to live, and even help to build a house for them. He ended his brief words of welcome by offering his guests gifts of fowl, eggs, and yams.

It was our turn to speak. Addressing Chief Ganaa and his people first in Moré and then in English, Monsignor Morin thanked them on behalf of us all for their cordial welcome and generous gifts. He assured the old chief that through the missionaries' presence and work, God intended great blessings for him and all his people.[2]

When at last the formalities had ended, Colonel Whittal and Captain Armstrong shook hands with each of us and wished us well in the days ahead. Then they took their leave of the chief, got into their car and turned back toward Lawra.

Meanwhile, the chief had ordered some of his people to carry our belongings up the hill to the rest house, which was to be our temporary home until a site could be chosen and a permanent dwelling constructed for us. The rest house consisted of two large circular adobe buildings with grass roofs and a kitchen. There were no doors, no windows, no furniture, and — except for some big earthen water jars — no cooking utensils.[3] Women came from the chief's compound and filled the jars with water. As for food, chicken, rice, and yams could be bought locally with cowrie shells. When the chief learned that the missionaries could drink pito (the local beer brewed by the women from millet or guinea corn), he sent some up to us. It was a gift we greatly appreciated on that very hot, dry day. Word spread quickly among the people that these newcomers were not like the others who pray. They referred to the Muslims, who are not allowed to taste any fermented drink. Though not the noblest of distinctions, perhaps, being labelled pito-drinkers did serve to set us apart from the Muslims and establish us in the minds of the people as a more congenial breed of *mwinpuorobo*.[4]

4

Jirapa

When the chief and his elders and headmen returned home after welcoming the white-robed strangers who had come to stay and supposedly help them to learn more about God, there was great speculation among them and all the people on the true reason for their coming. Recent history, especially the devastating wars led by Babatu and Samouri across their lands and the forced recruitment of men, women, and even children by the British and French during the First World War, had left them scarred and suspicious of foreigners, black or white.[1]

Some suggested we might be Zabog people, warriors from across the border come to lure away their young men and make slaves of them in far-off lands from which they would never return. Others disagreed with this in part: while they did not think we had the look of warriors, we might well be slave traders in disguise. But many of the people, after seeing us for the first time that day and observing our beards, had decided we were just plain traders. They referred to us as "Patachi" (Portuguese), which was a term used by them to designate all foreign traders at the coast, most of whom were really Lebanese and Syrians. They had no experience of philanthropy and found it impossible to believe that men could leave home and country just to help them — people of a different race — whom they had never seen before and with whom they had no personal ancestral ties, and for no apparent benefit to themselves. There had to be some ulterior motive.

As for the Jirapa naa, he kept his own counsel. He had heard good things about these white men today, of how they had come to make them all happy and better people. He would like to see how they did that. There was no denying they came with the highest recommendations of the ruling power, a power to whom he owed a great deal personally. Though he too had some reservations about their sincerity of purpose, he did not want to risk losing them to another village. Not yet, anyway. He would go along with the recommendations of Colonel Whittal and Captain Armstrong and make good his promise to help the strangers. But he would keep a close eye on their movements all the while he was doing it.

On Sunday, 1 December, the mission site was chosen with the approval of the chief, his elders, and the two *tendaama*, Taabe and Moyanga.[2] The site was one of several that had been offered. Other options included a plot on the road to Tizza, another on the road to Gontag, and one near the site of the present secondary school. We chose the actual site for several reasons. Though they were all in the immediate area of Jirapa, this was the most central. It was about a quarter of a mile from the chief's four-storey mud compound, which housed him and his fifty wives, some hangers-on and their considerable assortment of wives. It was a wide-open space, superior to the other sites offered in that it lent itself better to eventual expansion. And last but not least, it was clearly the choice favoured by our host, the chief.

The advantage of being in Jirapa itself was that it was central to our mission among the Dagaabas. Jirapa was like the hub of a wheel from which roads — built by the people through forced labour by order of a former DC, Duncan Johnson (whom the Dagaabas called *"Muriyi"*)[3] — went out in all directions, linking the surrounding villages to it. It was the crossroads between Tizza, Duori, Babile, Nadoli, Gbare, Sigri, and Domweni.

Neglected land and of no use to anyone else, the soil was poor and full of brambles, stones, and a creeping plant with soft thorns called *gyira*.[4] The occasional rabbit or guinea fowl nested in it and evil spirits haunted it. We did not learn about the spirits until much later. Perhaps the Jirapa naa had in mind to pit us against each other. If they chased us away, he would be rid of us without having violated his promise to the district and provincial commissioners. And if we won, he would be delivered of a still worse problem. In the process, the true worth of the missionaries would be proven.

When I arrived on the scene the next morning (Monday), I found the chief himself tracing out the area the huts would occupy. The ground had already been cleared and levelled, and some men were busy digging the earth to make the mud walls while women brought water. There was much well-organized activity, with the result that in ten days' time the five round huts forming our provisional compound were completely roofed, plastered, and ready for occupancy. On Friday, 13 December 1929, only fourteen days after our arrival, the chief and his people moved all our belongings from the rest house to the new compound. In one hour, the move was completed. Two charcoal filters were set up for water and we were "in business".

As soon as the temporary compound was finished, work began on our permanent residence. The site chosen was at the north entrance of the present church. The cornerstone was laid on 12 December 1929.

From the beginning, Chief Ganaa had absolutely refused to let us pay the labourers for their work on our temporary quarters. But now he went even further, insisting that they contribute voluntary labour toward the construction of our mud-brick and thatch four-room house and chapel, and even that they provide the thatch themselves. Our objections to this arrangement were overruled by the determined naa and we were left with no immediate alternative solution. But in fact the people got tired of working for nothing on the whim of their chief, and progress was slow. They would arrive at the building site at ten or eleven o'clock and leave at two or three in the afternoon.

When Brother Basilide finally arrived to complete the community of three White Fathers and supervise construction, his deep Dutch regard for thriftiness would not left him rest until he had remedied the situation. Before long he had decided that the mission needed a permanent building-and-maintenance staff, not a merely temporary and "voluntary" corps of helpers. Under that pretext, he was able to hire the men he needed and train them.[5] Three months later, the first permanent mission house and chapel in Jirapa were completed.

Meanwhile, we were encountering several roadblocks in the way of our apostolate. The first of these was the natural suspicion of our motives on the part of the people. The fact that we seemed to be friends of the colonial power did nothing to lessen it. On the contrary. Many harboured real hostility toward us as a result. Even the children hid from us, warned by their elders of the various misfortunes that would certainly befall them — if not at our hands, at theirs — if they went near the strangers. Not all the people shared this hostility, of course, and Chief Ganaa was affable enough in his own way. But peer pressure was strong and no one lingered long in our company.

However, most men have been boys once upon a time, and we were no exception to the rule. We still knew a thing or two about the psychology of those energetic and inquisitive little bundles of "snips and snails and puppy dogs' tails", so adored by their mothers and often detested by their little sisters.

One day we brought a soccer ball out from our meagre stores and began to kick it around among ourselves. Though we couldn't see them at first, we knew that more than one pair of small eyes was observing us from afar. We ignored them and began to enjoy ourselves. (There is no law that says the apostolate cannot be fun.) In the measure that we did, the circle of observers began to draw closer. Fear slowly gave way to curiosity, which in turn succumbed to an almost uncontrollable urge to be a part of the fun. Even some of the grown-ups had stopped to watch and enjoy, laughing at our antics — it was no very graceful exhibition, trying to run with a ball while attired from head to foot in long robes! — and growing excited despite themselves at our efforts to steal the ball from one another as we whooped and hollered from one end of the makeshift pitch to the other.

Some of the braver lads drew even closer. Hector Awia and Ludger, the cook, invited them to join in. They still hung back, but when the ball suddenly escaped us and rolled toward them, the last strand of resistance snapped and they were on it in a flash. Pandemonium ensued as dozens of small bodies all tried to kick it at the same time. We intervened to bring order and impart a few very fundamental pointers on technique and the object of the game. Rules would come later.

That day the ice was broken. In the days and weeks that followed, the soccer ball continued to be an effective instrument of the apostolate. An indirect one, to be sure; but hadn't Jesus Himself used a cup of water to approach the Samaritan woman at the well and a lifestyle free of prejudice against the outcasts of society to draw people to Him? Just imagine what He might have done with a soccer ball!

A second roadblock impeding our work among the people was the language barrier. Nothing but application and perspiration would overcome this one.

The Dagaabas speak Dagaare, a tongue having nothing in common with Kassem, the language spoken in Navrongo, 140 miles to the west. Moreover, as there were no schools in the Northwest and no interest in the language outside the area in which it was spoken, it had never been written down. No dictionary had ever been compiled and there was no book of Dagaare grammar. Ludger, who was from Navrongo, spoke Moré and Nankam (besides his native Kassem), and he was soon able to understand and speak Dagaare well enough to act as interpreter. A bit later I had the good fortune to find in the chief's compound a Gurense-Wala man who spoke Kassem. His name was Laagi and he became our first Dagaare teacher.

Anyone who has ever had to learn a second language knows that there is no substitute for hard work. There are individuals who are able to pick up a language with relative ease. I have met quite a number of them; they are nearly all between the ages of three and four. They use the Direct Method to perfection, listening and repeating what they hear, being corrected, and repeating the correction again and again and again until it sticks in the little sponges they call brains. At that age they have no complexes and are not afraid to make mistakes. Communication is the important thing. They are indefatigable in their pursuit of a working knowledge of the language, most often exhausting their parents' patience long before they exhaust their own.

Something similar to that now occurred between Laagi and me as I set about trying to learn Dagaare in the shortest possible time. Each day he came to the mission to coach me in the fundamentals of the language, and each day when he had gone I went out and practised every word and phrase he had just tried to

teach me. They were practical things I needed in order to communicate with the workers and with the people who came to the
mission in increasing numbers to see these mysterious white men
who had apparently evicted the evil spirits from the site. At first
I learned enough to be able to ask questions. Like a modern-day
tourist using a phrase book in a foreign country, I knew what I
was asking (most of the time), but the relative unpredictability
of the answers usually meant that I ended up none the wiser for
having asked the question. In these encounters, the people were
patient, kind, and always good-humoured. They appreciated the
effort I was making to learn their tongue. It meant I valued them
enough to want to use their culture as the bridge between us
rather than oblige them to adopt mine. They had yet to see a
colonial official who did as much. (There were some, of course,
but they were the exceptions to the rule, and none of those had
been posted to the Northwest.)

Gradually, through Laagi's efforts and my own, my ear began
to identify speech patterns and to understand the answers to my
questions. In the evenings, like the parent bird feeding its young,
I would transmit to Father Paquet and Brother Basilide what I
had learned of the language during the day.

At the end of three and a half months, I felt confident enough
to make my first public speech to the Dagaabas. It was the feast
of Saint Joseph, 19 March 1930, and the occasion of the completion
and blessing of our new permanent mission house and chapel. We
had decided to buy a cow and some rice and to invite our workers
and their families to join us in celebrating the event. While the
food was being prepared, I began to explain to the people the
real purpose of our presence among them. My message was simple
and my speech short — a winning formula at any banquet.

"We have come to tell you something wonderful," I began,
"something you could never have imagined possible. God has sent
His Son to us. He has come on this earth to make us all children
of His Father. But if we are all children of His Father, then we
are brothers and sisters of the Son. And if we are all brothers
and sisters of the Son, we are also brothers and sisters of one
another. We are one family, the family of God.

"God loves each and every one of you, and He wants you to
be happy. He is happy. In His home, everyone is happy; and that

is why He wants you to be there with Him one day. He has sent us to Jirapa because He wants you to be happy even now, in this life. So we try to cure your diseases. We want to open schools, too, so that one day your sons and daughters may be able to enjoy a better life and help to make life better for you, too." The rest I left to the Holy Spirit.

Explanations had to be very simple to avoid losing my listeners in theological subtleties and myself in a syntactical labyrinth. Years before, the Muslims had come to the area and had told the people to pray and to abstain from all fermented drink, and that by doing these two things they would find God. (At this time, that was all the Dagaabas knew of Muslim teaching.) It would have been difficult to surpass that in simplicity.

We had invited Chief Ganaa, of course, and were relieved when he arrived with only a modest retinue. Had he brought his entire household, our poor cow would have provided scarcely the equivalent of a hamburger apiece to the assembled guests.

He rose now to speak. On behalf of all his people, he wanted to welcome us again to Jirapa and tell us how happy he was that we had come to live among them. He hoped that we would indeed improve the health of the people as there was much sickness in the place. Many were unable to farm their fields because of weakness resulting from disease, and every day people died from lack of medical care. The old remedies no longer seemed to work and the new ones prescribed by the traditional healers often seemed worse than the maladies they were supposed to cure. It was all very worrying. If we could help in any way, he and his people would know how to show their gratitude.

He too kept his discourse short, ending it by saying that all the Dagaabas believed in the Supreme Being, the Creator of the world, and that he and his people would surely come to learn to pray.

He did not say when.

5

Reaching Out

It had been clear from the start that eventually health care would have to be a priority of our ministry among the Dagaabas. On our visits to the villages around Jirapa, as in Jirapa itself, we were constantly made to witness the cruel ravages of disease; much of it, we felt, preventable. Yaws, guinea worm, dysentery, conjunctivitis, malaria, sleeping sickness, and leprosy were among the prevalent maladies. Taking our cue from the chief's speech at the blessing of the new mission house, we decided to seek government authorization to open a clinic.

The work would not be entirely new to us. At that time the White Fathers' program of studies in Algeria included a condensed course in tropical medicine taught by a very practical Sicilian physician, Doctor Sabidini. And I had also had some experience working with Father Dagenais in the dispensary at our Navrongo mission clinic.

We contacted Captain Armstrong at Lawra and offered to open a clinic at Jirapa if the approval and cooperation of the medical department could be obtained. The DC was favourable to our proposal. All such help was welcome, he said, and he would contact the director of medical services in Accra immediately to discuss the matter with him. At the same time, he informed us that a medical officer had been appointed to Lawra who might be able to help us.

A short time later, the principal medical officer, residing at Tamale, visited us and gave his wholehearted approval for the proposed clinic, promising to send over some medical supplies for it. He was as good as his word. On 28 March 1930, Doctor Seth-Smith of Lawra arrived with four cases of supplies for the clinic and a good quantity of Sobita solution to be used for injecting yaws patients.

Doctor Seth-Smith was a man dedicated to the welfare of the people and a credit to his profession. One short tour of the area was all he needed to see for himself the enormity of the problem. The amount of disease and suffering — nearly all of it borne resignedly — visibly impressed him. If the clinic caught hold among the people, and there was no reason why it should not, it might well be swamped. Before returning to Lawra that day, he told us that even though he would rely on us for the effective continuity of the medical care of the people, he would not leave us orphans. If possible, he would come to Jirapa every week to help.

At first a weekly clinic was started on the verandah of the mission house. The doctor would come, bringing medical supplies from Accra which he supplemented from his own stock, to train us in diagnosing and treating the most common ailments in the region. He would have us give the treatments ourselves in his presence.

"I want the people to gain confidence in you," he said. "I can be here only occasionally, whereas you will be here whenever they need you."

In the beginning many were reluctant to come, not because they feared our inexperience, but because they believed that all sickness (and every misfortune, for that matter) was caused by spirits — either evil spirits or the spirits of their ancestors whom they had offended in some way. They would consult the local witch doctor to find the cause of their problem and the means to put it right. It was only after repeated failure in this quarter that they would finally decide to try the missionaries and their medicine.

Our first medical case of importance, in terms of instant impact on the people, took place near the mission in a part of Jirapa called Zokyiere.[1] A man returned from the market and fainted upon entering his compound. His younger brother came running to tell us that he was dying. When I reached the scene, accompanied by our steward, Hector Awia, I found the man still unconscious, his face a sickly gray and his respiration weak. The smelling salts brought no reaction whatsoever. There was some brandy at the mission which was kept for medicinal purposes, so I sent Hector to fetch it. He had to make his way through a crowd of several hundred persons, including Chief Ganaa, to get out of the compound.

As the crowd looked on with a mixture of fear and curiosity, I began to speak to the man as though he could hear me. He was a person who came to church occasionally, so with that in mind I proceeded to instruct him in preparation for baptism. (There was still a possibility that he could hear me even though he could not respond.) I spoke of it as entering a new life: "God's way". The crowd was attentive to my every word and gesture. I had just finished baptizing the man conditionally when Father Paquet arrived with the brandy. We forced a small amount down the man's throat, and in a few moments the pallor left his face and he began to breathe normally. Suddenly he opened his eyes and began to speak.

The chief was dumfounded. When he had recovered from his initial surprise, he turned to his people, who were just as astonished as he was, and told them: "What the father has just said about God wanting to share His life with us must be true because this man was dead and he has come back to life!"

It soon became necessary to build a small dispensary. The mission house verandah was no longer adequate or suitable as patients began to arrive in ever-increasing numbers.[2] One of the reasons for this was our early success in treating yaws *(frambesia)*, a horrible and highly infectious tropical skin disease caused by a spirochete *(treponema pertenue)* and characterized by raspberry-like sores all over the body. The source of much suffering, in extreme cases it could cripple the limbs. Yaws was very prevalent throughout the country at that time. Yet with only seven weekly injections of Sobita solution, it was possible to cure it completely. (Today one or two shots of penicillin will do the same.)[3]

As word of our spectacular success in treating yaws began to reach beyond Jirapa, patients from all over the surrounding country started to come for treatment of every kind of ailment including sleeping sickness and leprosy — and not just one day a week, as in the beginning, but every day. As many cases of yaws were treated as it was possible for us to handle each day, and sometimes dozens of other ailments as well. It was not unusual for us to give 150 injections of Sobita in a single morning.

The daily routine of the clinic would begin with a prayer aimed at reminding our patients that the curative power of the medicines and the care dispensed was a result of God's great love for them as His children. We were conscious of our primary role as ambassadors of Jesus Christ to the people of the Northwest. And so there was a constant effort on our part not only to make them aware of it but also to keep ourselves from forgetting it as a natural consequence of the long hours spent treating the sick each day at the clinic or in their homes.

Part of our efforts to fight disease in the area involved frequent visits to the surrounding villages to treat those who were too ill or unwilling to come to Jirapa. We would take turns visiting them on our bicycles, a small medical kit strapped to our backs.

On one such visit, Hector Awia and I came across a large group of men and women sitting in silence around Nameri, the headman of the village of Konkwa. Even before we reached him, we could tell he was very ill. The sick man was sitting under a tree, held by his brother who sprinkled water on him to cool his feverish body. As the people expected him to expire at any moment, they were just waiting for the last flicker of life to extinguish itself before starting the funeral rites.

I got down off my bicycle and greeted the brother and those near him. No objection was made when I asked if I could examine Nameri, so I proceeded to do so, questioning his relatives about the symptoms of his illness. He was clearly dying of dysentery. (In those days, dysentery was a frequent killer in Africa.) As I prepared to give him an injection of Emetine solution, I suggested to the brother that he cover the sick man rather than chill him with water. All this time the people continued to watch quietly, but the quality of their silence had changed.

Before leaving, I prescribed a diet of rice water for the patient, to be followed later by unseasoned rice. I do not know whether it was just to humour me or because they had been impressed by the syringe and needle, but they did as I told them despite the fact that Nameri did look as if he would die at any moment. For the next few days I visited him morning and afternoon in his compound. At the end of that time, Nameri got well.

All the witnesses — and there were many — agreed that this was indeed a "miracle", for a man on the very brink of death had been pulled back and restored to health. I replied that God was the real master of life and death, not any mere mortal, and that the life that comes from Him is stronger than death. From that day on, Nameri and his villagers became friendly toward the missionaries.

Among the many ailments we treated at the Jirapa mission clinic in those early days, some were curable, others were not. Conjunctivitis was one of the easier challenges we faced. People would be brought to us with swollen, pus-filled eyes, unable to see out of them. After a few days of treatment with nothing but hot compresses, they returned to their villages with clear vision and a new lease on life.

For malaria, we had quinine which gave relief in most acute cases. Limited supplies of epsom salts, bismuth, and Emetine solution were available for intestinal disorders. In some cases of pneumonia we used what was called "fixation abcess treatment", in which turpentine or the like was injected just beneath the skin on the leg. (Penicillin and sulfa drugs had not yet been discovered.)[4]

Among the most heartbreaking cases we were called upon to treat were those of leprosy. Sulfon treatment, which would be so effective in arresting the dread disease one day, was still a long way off. All we could do was to give our leprosy patients injections of chromogrol oil as we had been taught to do and bandage some of their sores. We did not notice much improvement from the chromogrol oil treatments, but the afflicted seemed to draw benefit of another sort from the care we gave them. They found it wonderful that anyone should show practical concern for their welfare.

Sleeping sickness *(trypanosomiasis)* was also prevalent in the area then. On one occasion, there was a severe outbreak of it in

Gbare village. I alerted Doctor Brennan, an Irish Catholic who had succeeded Doctor Seth-Smith as medical officer in Lawra. He came immediately, examined the entire village, and found that forty-six per cent of the seemingly healthy inhabitants were infected with the disease and didn't know it. These and the more advanced cases were given a series of treatments that eventually put an end to the Gbare epidemic.

When Doctor Brennan notified his superiors of the situation and of the danger of the disease spreading, the government decided to act boldly and decisively. They contacted French officials across the border and quickly reached an agreement to mount a combined effort to search out and destroy the breeding grounds of the tsetse fly, principal carrier of the sickness. As this fly breeds in shaded still water and stagnant pools, the underbrush was cut to expose the water to the sun and kill the larvae. Within a few years, sleeping sickness had been eliminated from the whole area on both sides of the border.

Many were cured of their maladies through our medical efforts in that first Jirapa mission clinic. Whenever that happened, our satisfaction was as great as that of the patient in question, and we could understand something of the beauty of the physician's calling. The medical profession and the priesthood, after all, have much in common. Perhaps the most important is that they are best served — and the people, too — when they are viewed and practised as vocations first and professions second.

On the other hand, many who came to us for help were not cured despite our best efforts. Often they were brought to us by their families as a last resort, when it was already too late to do anything effective for them. But even then they were grateful for the efforts made on their behalf and the kindness shown them. One of the characteristics of the Dagaabas, we were to find, was their well-developed sense of gratitude.

I remember my surprise when the husband of a woman who had recently died, despite our attempts to save her, appeared at the mission one day with a gift of a fowl and some yams. He was from nearby Nyenne, and he had come to thank us, he said.

"How is it you thank me and yet I was not able to save your wife's life?" I asked. The surprise must have shown in my voice because he looked at me kindly for a moment before replying.

"Did you not visit her several times and do all you could for her?" he said finally. "That is what I have come to thank you for."

It was humbling many times to see the capacity these people had for patient suffering and the appreciation they showed for any little service extended to them. They had come to understand that the missionaries were different from government officials. Dedicated as many of them were to their welfare, government officials were paid functionaries. They were conscious of doing a job they did not particularly like, but one that might get them promoted to a more congenial post the next time their name came up for consideration. Most did not mix with those of a different colour or social class, except when performing their functions. And they had a way of disappearing for good after a few years.

The missionaries were different. They came and they stayed. They had left their home countries, which the people felt sure must be very rich and very comfortable, to come and help them. They spoke their language, visited them in their homes, took care of their sick, and attended their funerals to offer their sympathy. They even drank pito with them. The people were grateful, though they did not always understand why the missionaries did these things. This sense of gratitude gives one a clue to the reason (in addition to God's grace) for which the Dagaabas would prove so receptive finally to the Good News of His love for them.

6

Spirits

The Dagaabas were a God-conscious people, yet they never prayed to Him directly. They always approached Him through intermediaries: either the spirits of their ancestors or the *tengaama* (the spirits of the land or earth).

It was not difficult to speak to them about God because, as Chief Ganaa had reminded us, they believed in Him and had always done so as far back as they could remember in their collective history. Common daily exchanges among them included "God be with you", "God guide you", "God knows", etc. The idea of God as Creator was not new to them either. He was the All-Powerful Supreme Being, Master of all creation, whom they respected rather than loved. He was too "big", too important, too aloof, and too far away — "in heaven" — to have anything in common with them or to permit them to address Him directly. In the relationship that existed between the Deity and the Dagaabas, there was no possibility for love to intervene.

Though they were very conscious of the concept of sin, the idea of Redemption was unknown to them. They tried to do what was right, and in this they were guided by strict laws reinforced by punishments to suit infringements, all according to local tradition. Wrongs had to be put right by sacrifices and fines. Yet in all this concern for moral uprightness, they were less preoccupied with the Divinity than they were with trying to pacify evil or disgruntled spirits.

For example, if a couple were caught in the act of adultery or fornication in a field, they would be punished not because they had sinned against God in any way but because they had profaned the earth whose spirit was a very powerful and vengeful one.

If someone was seriously ill or dying, the elders would be summoned to the person's bedside to try to get him to confess what he had done wrong. He would have to make amends for the wrongdoing before entering the company of the spirits, otherwise he would face exclusion from that company and be sent back to earth, perhaps in a different life form — that of an animal, for instance. Hence the taboos on killing and eating the flesh of certain animals. Again, the point was not that one had perhaps offended God, but simply that one who broke the rules of the game was barred from the club.

Belief in the power of ancestors and evil spirits led to a deformation in the understanding of what constituted a sinful act. Because they believed that misfortune of any kind had its source in the displeasure or anger of spirits, a "sinful" act was not necessarily always an intentional act. Spirits were easily offended; they were jealous of their prerogatives and especially sensitive to neglect, whether deliberate or not, on the part of those who served them.

Sometimes it was not clear if it was the ancestors or evil spirits who were causing a particular misfortune. In such a case, the witch doctor would be consulted to determine the cause and to prescribe sacrifices of appeasement. These latter usually consisted of a chicken or perhaps a goat. If it was a family or community matter — a serious crime, for instance, or a plea for rain in time of drought — the sacrifice of a cow might be required.

There was one particular evil spirit, called *suobo*, that held great sway among the Dagaabas and Sissalas. They believed that the suobo took possession of a human being (usually, as it turned out, a defenceless old woman) whom it then used to enter the compound of its enemy at night for the purpose of eating his or her soul, thereby causing death. They visualized the soul as a person's double, free to leave the body and wander about whenever the person slept. The one possessed by the suobo had the power to capture the unwary soul and either devour it on the spot or keep it in reserve for some future punishment.

Whenever a death aroused suspicion, especially if it concerned that of a young or relatively young person, the kin and/or friends of the deceased would consult the witch doctor to discover the identity of the one possessed by the suobo. It was considered to be of the utmost importance for the whole community that the soul-eater be found and put to death before he or she could kill again. For this purpose the witch doctor used a procedure called "carrying the mat".[1]

The mat in question was composed of a piece of sleeping mat about six feet long rolled around a reed or stick to make it firm for carrying. Two people, one at either end, carried it on their heads while the witch doctor walked along striking it with a reed held in his left hand. The mat was supposed to lead them to the guilty one or to any place where the suobo had stashed the souls it had been catching. Sometimes the mat led them to climb trees, scale rooftops, or (as happened once, I was told) to crawl into a crocodile hole on the bank of a river! If the possessed one was present when they reached the place to which they had been directed, the mat-bearers would be "irresistibly" drawn to the person. A sideways motion of their heads in the direction of the culprit and beating the mat three times over him or her (allowing it to come in physical contact with the accused) would announce that this was the one responsible for the untimely death under investigation. If the one being sought was not there when the mat-bearers arrived, it was enough to strike a piece of clothing or some other possession belonging to the person to indicate guilt.[2]

There was a saying to the effect that a rich man or someone with relatives and friends would never be accused of being possessed by the suobo because they had the means to defend themselves. Poor persons who had no relatives and were alone in the world, especially poor widows, were the ones most vulnerable to persecution as witches or wizards.

One day a young woman of about thirty years of age came to see me at the mission. Her body was covered with cuts and bruises, obviously from a severe beating. Since the language she spoke was unfamiliar to me, I could not understand what she was trying to say. I assumed it had something to do with her wounds. Indicating by gestures that she should wait, I went off to fetch what was necessary to wash and treat them. When I returned a short time later, the woman was gone. Given the pitiable state she was in, I was surprised at her abrupt departure. Hector Awia was there, looking (or so it seemed to me) a bit uncomfortable. I asked him where the woman had gone. There was a slight hesitation before he spoke.

"She did not go away," he replied, "the people chased her away. They say she is a suobo. She was going to eat up your soul until you became ill and died, Father. They wanted to protect you."

It was only later that I learned the rest. She had been chased for two miles into the bush and there stoned to death. For fear the suobo might enter one of them, her pursuers refused to touch her body. Instead, they used sticks to prod it into a shallow pit they had dug, covering it over with earth and leaves.

We immediately informed the DC in Lawra, who was somewhat less than enthusiastic about investigating the incident. He cut off any further discussion of the matter by stating categorically that the chiefs did not allow witch hunts to take place anymore.

Later on, the chief regional commissioner in Tamale sent me a letter chiding me for my naiveté in believing the stories the catechists told me. I replied to the letter point by point. Since I had carefully recorded every single incident of suobo "possession" that had come to my attention, I had ten typewritten pages of documentation (single-spaced) to send him. At the end I added:

"We know the local language and do not rely on an interpreter. We have the advantage of direct access to the people. They are not afraid of us. These incidents of the suobo can be vouched for not only by catechists and other Christians but by animists as well."

The documentation must have impressed the Tamale official, who had been rather uncooperative until then, because he replied in an apologetic tone that he had never doubted the sincerity of the missionaries, and he instructed the DCs under him to be more friendly and cooperative toward us in the future.

Meanwhile, we had decided that if we could not fight the suobo directly, we could at least rob it of some of its prospective victims.

There was a vacant compound on the mission property which had been there before our arrival. Its original tenants, a Mr. Wotare and his family, had moved to a new compound built for them by the mission a few months earlier. Wotare's old house and compound would become the refuge for the so-called witches of the area.

We informed the DC that we were going to open a hostel for these people on mission property to guarantee that what he assured us did not happen would not happen quite so often in the future.

Word soon got around to the villages that the white men of God had a place of refuge for persons falsely accused of being witches. In a short time the "refugees" began to arrive. Many women, most of them old, came to the compound and enjoyed relative peace and security there. Occasionally a man would appear at the mission seeking our protection, but men seemed much less vulnerable to this type of persecution.

One day the chief came to see us with something on his mind. We were foreigners, he told us, and did not know his people. Those we had given refuge to were bad people and until we got rid of them our lives would be in great danger. They might go into our rooms at night while we slept and eat up our souls until we died.

We listened respectfully to what he had to say and thanked him for his concern. But we assured him we were not afraid and urged him not to be either, because those who came to the refuge were not the bad people they were reported to be. We visited them regularly and spoke with them. We had listened to their stories, one by one, and knew only that they were clearly innocent of the accusations made against them. The real culprits to be feared, we said, were those who had falsely accused them and condemned them to death. If any "possession" had taken place, it was of the accusers and not of their victims.

The chief was not convinced. When his momentary shock at this last comment of ours had subsided, a look of annoyance replaced it. The concentration of these people in the heart of Jirapa was proving to be a problem of another kind. Since they frequently ventured out to the market to buy food, something the chief did not want them to do, their very presence was disruptive and detrimental to the village economy. The villagers were afraid to go to the market if there was the danger of meeting "witches" there. Business was suffering; and if business suffered, so would revenues.

Years later, when there were up to fifty persons taking refuge at the mission at one time (some with their children), I gathered information on the villages they came from and especially on the people who had been instrumental in chasing them away. When the details were complete, we called a meeting of the chiefs of all the villages concerned, including the Jirapa naa, and representatives of the various families of those villages as well. The British administration cooperated this time, sending an open-minded DC to investigate the cases one by one.

With each case, the headman of the village involved would try to prove to the satisfaction of the DC that the victim of persecution was in fact a witch. There was no proof, of course, and where witnesses did not contradict one another outright in their testimony, they were invariably reduced to confusion when shown that they might just as easily have been accused of the same crime on the basis of their own relations with the "murdered" person or through a different interpretation of incidents from their lives than the one they claimed.

When the last case had been heard and the DC had declared all of the accused innocent, he gave the assembly a warning to carry home with it.

"These people have been guilty of no crime. They must not be prevented from returning to their villages and homes if they wish to do so. Let it be known to all that they are free and protected by law."

But he gave more weight to his decree by convoking a meeting of all the village headmen at his headquarters in Lawra. When they had all assembled, he proceeded to let them sit in the blistering sun for three days to soften them up and make them feel uneasy. At last he called them together, warned them yet more strongly on the matter, and allowed them to go.

The DC's deterrent action served to reinforce the British colonial government's law prohibiting the practice of "carrying the mat". Thereafter, whenever the odd case came up, the people knew they could go to the DC for help and he would apply the law.

As a result, most of those in our refuge did return to their villages, except for one couple and a woman with three children. In their cases, we had been unable to discover the identities of those responsible for driving them from their villages. The DC and Chief Ganaa had decided that if any of the refugees wished to remain at the mission, their families could no longer have any claims on them. And if they should marry, the dowry was to go to the mission!

Later, one of the girls, Madeline, did marry. As superior of Jirapa mission, I accepted the dowry solely because of the principle at stake. But since the mission had in fact brought her up and provided for her, and the head of the family normally accepts the dowry given for his daughter, it was fitting that the mission accept Madeline's dowry.

All through this difficult period, the Dagaabas were constantly amazed at our lack of fear or concern at the grave danger posed by the proximity of the witches' refuge to the mission house. They came to believe, correctly, that we enjoyed the protection of a Spirit more powerful than the suobo. As they no longer "saw" any evil spirits hanging about the area, they said that our Protector must have chased the suobo from the once-haunted site of the mission.

In time, faith in a God all-powerful yet infinitely loving would disperse their continual fear of spirits. That moment was not as far off for some of them as it perhaps seemed to us at the time.

NORTHWEST GOLD COAST
1929

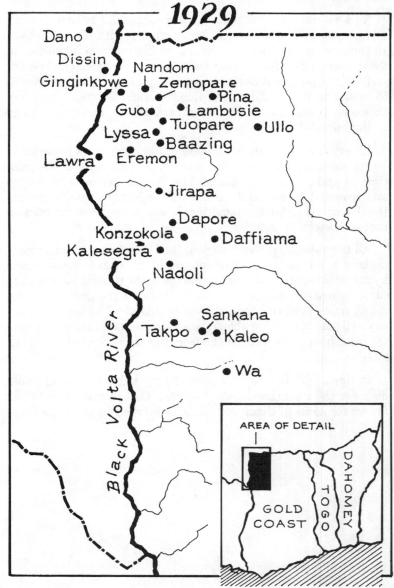

Dano

Dissin

Nandom

Ginginkpwe · Zemopare

Pina

Guo · Lambusie

Tuopare · Ullo

Lyssa · Baazing

Lawra · Eremon

Jirapa

Dapore

Konzokola · Daffiama

Kalesegra

Nadoli

Sankana

Takpo · Kaleo

Wa

Black Volta River

AREA OF DETAIL

GOLD COAST

TOGO

DAHOMEY

7

First Fruits

During the first eight months at Jirapa, we lost no opportunity to impress upon the people our principal reason for being there. We were messengers of Jesus Christ sent by Him, as He Himself had been sent by His Father, to expand and enrich their knowledge of God and to call them to a new dignity as members of His family. It was in learning to love as well as respect Him and, in Him, one another that their God-given potential to enjoy His love and share His happiness forever would be fully realized one day.

People came to Mass occasionally, even in the early days before anyone in the Northwest had shown any interest in becoming a Christian. Some of these were persons who had been cured of illnesses or treated in some way at the mission clinic. Others were attracted by the solemnity, to which they were accustomed in their own sacred rites, or the ornamental trappings (poor enough by any standard but theirs), or simply out of curiosity. The chief was one of those who attended Mass daily, though it would have been difficult to know why. I always suspected it was because of his promise to the district and provincial commissioners to be good to us. Once he was especially good to us when he showed up at Mass accompanied by thirteen of his fifty wives. It was his presence that kept attendance down, however. The people of Jirapa were afraid of him. He was a wily man whose reactions were not always easily predictable.

But the main reason for the hesitation of the Dagaabas to embrace Christianity was their natural cautiousness. The decision to break with the "old ways" and risk incurring the anger of their ancestors was a big leap they were not yet ready to take. Who could be certain what lay on the other side? A commitment to Christ demanded a new way of life, and they were not prepared to give up their ancestral beliefs and well-worn customs so easily.

Then, in August 1930, less than a year after our arrival in Jirapa, the first tender shoots of a future harvest suddenly appeared. Two brothers, Kyefondeme and Yelesigra, announced their desire to become Christians. They belonged to a family of six brothers whose father, Gala, was a prominent member of Jirapa society. The area where they lived was called Galayiri, that is, "Gala's home".

Like many others at that time, four of the brothers were employed as labourers at the new mission. Kyefondeme, who was one of the chief's headmen, had worked as a mason during the building of the first mud-brick mission house and chapel. Yelesigra had also had daily contact with the missionaries as a labourer.

On the day of their decision, the two brothers went to inform their cousin, Chief Ganaa, of it.

"We have been watching these white men ever since they arrived," they told him. "We have listened to all they have told us about God, of what He has done for us and of what He wants to do for us. And we have decided to leave the way we have known until now and follow their way."

Ganaa's reply was brief but generous. "You are old enough to know your own minds," he said. "Personally, I have no objections, though I cannot say what the reaction of the people will be." And he added that he might join them one day.[1]

Elated, the brothers made their way to the mission to tell us of their decision and to ask to be instructed in the Ngwinsore (Way of God).

Through these first two Dagati converts to Christianity, many more would be brought to follow Christ, among them three more of their brothers: Bagile, Dosogla, and Ninang. Kyefondeme was especially effective in attracting adherents to Christ. He was a born leader and would become our first head catechist. A quiet, unassuming man by nature, he taught as much by his life and example as by his words.

Of the six sons of Gala, Bagile was the eldest. He was already head of his compound when we arrived in Jirapa. It was a large one, inhabited by his four wives, his children by them, and four of his brothers and their wives and families. The remaining brother, Dosogla, lived with his four wives and their children in his own compound about half a mile away.

Bagile was an industrious and clever man whose hands were seldom still. Whenever he travelled, it was always with an axe slung over his shoulder which he would use to carve stools in the form of wild animals from any block of wood he could find along the way. If there was nothing to carve, his fingers would be busy spinning cotton thread. He was also a good mason when it came to building the traditional compounds. When the five huts forming the temporary mission compound were built on our arrival, it was he who laid out the foundations. He did this in a remarkable way. Once the brambles and stones had been cleared, he examined the spot for a moment. Then, putting his right foot forward, and free of any exterior assistance, he began to trace in the dust a perfect circle about fifteen feet in diameter. He repeated this feat for each of the five huts. (While the bricks were being made, he kept busy at his wood carving.)

Bagile was a *kontoma* priest, and a popular one. He inspired confidence in his quiet way, much as his younger brother Kyefondeme did, and got along well with everyone, with the result that people came from far and wide to consult him. The kontoma were benevolent spirits, somewhat like the household gods of Roman antiquity, whose job it was to protect the home and its inhabitants from the influence of evil spirits. The priest, when asked, would make a kontoma figure which the petitioner then took and installed in a place of honor in the family compound. Sacrifices were offered to it regularly. In return for the service, the priest was given a sheep or a goat. The emblems of his office were iron bangles which he wore on his ankles.

When Kyefondeme became a Christian catechumen, he persuaded Bagile to break with the animistic beliefs and pagan traditions of the Dagaabas and follow Christ instead. This involved a considerable sacrifice since he not only had to renounce the thriving practice of his kontoma priesthood, but he also had to send away three of his four wives. One of these had grown children to look after her. The two other younger ones went home to their father's house.

By the time Bagile entered the first catechumenate at the mission, he was already fairly old, so that it was not easy for him to grasp some points of Christian doctrine or to memorize prayer formulas. But he showed great good will, tenacity, and patience, and attended religious instructions faithfully. When tested on his knowledge, it was clear that he retained and understood the essentials of doctrine and had the gift of faith. He too would become a model for the early Christian community of Jirapa.

Another brother, Dosogla (meaning "black man"), was a prosperous farmer and an influential man in the region. When he too became a Christian, people were furious and some of them threatened to kill him if he did not forsake Christianity and take back his wives. But Dosogla had made his decision and no amount of effort at intimidation could shake him from it. Two or three years after his baptism (which took place in 1933), he fell ill with a serious case of diarrhea which no medicine seemed able to cure. He was convinced that someone had poisoned him, as his enemies had threatened to do so many times since his conversion, but he forgave them and prayed for them as he lay dying.

At his large funeral, some of the people began to sing dirges directed against his brother Bagile. "You gave up all to follow the white man's religion. You were rich and influential; now you are poor and worth nothing," they taunted him. "What did Christianity profit you?"

Bagile grew angry when he heard these songs being sung at his expense, but there was little he could do about it. When he could stand it no longer, he left the scene and took refuge in the mission chapel. He was just leaving it as I returned from the town. Surprised to find him there, I asked him why he had not stayed at his brother's funeral. He told me calmly what had happened and of his anger against the people who had mocked him publicly. He had let them get the best of him, he admitted, but it would not happen again. In the chapel he had prayed for strength and the Lord had made him understand that He too had suffered in much the same way. "If these people can make me more like Christ," he told me, "I'll be happy." Even a seasoned Christian could not have offered a better response to the situation.

All but one of the six sons of Gala embraced the Christian faith, and that one asked to be baptized before he died. He had followed a long catechumenate during his lifetime, never quite able to make up his mind. But when the moment came, he was well-prepared for it. He and his brothers left a solid Christian heritage that has passed from one generation to the next.

The courageous brothers Gala had a counterpart in the North named Poreku. He had been born and raised in Tizza, but the family had later moved to Zemopare in Ko district. At home he had little opportunity to display his talents, being a second child much overshadowed by his elder brother who was head of the four-family compound and the leading witch doctor or fetishist of the area.

But Poreku was an enterprising young man with a resilient spirit that would not permit him to be dominated for long. As soon as the farming was done, he would head north to Mossi country to buy quantities of cloth from the Mossi weavers and sell it at a profit in Dagati markets all over the Northwest. Thus he earned himself a bit of cash and acquired considerable knowledge of the region and its people.

On one of his marketing trips, Poreku learned that the white men had come to Jirapa. Not only did they cure people of illness, he was told, but they had been sent by God to teach the Dagaabas a "new way" to serve Him because He loved them and had sent His Son down on earth to prove it. Poreku was intrigued. Then and there he decided to go and see these white men to find out what it was all about.

On his way to the mission, all sorts of questions about what he had been told came to his mind, so that once we had been introduced they came tumbling out one after another. Did God really have a Son? And had that Son really come down on this same earth we were living on? Where? When? How was it that they had never heard of it before? What about the spirits? If God's

Son was killed, were they stronger than He was? What does God want of us now?... When, among other things, I told him that the Ngwinsore did not authorize polygamy, Poreku's vivacity dimmed and he seemed a bit sad.

"I would like to become a Christian," he said after a long moment, "but how can I? I have five wives."

It was not hard to detect the genuineness of his disappointment. The simplicity and artlessness of this man gave one the feeling, even after barely an hour's acquaintance, of having known him all one's life. His predicament was not unique by any means, polygamy being the rule rather than the exception in Dagati society. For this reason and several others, the introduction of Christianity would produce an authentic revolution in values in the Northwest, often demanding real heroism on the part of these early converts from traditional religious beliefs.

"I know that the problem is not a small one," I said sympathetically, "but let's not try to solve it right now. Go home and start praying to God for His help, and come to the mission as often as you can. I am sure you will find the way and the strength to do whatever He wants you to do."

Poreku went directly home to Zemopare, twenty-two miles away, and related to his wives and children all that the white man at Jirapa had told him. They listened attentively, punctuating his report from time to time with exclamations of surprise, amazement, or incredulity, as they always did when he returned from his trips and told them of all he had seen and heard. But when he announced his intention of going down to Jirapa each week to learn how to pray, and invited any of them who wished to do so to accompany him, the wives were silent. Only Dery, his eldest son, then about 12 years old, expressed interest in doing so.

One of the barriers to Poreku's own going was his elder brother, Ngmankurinaa, who disapproved of it.[2] The least of his objections was that the decision had been taken too hastily. But despite his brother's disapproval, Poreku began to go down to Jirapa to learn how to pray. Each week he would make the forty-four mile round trip on foot. And each week he would return more convinced than ever that he had made the right decision. He was very impressed by what he was learning, so impressed in fact that he did not hesitate to risk incurring his brother's wrath by openly trying to influence his relatives and friends to follow his example by giving up their animistic practices and going to Jirapa to enroll as followers of Christ.

Ngmankurinaa was infuriated by the way Poreku seemed to defy his authority as head of the compound in this matter. But when he discovered that he was trying to lead others in the village to forsake traditional worship too, he grew alarmed and determined to put a stop to it once and for all. It would not be easy; he knew his younger brother to be a strong-willed individual whose mind it was almost impossible to change once he had set it firmly on an objective. If the authority of the head of the family was unable to sway him, perhaps that of the spirits could.

The next time Poreku returned from the mission, Ngmankurinaa was waiting for him. "I have consulted *Konkpenebie*," the witch doctor told him solemnly, "and the spirit has instructed me to warn you and your kontoma to stop going to Jirapa at once!"

Poreku became very angry at this transparent effort on the part of his elder brother to impose his will and stormed out of the room leaving Ngmankurinaa to wonder if his ruse had succeeded or failed. When after some time the issue still remained uncertain, he decided to press the advantage of his office. This time he called Poreku and proposed that they consult the ancestors on the matter by sacrificing a chicken to them. (He could not conceive of the ancestors being in favour of his brother's rebellion against traditional beliefs. Poreku, meanwhile, was just as convinced that if the missionaries were right about God — and he had no reason to doubt it — He was not likely to let a dead chicken stop anyone from learning more about Him. But he agreed to the sacrifice just the same and even provided the chicken for it.)

Ngmankurinaa began the incantations while his nephew-apprentice, Dery, held the chicken firmly in his two hands. When he had finished calling upon his *tengaama*, the *kolle*, the hills, and finally the ancestors, he slit the chicken's throat and set it free. It jumped about for a brief time, then fell over on its back and died with its feet in the air.[3]

The expressions on the faces of the three registered perfectly the reply of the ancestors. Poreku and his son smiled with delight while the witch doctor stared in utter dismay at the traitorous fowl. There was nothing more he could say; the ancestors had spoken by means of an indisputable sign.

The weekly walking trips to Jirapa mission continued, but now that the ancestors had pronounced in his favour and Ngmanku-rinaa's opposition had been effectively neutralized, Poreku no longer found himself alone. His brother-in-law Kabiri, his cousin Naatee, and his son Dery began to accompany him.

On the feast of Christmas 1930, Poreku, Kabiri, and Naatee were among the first small group of catechumens to receive the medal of the Blessed Virgin Mary, marking the initial step in their progress toward baptism. It was a happy, hopeful Christmas for us missionaries, in contrast to the first one we had spent among the Dagaabas when we had been barely a half-dozen Christians to celebrate the Saviour's birth. But our happiness could not match that of our catechumens. They now had a visible emblem of their desire to follow Christ.[4]

Poreku, who from the very beginning of his contact with Christianity had revealed an apostolic side to his nature, soon began to develop this gift. Many began to follow him to the mission each Sunday, eventually enrolling as catechumens. When he invited them to come together to pray in his home, a good number accepted the invitation. Once he had called them to prayer when a plague of locusts was devouring the land. They had begged God to spare them, and the locusts had not dared to touch the crops of anyone who had prayed there that day.

As Poreku's prestige grew and his fame spread even across the border, some began to fear that he was becoming too powerful. One of these was the paramount chief of Nandom.

Early on in his catechumenate, Poreku had come to speak to us about building a chapel at Zemopare. Twenty-two miles one-way was a long distance to cover on foot to assist at Mass and instructions each Sunday. With a chapel at Zemopare, many more people would be attracted, and a priest could make the weekly trip easily enough from Jirapa on a motorcycle. Poreku offered to organize the people to build it. We agreed that it was a good idea and work got underway.

It had not progressed very far when the DC intervened to halt it. He had been advised by the paramount chief of Nandom that the chapel represented a political move aimed at eventually changing the balance of power in the region. The British were very sensitive to such accusations, being the guardians of the status quo in local politics. They did not suffer rebels easily.

As soon as I learned of the DC's intervention, I went to see what the problem was and to intercede with him about it. It was not an easy interview by any means. Poreku's apostolic zeal had generated quite as much opposition as it had enthusiasm. After much dispute, during which I tried my best to assure the DC that the chapel had no political significance but had been conceived solely as a means to fill a spiritual need in the area, he finally relented and retracted his order. Work on the chapel could resume.

Since Zemopare fell under the authority of the paramount chief, I decided to discuss the matter with him as well. It would be the first of many discussions between us on the subject of Poreku and his ambitions. Over a pot of pito, the chief laid out his case against him. Basically, he was convinced that Poreku was power-hungry. The proof of this lay in the way he was recruiting followers. As Ngmankurinaa had feared from the start, his brother's example and zeal in spreading the Good News of Jesus Christ was becoming a real threat to the survival of traditional religion and social institutions. Thousands in the North were breaking away from their ancestral heritage to pray with the Christians. They all followed Poreku to Jirapa. But now, the chief believed, Poreku wanted to establish his own power base by building a chapel at Zemopare and setting himself up as rival to Nandom. The chief would not stand for it! Why could not Nandom have a chapel? Then the people would not all flock to Jirapa or Zemopare.

Why not indeed? The chief had a point. Certainly Nandom would be a good place for a chapel. It was a growing population centre and a crossroads. Besides, until this "crisis", the Nandom naa had not been favourable to the introduction of Christianity among his people. It would be foolish, now that circumstances had opened a breach in his defenses, not to take advantage of it. Acceding to his request could do us no harm, at any rate, and it might even help to diffuse some of the hostility toward Poreku.

Accordingly, after talking the matter over with Father Paquet and submitting it to Bishop Morin, it was agreed that Nandom would also have a chapel.[5]

The respite I had hoped to win for Poreku was short-lived. There was, of course, no pause in his efforts to assimilate and spread the teaching he received each week at the mission. But it was his example, more than his words, that attracted disciples to him. As the number of these continued to grow, the old antagonism of his enemies regained force. The chiefs and elders of the villages, alarmed at what they saw to be a threat to their authority and to the stability of the area, now closed ranks against him. They gathered together to discuss what they could do to put a stop to the spread of the new ideas and practices Poreku was promoting so ardently in their territories. In the well-founded hope that he would add the weight of his office to their complaint, they advised the paramount chief of their fears and findings. Obviously, he had not been persuaded by my attempts to justify Poreku's evangelical zeal to him. Like many a politician before and after him, he could only see the zeal of another as a threat to himself. So he brought Poreku before the DC to accuse him (all falsely) of disobedience and of trying to stir the people up against the chiefs.

It was April 1933. The DC, for much the same reasons as in the chapel incident earlier, found in favour of the plaintiff and sentenced Poreku to prison for three months at hard labour. If that failed to cure him, at least it would serve as a warning to his followers. Perhaps Poreku was thinking of that as he was led off. At any rate, before he disappeared from their sight, he offered them the only encouragement he could think of — the pledge of his own perseverance. "Don't worry," he told them as the guards took him away. "They can't stop me from praying."

May is the month when people plant their crops in our part of Africa. The rainy season has begun then, and farmers can usually count on showers every few days to restore the parched earth and coax another yield from it. But from the day that Poreku entered prison, the rains ceased in the whole of the Nandom chief's realm.

As the weeks passed and the heavens remained sealed, the people began to grow more and more desperate for rain. Their crops were withering under the burning sun, and the threat of famine in the coming year occupied their thoughts a little more each day. Sacrifices were made repeatedly to the spirits throughout Nandom area, but to no avail.

Meanwhile, prison had not dampened Poreku's enthusiasm for sharing the Good News. It had merely presented him with new opportunities and new material to work on. Soon he was catechizing his fellow prisoners. Whenever possible he would send word to his followers on the outside to bolster their faith, telling them that as Christ had suffered for us, so they should not be surprised if those who followed Him had at times to suffer too. The same forces that had opposed Jesus during His ministry were at work now among His followers in Nandom.

A month passed and then two, and still there was no sign of rain. The chiefs and elders were finding themselves doubly affected by the situation. Not only were their crops ruined, but the people held them responsible for the disaster. Their efforts to blame Poreku impressed no one since it was the generally-held opinion that those who had procured his imprisonment could also procure his release if they wanted to. Their authority was in as much danger now as it had been when Poreku roamed free, but at least there had been rain then.

Finally, swallowing their pride in the face of necessity, they went to see the paramount chief at Nandom to plead for the release of Poreku. The chief was as aware as they of the gravity of the situation and just as anxious for rain. But he had not been prepared to be the first among them to yield on the matter. He was relieved that they had finally petitioned him. He went to the DC the following day and, after the usual civilities followed by the discussion of several pending matters of minor interest to them both, brought up the case of Poreku. He felt, he said, that Poreku had learned his lesson and could be safely set free.

When the order came through to the prison authority the next day, and he suddenly found himself at liberty again after so many weeks of internment, Poreku's heart leapt for joy. Without a second thought, he headed for Jirapa to thank God for having kept him faithful to Him throughout that difficult period. He had not lost heart. He had not cursed his opponents. He had not even prayed for his own release. Instead he had turned his punishment, for crimes he had never committed, into a witness for Christ. And God had confirmed that witness by a sign in the heavens. Poreku was ecstatic. He had seen the hand of God.

That day, rain fell on the whole Nandom area.

Many months later, Poreku returned from one of his weekly trips to Jirapa in a very serious mood. He called his wives together and, instead of briefing them as he usually did on his latest discoveries about the Ngwinsore, informed them that he had reached a decision: he had made up his mind that nothing was going to stand in the way of his becoming a full-fledged Christian. Therefore, he was sending his four younger wives back to their parents' compounds. They would be free to take new husbands. His sole wife from that moment on would be his original one, the mother of his son Dery.

When the news reached the ears of Ngmankurinaa, he objected strenuously to his brother's decision to send his wives away. This was pure Christian perversity and an insult to Dagati tradition not to be tolerated. He feared his brother's "spirit" which could apparently hoodwink ancestors, halt locusts in their tracks, and open and close the heavens with equal ease. But enough was enough. He had watched as more and more of his own people fell under Poreku's spell and followed him off to Jirapa. If he succeeded in carrying this plan through, there would be no further barrier to his becoming a full Christian. He was already such a menace to the old ways as a "half-Christian", what would he be like if ever he got the full dose?

The two brothers confronted one another once again, but this time there would be no chicken to decide the issue.

Ngmankurinaa was adamant. The ways of the ancestors were being violated at great risk to the well-being of the clan. Besides, the prestige of their family was in jeopardy.

Poreku stood his ground, as adamant as his elder brother. There was no God but God, and His will took precedence over ancestors, spirits, clan, or family. That will did not permit a man with more than one wife to become a baptized Christian. That was why he was sending away all but one of his wives.

"I forbid you to do this!" Ngmankurinaa stormed. "These women do not belong to you alone. They belong to our clan and to our compound. You cannot send them away!"

The younger brother looked at the grotesquely angry face before him and felt all his own anger, tension, and hatred begin to drain away like pus from a wound. He had suddenly become aware that what he was staring at in those contorted features was not the arrogance, callousness, or authoritarianism he had supposed and always resented in his elder brother, but a kind of naked desperation because the old ways were dying and their sole legacy was fear. In that moment of revelation, Poreku felt a great pity for his brother and an urge to reach out and pull him back from the brink. But unless the man himself chose to be freed, he knew there was nothing anyone could do except leave him to God.

Ngmankurinaa, meanwhile, continued to shout and threaten. "Do you hear me?!" he cried. You have no right to send away your wives! The spirits forbid it! The ancestors forbid it! *I* forbid it!"

Poreku eyed him calmly, waiting for a pause in the tirade. When at last it came, he pounced on it.

"Then marry them yourself!" he said, and walked away.

It was obvious that he could no longer live in peace in his brother's compound, so he made arrangements to go to another village some distance away from Zemopare where he eventually built himself a house.

Ngmankurinaa's anxious appreciation of his brother's potential as a "full-Christian" proved to be perceptive. After his baptism at Nandom (together with his wife and children) in 1936, he grew even more ardent than before in living and spreading the Good News. Many more wonders of divine grace were worked through him so that he became in time one of the best-known, best-loved, and most effective apostles of Jesus Christ in all the North.[6]

*
**

A few miles from Zemopare lay Tebano, until then just another of the many villages of the Northwest untouched as yet by Christianity. That would change with the opening of the new mission station at Nandom in 1933, when the missionaries would begin to visit it as they did all the surrounding villages. But for the moment Tebano remained aloof and largely uninterested in what was happening around Jirapa to the south. Life went on as it always had for as far back as anyone could remember, and no one expected the future to be much different. Change was not a word often heard in Tebano.

Then one day the missionary came, his arrival heralded by the strange racket of his motorcycle approaching through the bush. The people rushed out to see what the origin of this din could be, curiosity overcoming their initial fear. The white man greeted them in their own tongue and, as custom dictated, went in search of the chief to pay his respects to him. Afterwards he returned to the people and spoke with them for a little while about God. They were impressed and pleased that this stranger could speak their language, though they did not grasp too well the meaning of his message. After telling them he would return in a few days to treat their maladies, he was off again in a deafening roar that had many of them holding their ears. It would be quite some time before the first conversions to Christ would take place in Tebano, but life there would never be the same again.

Some months passed, during which the visits of the missionaries to the village became regular and accepted. As in the Jirapa region, there were many illnesses to be treated among the villagers and many baptisms to be administered to persons on the point of death. But unlike Jirapa, there was no rush to forsake traditional religion and embrace Christianity. The one chosen to be the apostle of Tebano had not yet appeared.

One day, as the visiting missionary was attending to the sick who had lined up to consult him, someone came to inform him that an old woman was dying in a hut nearby. Promising the patient whose sore he was dressing that he would return shortly, he grabbed his stole and hurried after the messenger. A group of the woman's friends had already gathered outside her hut in anticipation of what now appeared to them to be the inevitable outcome of her illness.

As he left the bright sunshine and entered the dwelling, it took a few moments for his eyes to adjust to the comparative darkness inside. Slowly the figure of the dying woman lying on a pallet began to detach itself from the gloom. He recognized her as one of the women he had seen and spoken to several times on past visits to the village. She was a widow, he knew, whom he judged to be somewhere in her sixties. Listening to her breathing and examining her face, he agreed with those waiting outside: it did not seem likely that she would survive her illness.

The old woman had been aware of the young missionary's arrival from the first moment he entered her hut, even before he had become aware of her. Her eyes had fastened on the white-clad figure, as they did now, hardly blinking. Though too weak to speak, she seemed to be trying desperately to communicate some message to him through the intensity of her gaze.

The priest knelt down at the bedside and felt her brow as he greeted her quietly. It was hot to the touch and there was fever too in the luminous eyes that remained fastened on him. He felt for her pulse and could not find it at first. Then he caught it, faint and fluttering, as if some small bird with a broken wing were caged within her and struggling feebly to escape.

"Grandmother," he said at last, "you are very ill. I will do what I can for you, but your body is very tired. You have borne many burdens and now the Almighty One is about to lift them from your shoulders and give you peace."

She lay there, her tiny hand in his, as he went on seeking words from his meagre store that would move her to reach out to God and, if not welcome His coming, at least not resist it or fear it unreasonably. She was listening to him, he felt sure, and so he made a very special effort to pronounce distinctly, repeating in broad outline the story of salvation and trying to will her to see the importance of it for her at that moment.

"Jesus died for you, Grandmother, because His Father, the Almighty One, loved you so much He did not want to lose you, ever. Do you love Him in the same way? Do you want to be with Him forever?"

The young missionary sensed rather than felt a slight pressure as the old woman responded by trying to squeeze his hand. He repeated the question in another way to be sure of her response.

"Do you want to become a Christian?"

Again the pressure was felt, stronger this time. Taking a small canteen of water from his pocket and placing the stole around his neck, he began to prepare her to receive the sacrament.

When he left her a short time later, the luminous eyes were closed and the old woman had fallen into a heavy sleep. He returned to his waiting patients and continued to treat their bodily ills.

On his next trip to the village, the priest inquired about the old woman and was surprised to hear that she had not died of her illness. In fact, she was well again. This first grace was to be the beginning of a long chain of heavenly favours for Tebano. Not only had the widow, who was now called Maria, stolen her way into the fold of Christ, but baptism had made an apostle of her.

As soon as she felt strong enough, Maria began to go to the mission at Nandom each week to complete her instruction in the faith. She did so with enthusiasm; and after the required time and examinations, she was admitted to the reception of the sacraments. Then things began to happen in Tebano.

In the course of her instructions, as she was gradually exposed to the person of Jesus Christ, His life and teachings, she had fallen in love with Him. She could not imagine a better or more noble person, nor one that appealed to her more as a woman and a mother. Out of that love grew a zeal, neither tempestuous nor fanatical, to share with others what she was experiencing of inner peace and happiness for the first time in her life. It was too much for one heart to contain.

Through calm persistence, she wore down the opposition of the elders of her household to her request to teach the children about God. Each night, by the flickering light of the fire, Maria would gather the children of the compound around her and keep them spellbound with her tales of Jesus Christ and His heavenly Father. Often a few adults would hover in the shadows, just within hearing distance of the old woman's voice, and allow themselves to be drawn slowly into the circle of light.

From teaching them about God, Maria proceeded to teach the children to pray to Him. Again with the elders' permission, she invited them to gather around her twice a day — in the morning and before retiring at night — to praise, thank, and petition this loving and caring Father they were coming to discover through Maria's efforts and the inspiration of the Holy Spirit. She even taught them to recite the rosary and led them in doing so each evening at nightfall. She was becoming the de facto catechist of Tebano.

One day, as Father Alfred Richard arrived in the village on one of his periodic visits, he was stopped by the excited cries of a woman running toward him. A young mother had just given birth and was dying. Leaping off his motorcycle, he hurried to the hut indicated, praying that he would at least be in time to baptize the woman if he could do nothing else for her. His anxiety was needless. At the hut, he was met by Maria.

"Father," she said, "I was at her side when she passed away. She accepted Jesus and I baptized her before she died, along with her infant who has just joined her in death. The child has been born twice in one day! We, her family and I, have offered a prayer for them and we have also offered one of submission to God's will."

That evening, as the priest knelt before the Blessed Sacrament in the dimly lit mission church, he could not get Maria out of his thoughts. The change in her had been as remarkable as her recovery from her illness. Illiterate, a devoted adherent of the traditional religion of the Dagaabas for some sixty years, and a woman, she had become in a short time a valued co-worker in the Christian apostolate, with increasing influence in her village. Though she possessed only the basic religious truths, her faith and spiritual wisdom outstripped that of most other Christians.

Maria continued to instruct the children of Tebano and to do whatever she could to render service to her neighbours or to dedicate herself to worthy causes whenever possible. The people of the village began to appreciate her dependability and to approach her in their needs. Something there was that lit up her life from within, something to which not all of them were blind.

In the early 1940s, cerebrospinal meningitis ravaged the country. People, especially children, were dying by the hundreds. Ten thousand afflicted persons received treatment for it at our dispensaries in a single year. Because of the efficacy of the sulfa drugs with which we were treating our patients, only a thousand deaths occurred from the epidemic in our area. This was considerably less than the number of fatalities in other parts of the country.

At Tebano, as in other villages, fear approached panic. The elders consulted the witch doctors who prescribed sacrifice after sacrifice as the only means of warding off the deadly plague. In Maria's compound, the elders had all but decided to sacrifice a cow when she learned of it. Going before them, she proposed an alternative solution.

"If you follow my advice, not a single child in this compound will be stricken by the terrible disease," she promised them. "Morning and night, you must all join the children and me in praying to God as long as this plague lasts. Do this and I guarantee we will all be spared."

There was, of course, some hesitation and debate over the proposal. But they had so often witnessed the excellent results of Maria's intercession on previous occasions that all finally agreed to do as she said. If she failed to avert the catastrophe, however, they threatened to expel her from the compound.

Maria was not worried. If God had rescued her from death once, He would certainly not abandon her now. Within a few days, her new "converts" had all learned, willingly or not, to pray the rosary. True to their promise, they gathered with her and the children each morning and night to beg God, through the intercession of the Virgin Mary, to save them from the epidemic. All around them, in other compounds, children were stricken with the malady and, in most cases, died. But in Maria's compound, not one child fell ill. With the coming of the rains, the plague ended.

The elders whose children had been spared approached the old widow to thank her. But Maria shrugged off their thanks and directed it to where it belonged. "It is to God that you must be grateful," she told them. When they insisted on doing something to show their gratitude, she hit upon a solution that satisfied them.

"Collect among yourselves a little sum of money, whatever you can give, and I will take it to the mission at Nandom as your offering of thanksgiving to God."

They agreed to this, and the following Sunday morning Maria took the collection from the villagers to Father Richard at the mission.

"This money comes from the people of my compound, Father," she explained. "They have asked me to give it to you as an offering to God who protected their children from the terrible sickness. Could you offer a Mass of thanksgiving to Him on their behalf, please?" In her other hand, she clutched her own widow's mite: a hen for the missionaries' table.

"Certainly, Maria," the young priest replied, accepting the five shillings from her. "Nothing would give me greater pleasure. We'll make it a High Mass, and you can invite the people of your compound to attend."

The old woman smiled and thanked him. She would tell them, she said, and they would be pleased. But whether they would attend or not, she could not be sure. Only one thing was sure: Maria would certainly be there.[7]

For the old widow of Tebano, whose life had begun at sixty, each new day was a little miracle and an invitation from God to give thanks. She too became one of the early apostles of the Good News in northwest Gold Coast, living proof that God is not bound by human prejudices or traditions when it comes to selecting His special messengers.[8]

8

Loaves and Fishes

Toward the end of the rainy season of 1931, the Good News of God's love for them spread like a brush fire among the Dagaabas, and the number of those coming to pray at Jirapa on Sundays increased rapidly. Men and women from villages in every direction came to hear the missionaries talk about God and to learn to approach Him directly and without fear.

The interest of the people stemmed from many sources: the priests' visits to their villages, the enthusiasm of the first group of catechumens undergoing instruction, the health care they received at the mission clinic, and, last but certainly not least, the impulse of the Holy Spirit. In the short space of two years, Kontombilitang (site of the Jirapa mission and, prior to our arrival, reputed habitat of evil spirits) had become a centre of worship and knowledge of God.

It was during the rainy season of that year that Father Paquet fell ill with diphtheria and had to be transported to Navrongo. There was a doctor and a small government hospital near there, at Zuarungu. The only mechanical means of transport available was my BSA motorcycle, so I put him on the back of it and we set off.

The plan was to go as far as the village of Han (Hian), about twenty-five miles from the mission. There Captain Armstrong would meet us with his car and take my ailing companion as far as Tumu, some forty miles further on, where "McCoy's ambulance" would resume service. At Tumu, the road had been washed out, making it impossible to go on from there by car.

The poor condition of the roads due to the rains already curtailed our speed somewhat, but just outside Jirapa we were forced to slow down even more by a heavy shower that soaked us to the skin. It was miserable going for the strong, let alone the weak.

At Han the DC was waiting for us. He quickly transferred Father Paquet to his car and they set off immediately for Tumu, with me following them at a safe distance. The sun had come out again, drying my clothes and improving my disposition, though it did little to improve the road. I hoped it was lifting Father Paquet's spirits a bit too, for the worst of the ordeal probably lay ahead, after Tumu.

I was right. As we continued our journey eastward after taking leave of the DC, things got progressively worse. Bridges were out in several places, forcing us to wade through chest-high waters with the motorcycle held over our heads. At one point, after night had fallen, the headlamp suddenly went out, plunging us into total and impenetrable darkness. Before I could come to a complete stop, I felt the road take a sharp downward angle and the motorcycle accelerated. The next thing we knew we were lying on the ground, surprised and shaken but otherwise unharmed. We had fallen into a deep gully where a culvert had been washed away sometime earlier. I found the motorcycle again and, with the help of a flashlight, examined it for damage. As far as I could tell, there didn't seem to be any. With a good deal of difficulty, we managed to climb out of the gully and continue on our way cautiously, using the flashlight as a headlamp. No further mishaps of that nature occurred, and several hours later we arrived in Navrongo.

The next morning, Father Paquet awoke from a restless sleep with a temperature of 104 degrees (40 degrees centigrade). We bundled him into Monsignor Morin's car and took him to the doctor at Zuarungu, east of Bolgatanga, where it was decided he should remain temporarily in the hospital there. In fact, it would be a full year before he would be well enough to return to active service.

As I headed back to Dagati territory and the mission, I wondered how I was ever going to manage the instruction of our five thousand catechumens all by myself. Monsignor Morin had promised me a replacement for Father Paquet, but he would not be of much use in that area until he learned the local language, which could take several months at least. (At that time, the only white men in the Gold Coast who spoke Dagaare were Father Paquet, Brother Basilide, and myself.)

Monsignor Morin was true to his word, and within a week Father Eugène Coutu arrived from Wiagha to help me. His first Sunday at Jirapa (26 July 1931) was spent registering the names of newcomers as best he could. That kept him busy for a good long time.

Meanwhile, I confronted the problem of feeding the five thousand the spiritual food they had come for. I felt as inadequate to the task as Andrew had judged the five loaves and two fishes to be to feed the five thousand men ("not counting the women and children") who had flocked to hear Jesus at Bethsaida nineteen centuries earlier. Now the Lord would have to perform a new miracle, and this time He only had one "poor fish" to work with.

The miracle that Sunday was that I survived it. Dividing the crowd into smaller, slightly more manageable groups, I passed from one to the other repeating the same instruction again and again. It took a lot of time, of course, and with the heat and humidity of the rainy season added to it, I had to struggle with myself sometimes to keep from shortchanging my audience. They, after all, had suffered as much or more inconvenience to receive their instruction as I had in providing it. Most had walked many miles to get to the mission and would walk them again to get home. And all had waited patiently, especially the last groups to be instructed, until I could give them my attention. But I did not fancy having to repeat the feat of that Sunday week after week until Father Coutu could become proficient enough in the language to help me.

The following weekend, more newcomers came to be registered. We were witnessing the first stages of a new Pentecost, but as yet there were no disciples. That was about to change. As I gazed down from the mission verandah at the lively multitude below me, where only a year before there had been no one, I breathed a prayer to the Lord of the harvest that what I was about to try might work. Then I set about it.

Again I divided the crowd into smaller groups. But this time I singled out five or six "veterans" such as Kyefondeme, Poreku, and Anglieremwin, and took them aside. They would be the new miracle of the loaves and fishes. After indicating to them the points to be covered that day, points they were already familiar with, I sent them to instruct the groups of more recent catechumens.

That Sunday the Dagaabas entered upon a new phase of their evangelization. The fact that their teachers were now men of their own race and ethnic group made an impression on them. And the novice catechists were no less impressed by it. From being merely recipients of a precious message of life and liberation from fear, they had become its dispensers.

These new assistants of mine — I was to choose more of them in the following weeks — were intelligent and quick to assimilate, with excellent memories and good pedagogical methods adapted to their audiences. They were also imaginative in their explanations, finding apt comparisons from daily life to clarify difficult concepts. I would wander around from group to group each Sunday, listening in on the instruction being given, and be amazed at the catechists' grasp of the material and their inventiveness in presenting it. Sometimes I stayed to learn.

Nothing happens by mere chance in life, nor are our sudden inspirations without prior preparation. The goundwork for all that occurs to us is laid well in advance. So it was in the case of this initiative of mine. While on retreat the previous year, I had read an account by a bishop in the Belgian Congo (now independent Zaire) of his catechist training program. It was a new idea in those days and I was attracted by its possibilities. But it was too early for that at Jirapa. At that moment we had barely a handful of catechumens and little indication that more would be forthcoming soon. I had filed the idea away in my memory and necessity had retrieved it.

It was true that my assistants were not catechists in the full sense of the term; as yet there were no baptized Christians in Jirapa. But under my coaching, they were fulfilling the same function with much the same results.

Most of them were still polygamists since we did not force the issue until the catechumen had acquired enough knowledge of Christianity to be able to weigh both sides of the question himself and come to a decision freely. That moment might occur early in his four-year catechumenate or later, though he could not proceed to the second stage of it until he had in fact sent away all but one of his wives. Many were baptized on their deathbeds in those days.[1]

One typical case was that of Anglieremwin, Poreku's good friend who lived in Konkwa (a section of Jirapa). He was related to Chief Ganaa and enjoyed his confidence. His name meant "Who can become God?" or "Who can take God's place?" At a time when people were afraid to speak openly with us about their customs and beliefs, Anglieremwin was not. He was his own man, and he trusted us. Much of the information concerning what people were thinking and saying about us came from him.

Anglieremwin had several wives. When he joined the first catechumenate, he already knew that he would have to renounce all but one of them before he could hope to be baptized. In the meantime, he prayed for strength and wisdom and learned all he could about the Ngwinsore. He was upright and honest, true to himself and to others. When it came to choosing my first assistants, I did not hesitate to call him.

Sometime later he succeeded to the office of tendaana or "priest of the Earth", to whose spirit he was required by tradition to offer sacrifice. This posed an additional obstacle to baptism since Christians were not permitted to offer sacrifice to spirits. Eventually he decided to hand over the sacrificial functions of his office to another. One hurdle had thus been cleared. But the question of his extra wives proved more difficult. He and I had many conversations about it and I agreed with him that it was indeed a difficult decision to make. I encouraged him to continue praying and not to lose confidence in God's love for him. Each time we had this conversation, Anglieremwin would reiterate his desire for baptism and tell me that if I ever heard he was dying, I should not hesitate to baptize him.

He lived to be an old man. All of his children had become Christians, thanks to his efforts. From the earliest days of their catechumenate, he had watched over their training and nurtured their progress. He had seen to it that they prayed regularly, he himself praying with them.

One day I received a message from him to come immediately. I hurried to his compound and found him ill and very weak. But the desire to become a baptized member of Christ's Body before he died was as strong as ever. There was no problem now. And he was well-prepared. I baptized my old friend, giving him the name Joseph, and a few days later he died peacefully in the Lord.

Not all of my early assistants were polygamists, of course, though most of the married ones were. This did not hinder them from being effective instruments in God's hands for the spread of His Kingdom in the Northwest. But the initiative needed to be taken one step forward.

The next time Monsignor Morin visited Jirapa, we discussed the idea of training catechists as the White Fathers were doing in the Congo. Our first small experiment had gone well, but we now needed a more formal approach. With the increasing numbers arriving weekly to be registered as catechumens, the missionary personnel available, even with a few reinforcements, would never be sufficient to handle them effectively. Besides, people learn best by example. In a country devoid of Christian tradition, the sight of men and women like themselves, living the Christian faith they taught, was worth as much or more than any number of formal instructions. Had not Jesus used the same method in His ministry, preparing and sending out disciples chosen from among the people to preach the Good News by word and the example of their lives?

Monsignor Morin agreed that it was a good idea and that a catechist training program should be initiated as soon as possible. My experience with assistants had shown us that it was not necessary to postpone it until we should have baptized Christians to choose from.

Accordingly, a group of a dozen young men, all illiterates, was selected from among the catechumens preparing for baptism. They would be the first catechist trainees. Those chosen had first to agree to their selection after consultation with their families, for it was to be a purely volunteer service with little or no financial remuneration. Married students would bring their wives with them. In some cases the candidates were chosen by the village they were meant to serve eventually (usually their own), which then offered them sponsorship. Such cooperation was imperative for the support of the student catechists. During their training they would have to remain at the mission and take care of their own needs. The mission could contribute only ten shillings a month toward their upkeep at the time.[2] Thus they depended on their villages or families for their food, which they collected from home every few weeks. During the farming season they would be allowed home for a brief "holiday" to help with the crops.

The qualities we sought in making our selection involved the will, heart, and mind of the candidate.

WILL: He had to have a keen interest in learning the Word of God, indicated by regular attendance at the weekly instructions and active participation in them. He also had to show dedication and leadership by his efforts to bring the Good News to others and to help them to understand the purpose of Christian living.

HEART: Genuine concern for the things of God and the welfare of the people was also essential, together with a readiness to sacrifice himself in the interests of both.

MIND: Intelligence to understand the things of God and the ability to impart that understanding to others was a further requirement. The potential student catechist would be tested by asking him to repeat and explain to another group of catechumens a lesson just imparted to his group.

These qualities were assessed regularly throughout the years of training.

On 16 November 1931, the catechist training program opened with a dozen students and myself as their professor. Both student body and staff would double in number before long. Father Coutu was needed back in Wiagha, but he had been replaced the week before by Father Joseph Larochelle who would eventually become director of the catechist program. For the next few months, however, all of his efforts would be concentrated on learning Dagaare as quickly as possible.

I began the course with simple catechism lessons and practical instructions on how to administer baptism. Baptism in danger of death was a regular occurrence then, so it was necessary that the future catechist know how to administer it in an emergency.

They were all eager to learn and kept me on my toes. I marvel to this day at their ability to understand my Dagaare. The language was still relatively new to me and I spoke it with a foreign accent that made me a sought-after source of entertainment among local children. My vocabulary, while growing, was still limited so that I did not always make the most fortunate choice of word when trying to express myself. I did the best I could and plowed ahead, convinced that if God had wanted perfection, He would have sent somebody else.

Because I was still alone to handle the bulk of the mission work, which increased with each week's influx of new catechumens, I was unable to devote much time to preparing my classes. At any given time I was just one step ahead of my students. It was quite an undertaking to translate Christian doctrine into Dagaare. Nothing existed in print in that language at the time. In fact, the language had never been written before we arrived, and the people had never been to school. Sometimes a Latin word had to be used because we could find no equivalent in Dagaare. "Sacrament" and "grace" are two examples that come to mind of concepts that were totally new to the Dagaabas.

When translating the catechism, I used to get five or six of the best student catechists from different areas of the Northwest to assist me in discovering how the same idea would be expressed in each of their regions. I would explain what I wanted to convey to the people and they would give me the best way to say it. I learned more theology translating the catechism than I had in my four years in the seminary at Carthage (Tunisia) simply because the idea had to be clear in my mind before it could be translated into Dagaare.

Thanks to the assistance of men like John Kyefondeme and Joseph Gbare from Tizza, who were among the first group of catechist trainees, it was already possible to produce the first catechism in Dagaare in 1931. The printing was done at the motherhouse of the Missionaries of Africa, then located at Maison Carrée, a suburb of Algiers.

By 20 December 1931, the number of catechumens enrolled at the mission had exceeded seven thousand and was still rising. On one weekend alone, 750 newcomers arrived from all over the Northwest. Monsignor Morin returned to assess the situation and suggested it was time to build a catechist training school. Existing facilities were not adequate nor could they be easily expanded to meet the need to admit more students. He obtained the necessary authorization from the government and work began under the supervision of Brother Basilide. The student catechists themselves, with the help of some of the catechumens, built the mudbrick and thatch classrooms during their two daily hour-long manual work periods.[3] Before the end of the year, some forty rooms were added as living quarters for the catechists, their wives and children.

Father Larochelle, meanwhile, made good progress learning the language, and within a few months he had begun to teach the students how to read and write their mother tongue. Besides these literacy classes and the two one-hour manual work periods, the daily schedule included classes in Religious and Spiritual Formation, Bible History, and Arithmetic. Time was also devoted to the catechists' wives. They were given religious instruction as well as training in hygiene and child-care. Some of them attended literacy classes with their husbands and gave catechetical instruction to groups of women and children.

As originally conceived, the training period for catechists was to last three years. But later a fourth year was added to enable them to learn English.

It was at this time (February 1932) that the concept of "Sunday everyday" came into being at Jirapa. This was a temporary expedient devised and employed by us to escape the confines of the mission compound and visit the people in their villages again. For months, ever since the flow of catechumens to Jirapa had begun, we had been virtual "prisoners" of the mission precincts, ministering to these new arrivals on weekends and occupied with training our student catechists during the week. Treatment of the sick at the mission clinic continued as usual. Meanwhile the villagers went unvisited. It did not strike us as healthy behaviour to sit back and let people come to see us all the time. It was never Jesus' way and it should never be the missionary's either, at least not habitually.

Consequently, each day of the week was designated "Sunday" in a different area outside Jirapa. Father Larochelle and I would take turns visiting them to conduct special sessions of prayer and religious instruction for the people, sparing them the necessity of making the long trek to the mission on the weekend. No catechists had completed the training program yet, so they were of no help to us initially. On 26 March of that year, however, the students started to go out to give instructions in the villages on weekends, thus freeing us to serve other areas during the week.

They were sent out two by two on Friday evening, spending the night in a village along the way. On Saturday they would conduct prayer services and give instructions in perhaps two villages, and then push on to another and repeat the process on Sunday. As often as not, the shade of a tree served as the first "catechist centre" in the places they visited. Sunday afternoon they would begin the long trip home to the mission. There were few roads linking the villages in those days, so they made their way through the bush on footpaths.[4]

These apostolic outings were not without incident. One of the most frequent sources of opposition and irritation was the "voluntary" labour recruiter.

At the time, Sunday did not exist as a day of rest in the Northwest, except for expatriates. In fact, Sunday hadn't existed there at all prior to the arrival of the missionaries. The people had a six-day week based on the six market days of the region. The names of the days were Tizzada, Babileda, Jirapada, Takorada, Lawrada, and Tangasaida. One of these, Takorada, means "Don't farm". There had been a serious drought once, and when the people had consulted the witch doctor about it, the juju had told them they should not farm on that day. They could do some light chores, such as hoeing groundnuts, but no serious farming. Takorada had replaced the original name of the day, Gbareda, which was the day of the market at Gbare.

The absence of Sunday observance protection meant that a group of catechumens gathered around their catechist for prayer and instruction presented a tempting target for recruiters of road workers. These recruiters, working in the pay of the chiefs (who were held responsible by the British administration for the construction and maintenance of roads in their respective territories), would pounce on the peaceful Sunday gathering and press the catechumens and sometimes the catechist himself into service. No payment was received for this work and the labourer had to bring his own food. Sometimes the people would resist.

We encountered much difficulty in our efforts to gain freedom for our catechumens to worship unmolested on Sundays. Finally, in mid-October 1932, we requested a meeting with the Jirapa naa to discuss it. He agreed and summoned his elders and headmen to take part in the discussion. In the course of it, one of the elders, a Muslim advisor to the chief, said to him: "Chief Ganaa, I think the fathers have a point. We Muslims have our day of prayer each week, and no one can force us to work on that day. It is recognized by everyone. I don't see any difference between that and what the Christians are asking for. Why should we not accept and recognize their day of prayer too?"

The chief seemed to agree with this fair-minded man. But though the problem did lessen noticeably after that, it did not disappear completely. We wanted nothing less than a full solution to it, however, so we decided at last to approach the DC.

The Labour Party then in power in Great Britain was opposed to the practice of forced labour in the colonies, so officially the colonial administration in the Gold Coast was opposed to it too. As the highest authority and chief representative of Westminster in the country, Governor Thomas in Accra was responsible for eliminating it in all its manifestations in preparation for implementing indirect rule. He had already done so in much of the South, but the North was another question. There the DCs did much as they pleased. Forced labour in the Northwest was as illegal as it was in the South, but it was tolerated there for various reasons, principal among which was the need for roads. The DCs did not know how they could get the roads built and repaired any other way. Because of the world economic crisis then at its height, money was unavailable for development.

Captain Armstrong listened to us with official British courtesy, if meagre enthusiasm. When we had finished, he had to agree that we did indeed have a case and promised to take it up with the governor. He could not very well oppose us on something declared illegal by the government he served and represented. Monsignor Morin, meanwhile, had taken the matter up directly with the governor. Eventually, thanks to the pressure applied by the missionaries, the colonial administration proclaimed Sunday a day of rest in the North and reinforced the prohibition of forced labour.

One day, toward the end of 1932, a government official visited the Jirapa naa to inform him of this sudden reversal of policy on forced labour. It was not altogether welcome news, for the naa had the habit of making use of the practice to farm his lands. Probably suspecting that we were at the bottom of it, he briefed the official on what was then happening at the mission. The latter hurried over and found the student catechists making mud-bricks to build their compound. Smelling an infringement of the law by the very ones who had done most to force its strict application, he asked through his interpreter: "And how much are you being paid for your labour?" One of the catechists paused in his work and replied: "We're not working for money." At that the official sneered. "That's absurd," he said. "I wouldn't work for nothing." ("No Pay, No Work" was the administration slogan.) The young catechist was not surprised to hear it. Government officials never worked for nothing. "We think differently," he replied with a smile. "We are helping our people. If there is to be any repayment. God will take care of it."

As time passed and my classes at the catechist school advanced, I became more proficient in Dagaare, but the material also became more difficult for me to explain in that language. I became increasingly concerned about my ability to get it over to my students. For example, when some of the first group were preparing for baptism and it came time to study the doctrine of the Eucharist, I worried about it constantly. This was a totally new concept for these people. How could I ever find adequate terminology to explain it to them? I wrote and rewrote my presentation before finally translating it into Dagaare. Then I rewrote it again.

The next day, before beginning my explanation to the morning class, I invoked the Holy Spirit as never before. But I don't think I really thought there was much He could do for me. I felt inadequate, so inadequate in fact that when I had finished my presentation, for the first time since the course had begun I neither asked questions nor did I take them. I merely murmured that I would reserve any questions for the next day when we would all be fresher (it was a very hot morning) and I could concentrate better in Dagaare.

After a good night's sleep, I returned to the 8 a.m. class the next day to face my humiliation. And I was indeed humiliated, though not in the way I had foreseen.

"What did you understand about the Eucharist yesterday?" I asked the class in general, not really expecting a response. To my surprise, Yacobi Kpiende stood up and said: "I understand it this way, Father." And the simple villager from Tizza went on to explain the doctrine perfectly — and better than I had done — using examples and comparisons from Dagati life. I was dumfounded. I felt Yacobi must be some kind of genius. Then another student, Paulo Nora, stood and offered his explanation. Again I was astounded. He too had understood it all perfectly.

I realized then that all my worry had been in vain. I had been relying too much on myself, as if success depended on me rather than on God. This was His work and He had just reminded me that the Holy Spirit was equal to it. I felt humbled and exhilarated at the same time.

One of the students at the catechist school was Dery, the young son of Poreku. He had come to the mission when he was twelve, sent by his father to become a catechist so that he could return to his village one day and teach his people about God. He had exchanged apprenticeship to a witch doctor for discipleship of Christ. Dery was shy, however, and did not tell me his real purpose for being at the mission the night I discovered him there.

I remember it was raining very hard that night. I was just getting ready for bed when the sound of voices reached my ear above the din of the rain. They came from somewhere just beyond my window. I took my flashlight and went out on the verandah. In the pitch-black African night, it was impossible to see anything with the naked eye.

"Who's out there?" I called, flicking on my flashlight and sweeping the mission yard with its beam.

Two small forms, huddled together beneath a ga tree a few feet from the house and trying in vain to keep from being thoroughly soaked, looked into the light with startled eyes and identified themselves. One was Dery; the other, his younger brother.

"What are you doing?" I asked.

Dery answered this question with determination, as if he had been expecting it for a long time and was prepared for it.

"We have come to learn about God."

"That's fine," I replied, "but what are you doing there? Have you nowhere to stay?"

"We went to Hector Awia's compound, but there were already too many people there. It was impossible to get in. We thought you wouldn't mind if we slept here," he said, evidently resigned to spending the inclement night in the largely symbolic shelter of the tree. "We didn't know where else to go. We won't make any more noise, Father. We promise."

I looked at them in the glow of the flashlight and knew I could not leave them there to catch pneumonia. They were clad in loincloths and nothing else. And it was certainly too late and too wet a night to go seeking lodgings for them elsewhere.

"Come with me," I said. "You can stay in the mission tonight, and tomorrow we'll find somewhere else for you to stay."

Timidly at first, the two small boys crept out from under the ga tree and followed this tall stranger into the mission house. It was poor enough, but to them it was full of delicious mystery. This would be a night they would long remember. After drying them off and giving them something to eat, I took them into our small parlor and told them they could sleep there.

Very early the next morning, they were up and away. I was extremely busy then with the student catechists (it was before the arrival of Father Larochelle), so I promptly forgot about our young nocturnal visitors for awhile.

Dery, in the meantime, had determined to find a job at the mission to support himself so that he could remain close to the catechist school. He found one with Brother Basilide who put him to work carrying oyster shells to the kiln where they were burnt to make lime.

One day a few months later, I happened upon Dery sitting with a book in his hands. The way he was looking at it, one would have thought he was reading it. But I knew he could have had no opportunity to learn that skill since there were no schools in the Northwest, other than the catechist training school. Apart from the student catechists and some of their wives, whom Father Larochelle was then teaching to read and write, no other Dagao in all the land possessed that knowledge.

The book he held was a copy of the Dagaare catechism just recently published. I asked him what he was doing with it.

"I am studying it," he replied solemnly.

"Really?" I said, not believing him. "Let's see then. What does this page say?"

To my surprise, he told me; and his answer was word-perfect. I pointed to another page and another. Each time the response was perfectly accurate. But I was not ready to believe that this little bush boy from Zemopare, with no formal education, could really read. I knew the prodigious memories of some of these people and supposed I was witnessing such a phenomenon in Dery. He had obviously learned the texts by heart listening to the catechists. So I decided on a fool-proof test.

"Now read that page backwards to me," I told him, "from end to beginning."

He did not even look up to question me by a glance or to check to see if I was wearing my sun helmet. He may have thought it a curious way to learn about God, but his apprenticeship to his Uncle Ngmankurinaa had accustomed him to receiving — and obeying — strange orders. Without so much as a pause, he read it back to me exactly as I had told him to do.

I was very surprised indeed.

"Where did you learn to read, Dery?" I asked him at last. (Had I asked him that question in the first place, I would have had less reason to doubt his word.)

"I have been learning from the student catechists in the evenings, Father," he replied.

It was true. He spent his days carrying oyster shells to the kiln and his evenings learning to read and write. It began to dawn on me that this was an exceptional child.

"Why have you been learning to read?" I asked.

It was then that he told me of his desire to become a catechist and return to his village to serve his people in that capacity.

That very day I spoke with Father Larochelle about him and we decided to let Dery join the catechists-in-training despite his youth. He would be entering the program late, but there was no doubt he could catch up to them easily enough. In fact, he was not far behind. Unknown to us, each evening after work he had been picking the catechists' brains of all they had learned that day.

To provide for his food and upkeep, he was given a new job as houseboy at the mission for the duration of his studies at the catechist school.

*
**

Dery's singleminded pursuit of his ideal was common to all the students at the school. They were prepared to make sacrifices for it and often did.

Times were difficult then all over the world. The Great Depression had hit like a tidal wave, leaving badly crippled economies, ruined investors, and bleak poverty where before there had been prosperity. There was no one who escaped entirely unscathed, no area that did not eventually experience the repercussions of it... not even Jirapa.

The missionaries, of course, were dependent (and still are) on the generosity of family and benefactors in North America and Europe to maintain themselves and their projects. When these sources began to dry up, the already precarious state of our material existence and that of our missions worsened noticeably.

Toward the middle of 1932, Monsignor Morin arrived at Jirapa with the bad news. There was no more money for the catechist training program. The motherhouse of the Missionaries of Africa in Algiers, as well as the Propaganda Fide in Rome, had had to cut back on funds regularly allotted to the prefecture apostolic.

Everyone would have to tighten his belt and hope for better times. The school was not being closed, but he could no longer guarantee the paltry ten shillings a month to the catechists. He would tell them so himself.

The next day an apologetic Monsignor Morin addressed the catechists and their wives. He was aware, he said, that the financial help he had been able to give them until then had been little more than a token. Now, even that token had become more than the mission could afford. He was there to tell them that he could no longer fulfill his promise to pay them their ten shillings. If they chose to leave — for they were free to do so, of course — neither the Church nor the missionaries would blame them. It was clear to all that their first priority had to be their families and the need to support them somehow. Perhaps when better times came, they would be able to return and take up where they had left off.

When he had finished speaking, there were a few seconds of silence during which the assembled catechists exchanged glances. Then one of them, Joseph Gbare, stood up.

"Monsignor," he said, "when we came here we were not looking for money. We came to help our people. If you have money to help us, fine; if not, that's fine too. We won't stop our studies just because of that."

The others all agreed with him. The catechist training program proceeded on schedule.

What Gbare had said expressed well the sentiments of those early apostles of the Jirapa mission. They were eager to learn, but not for the sake of learning. Their self-fulfillment would only come in spending themselves for their people. That was why financial remuneration, which was not unimportant to them in the situation in which they found themselves, was less important to them than their calling.

One day I sent two catechists out to visit and instruct the people in a certain village some distance from the mission. Before they set out, I wanted to give them each a small amount of pocket money for their needs. But their response was immediate.

"No, Father. Keep it for someone else who might need it more than we do."

That was the spirit that prevailed among our catechists and helped to make them such effective co-workers with us in evangelizing the Northwest.

Rain

Efforts to reach the people in the villages at regular intervals did little to reduce the numbers coming to the mission to pray and receive instruction on Sundays. First of all, the villages were too numerous and some of them too far away for the few available missionaries and a handful of student catechists to be able to visit them all. Secondly, no sooner had one group of catechumens stopped coming to the mission than another, more numerous than the first, sprang up to replace it from some new area as yet unserved. They were times of great movement and activity, in which Jirapa suddenly found itself the spiritual centre of the Northwest and the stage for yet more manifestations of God's eternally youthful Spirit.

When, at the end of April 1932, the expected rains failed to appear, the people began to worry. They were accustomed to such worries, however; droughts were frequent in the North and had been for as long as they could remember. All were subsistence farmers, barely eking out an existence on the land, so that lack of rain at the proper time could very well mean for them the difference between life and death. As April became May, and May dwindled into June, and still the sun beat down implacably from a cloudless sky day after day, worry turned to despair. Sacrifices were offered in all the villages to appease the spirits. When nothing happened, they were repeated and then repeated again, each time with diminishing expectations. Those who prayed at the mission (the catechumens) refused to join in the sacrifices to the spirits, even though their fields were as dry and parched as those of the others. Soon they were being blamed for the drought.

"If the spirits are angry," the people said, "they are angry at those who pray with the Christians and refuse to sacrifice to them."

But the catechumens would not be swayed, and the witch doctors could find no sacrifice acceptable to their unresponsive masters. Little by little, complaints against the catechumens died down as the people realized that only one alternative remained to them. Perhaps, after all, the God of the Christians held the key to the heavens. It was worth a try, at any rate. Anything was worth a try if it worked. Though not all agreed, many felt that the threat of famine in the coming year was too real to let religious principles stand in the way of a possible solution.

In the villages, the elders gathered — sometimes on their own initiative, sometimes on the initiative of the chiefs — to form delegations to go to the mission at Jirapa. They would see if the missionaries could be more persuasive with their God than their own specialists had been with the spirits.

One such delegation stands out in my memory. It was about eight o'clock on the morning of 5 June 1932 when Hector came looking for me to tell me that a large group of elders from Daffiama was asking for me. They had come bearing gifts, he told me, and looking uncomfortable about it. I went out to receive them where they stood, in front of the mission house.

Despite the early hour, there was already considerable activity around the place. The day promised to be another oppressively hot one, and people were intent on accomplishing as much as possible while it was still relatively cool. Not a cloud could be seen from one horizon to the other.

When I reached the group, I saw that Hector had been right. Some thirty persons stood about uneasily awaiting me, clutching gifts of chickens, eggs, and a little produce. It was clear from the look on their faces that, though they had come to seek a favour, they weren't at all sure they were going to receive it.

After a brief exchange of customary greetings, their spokesman, a bold and unceremonious man, poorly equipped for a public
relations role, spread before me the gifts they had brought and
got right to the point.

"What we want is rain," he said.

Well, to tell the truth, I was annoyed. This wasn't even mini-
mally polite Dagati procedure. I decided to let my annoyance
show.

"What do you mean? Do you think I deal in rain?" As I spoke
I turned out the pockets of my cassock. "You see? *I* have no rain
to give you. The rain is God's and His alone to give, not mine.
Take back your gifts. God doesn't want your chickens."

There was a gasp of shock and a look of chagrin on several
faces in the delegation. Was the Christian God going to turn His
back on their plea too? The group withdrew a little distance to
confer. They had come expecting a straightforward transaction:
their gifts in exchange for a little rain, or at least some efforts
to obtain it for them. If the gifts were not satisfactory, the father
should have said so, and in what way, so that they could have
tried to correct their error. Instead, he had disconcerted them
by rejecting their gifts outright. Some wanted to return to
Daffiama immediately, before the sun got much higher in the
heavens. But other, cooler heads prevailed. Finally, another
spokesman came forward and addressed me.

"That man who spoke just now, don't pay any attention to him,"
he told me. "He doesn't know how to speak to a big man. We did
not mean to offend you. When we go to a big man for any reason,
it is our custom to offer him gifts. In this way we let him know
that we want to be friends with him. If he refuses our gifts, it
means he rejects our friendship."

He and his companions were watching me attentively now,
trying to discern a softening in my attitude toward them. Though
I was beginning to appreciate my mistake in regard to the gifts,
it obviously wasn't showing on my face sufficiently for them to
notice. The spokesman hurried on.

"You know our village. You know that we are poor people
there. Our gifts reflect that. They are not worthy of you, we

know. But we have no better ones to offer. Please, Father, accept them... and our friendship... and ask God to send us rain so that our people may not go hungry and die."

I was mollified by the humble good manners of this elder and mortified at my own faux pas. I looked at the gifts still spread before me. Then, offering him my hand, I said: "Please understand me. I did not reject your gifts because of their quality or their quantity, but simply because I did not know the true motive behind them. Thank you for your explanation. I am sorry for the misunderstanding. Certainly I accept your gifts and I gladly accept the friendship that goes with them."

There was a noticeable relaxing of tension as the elder and I shook hands. Even those who had difficulty with my pronunciation of Dagaare understood that I accepted their gifts at least.

"As for the question of rain," I continued, "of course God can give it to you, and He will. But first He wants something from you."

The Dagaaba were not accustomed to giving anything to God directly. All offerings were made to lesser beings who might or might not accept to act as intermediaries with Him on their behalf. That God should even know they existed, let alone condescend to require something of them directly, was enough of an innovation to cause shock.

"He wants you to promise Him three things," I said. "First, you must promise to stop making sacrifices to spirits. Second, you must allow your people freedom to come to pray at the mission whenever they want to do so. And third, you must not force your daughters to marry anyone against their will."

A loud murmur greeted my words. These might be God's conditions for giving them rain, but not all were agreed the exchange was a fair one. After much animated discussion among themselves, the spokesman returned with the delegation's response.

"The second thing God asks, we all agree to that," he announced. "We will not stand in the way of anyone from our village who wishes to pray with the Christians. And we can even agree to the third thing if God really insists on it, though we think He would not insist quite so much if He knew our daughters as we

Remy McCoy, in the habit of a White Father postulant; his sister Margaret (Sister Monica of the Sisters of Providence); and their parents, Michael and Sarah McCoy. Photo taken in 1920 or 1921.

McCoy family home in Mayo, Quebec (1920).

Canadian members of the ordination class of 28 June 1925 (Carthage, Tunisia). Standing, l. to r.: Antoine Boivin, Jacques Desmarais (1900-74), Edouard Fafard (1899-1973), Auguste St. Pierre (1898-1981), Olivier Bédard (1898-1966), Jean-Baptiste Durand (1898-1970), Paul Lefils (1902-80), Henri Côté (1900-82). Seated, l. to r.: François-Xavier Lapointe (1898-1973), Armand Landreville (1900-63), Antoine Caumartin (1899-1975), Jacques Boudreau (1896-1967), Remigius McCoy.

On his return to Canada after ordination, young Remy McCoy celebrated two "First Masses", one in his home parish in Mayo (19 July 1925) and the other a week later in Perkins, Quebec, at the invitation of the pastor, Father Morin (above, top centre). In this photo, taken at the Perkins gathering, Father McCoy appears between his father and Sister Monica (his mother had died the previous year). Other brothers and sisters present were Msgr. Edmund McCoy (second row, third from right); Joseph (third row, fourth from left); Rosalie, who would enter the convent later that year (standing beside Joseph and wearing hat); and Mae (Mary), holding her youngest son Edmund (behind Msgr. Edmund). Mae's husband, Edward O'Brien, is the first person on left in third row. Beside him stands their eldest son Redmond, while their eldest daughter Marion can be seen (back row, centre) just below Father Morin and between Joseph and Rosalie. The rest of the O'Brien children are in the front row (l. to r.): Walter, Kay, Monica, Patrick, Eileen, and Andrew.

Father McCoy and some of his students. Navrongo 1926.

Typical compound of the Navrongo area of northern Ghana. (Photos "Vivante Univers")

The government rest house on "Nasaalatang" (White man's hill) in Jirapa. It was here that the first missionaries to Dagao were lodged upon their arrival on 30 November 1929. (Photo by Michael Wood)

Chief Ganaa, first Jirapa naa (circa 1930).

Bishop Oscar Morin, vicar apostolic of Navrongo (1934).

Brother Basilide with one of his masons, Willie
Balembora.

Chief Ganaa's palace. The only multi-storied dried-mud edifice in the
Gold Coast at the time (1929).

The first church in NW Gold Coast, built in Jirapa in 1934 and dedicated to St. Joseph.

Interior of first church in Jirapa.
Sanctuary and part of nave.

Chief Yelpoe I, successor to Chief
Ganaa as Jirapa naa.

Sa ne Bie ne **Vorong** Song yuure enga.
Amina.

Mâ,.....,mâ nâ are Nawine ninge,mâ
eng nware Father zie,ka mâ bwòra na tung
n Katekisi tuma a ku Nawine,k'O nyè puu-
bo yagha a pwò.

Mâ eng nware ka n na tuna n tuma za
sing Father mine nà yele lè,ba nâ liéra
Nawine zu n zie n so.

Mâ eng nware ka n mengu na eru ania
tuuro Nawine sore vela.

Mâ eng nware ka n na sungna n taaba
zu,sing Nawine nâ bwòra lè,ka ba me tuuro Nawine sore vela.A zuing,mâ na sungna
ba ne n puro yèla za,ne n nware yèla za,
ne n eebo viele zu,ne n doghè yèla za.

Mâ nâ eng n nware nga,n bung kye era
ne n pwò za.

Mâ nâ bwòra na taa n nware nga vela,
n bang ka n yong kon twò taa.A zuing,mâ
pâ sòrò n Ma Virgo Maria,ane n Maleke-
Guuro,ane n Ninsong-Guuro,ka ba soro a
grasia nga Nawine zie,a ku mâ.

Mâ pâ de n menga za a eng Nawine nuu-
ri pwò,kye kyilla n tuma tonno O zie yong.

N pwotirong la lè,ka n yele.

annburozios Bunnu
....
Sargius Bayss

Original text, in Dagaare, of catechist's promise. Each catechist read
it publicly and signed it before a representative of the ecclesiastical
authority during the commissioning ceremony at the end of the formal
training period. A translation appears in note 5 of chapter 10.

Chief Karbo of Lawra (wearing chest medallion) surrounded by some of his elders and headmen.

Catechists Simon Beru (l.) and John Kyefondeme (r.) prepare food for St. Joseph's Day festivities (1949). Simon, then catechist at Eremon, was the father of Irenaeus Songliedong who later became a priest of the Wa diocese. John, the first Christian convert in the Northwest, was head catechist at Jirapa.

Remigius Francis-Xavier McCoy (ca. 1937).

A visit to Jirapa mission (1936) by the chief commissioner and the regional medical officer. Standing, l. to r.: Father Ubald Rochon; the chief commissioner and his wife; Doctor Brennan (reg. med. officer); Father Jean-Baptiste Durand. Kneeling: Fathers Gabriel Champagne and Stanislas Leblanc.

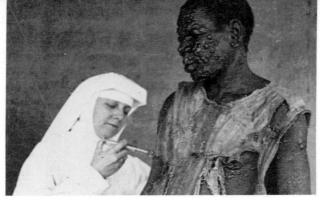

Sister Clementine (Gertrude Lapointe) treats a yaws
patient in the Jirapa clinic.

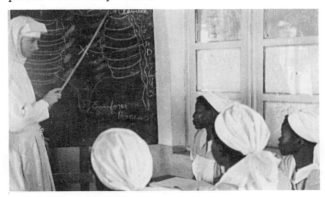

Sister Cyprian instructing student nurses at Jirapa
Hospital (ca. 1955).

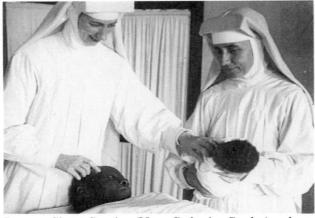

L. to r.: Sister Cyprian (Mary Catherine Swales) and
Mother Caltry (Thérèse Belzile) present a new-born
baby to its mother.

Distribution of medicines to leprosy patients at Jirapa
clinic. Seated: Sister John (Gladys Hayford). Standing:
Sister Evremond (Imelda Drapeau).

Recognition of the work done in NW Ghana by the
Franciscan Missionaries of Mary came with the bestowal
on Mother Caltry in 1959 of the African Society of
London's bronze medal "for services rendered to Africa".
The official ceremony took place on 3 April 1960. In
addition to the medal and a modest check of ten pounds
sterling, the women of Jirapa insisted on presenting her
with homemade gifts of their own.

NO. 216 /23/1937 SF.1C.

DISTRICT COMMISSIONER'S OFFICE,
LAWRA - N.'S.,
18th March, 1949.

WITCHES.

The Jirapa-na has been asked to hold an investigation of the twenty so-called witches now residing at your Mission .

2. Please give him every assistance over this matter.

3. When the investigation is finished, further discussions will have to take place concerning the future of these people.

ASST. DISTRICT COMMISSIONER
LAWRA

THE WHITE FATHERS, JIRAPA, ✓
    JIRAPA - N. TS.

K'A   Inf. copies to:-
                            THE JIRAPA N. A.
                        THE LAWRA CONF. N. A.

Gathering of Gold Coast missionaries in Canada on the occasion of the episcopal ordination of Father Gérard Bertrand, named to succeed an ailing Bishop Oscar Morin as vicar apostolic of Navrongo (1947). Standing, l. to r.: Emile Rioux, Maurice Chartrand (1911-67), Camille Lafrance, Charles Gagnon (1894-1967), Victor Desrosiers, Roger Germain (1909-74). Seated, l. to r.: Joseph Larochelle (1904-87), Bishop Morin (1878-1952), Bishop Bertrand (1911-76), J. Alfred Richard, Jean-Baptiste Dagenais (1881-1957).

Jirapa N.A.

22; 3. 49.

My good friend,

        I shall be coming up with my chiefs at 10. a.m in order that we might pick out those witches you spoke with the District Commissioner the and other day. And so I hope to get all of them grouped at one place.

        I am,

        Your good friend,

        Yelpoe Jirapa Naa his x mks

N. A. clerk

As these two documents (opposite page and above) show, the problem of "witches" continued to flare up from time to time despite efforts of the British colonial government and the missionaries to put an end to it. The first is a message from the DC's office in Lawra to the White Fathers in Jirapa, alerting them to the Jirapa naa's upcoming investigation of some "twenty so-called witches" who had taken refuge at the mission. The second document, a letter to Father McCoy drawn up for the Jirapa naa (Yelpoe I) by his clerk, notifies the priest of his arrival to begin his investigation of the alleged sorcery.

Newly-ordained Father Joseph Awia of Navrongo, flanked by his father, Hector Awia, and his mother, Odilla (ca. 1958). Joseph was the first Christian to be baptized in Jirapa, shortly after his birth there in 1930. His parents had accompanied the first missionaries to the Northwest the previous year.

Rt. Rev. Gabriel Champagne, first bishop of Tamale (1950-1975).

The McCoys (ca. 1945): Remy, May (Mary), Sister Monica, and Fred.

do. But as for the first thing He asks...." He looked down and shook his head slowly. "What will happen to us if we desert the spirits? We are afraid."

We were getting somewhere. Two out of three on the first try wasn't bad at all. But I was going for all or nothing.

"My friend," I said, "what will happen to you if you reject the will of God who is far mightier than any spirit? To offer sacrifice to mere spirits is an insult to Him. Is not God the Master of all, even of the spirits?"

"Yes, yes," the elder agreed hastily. "God is the All-Powerful One. But it is the spirits who deal with humanity. He is too big to be concerned about us."

The rest of the delegation had moved in closer, intent on catching every word of a discussion that concerned them all vitally.

"That is where you are wrong," I countered, "and where your witch doctors and fetishists have led you astray. God knows each and every one of you and loves you. He knows your needs even before you ask Him for help. He loves you so much, in fact, that He sent His only Son on earth to be born of a woman, to grow to manhood learning to work with His hands and to know weariness and hunger, even sorrow, as you do. But more: He suffered at the hands of unjust men and gave His very life for you because His Father was willing to pay any price — even the life of His only Son — to rescue you from evil. That is how much God loves you. The spirits can have no power against those whom God loves and who love and serve only Him in return."

My partner in dialogue had listened with sharp attention. From the expression on his face, I could see a question forming in his mind, so I paused to let him ask it.

"If, as you say, God knows our needs and loves us so much, why has He not sent us rain already?"

A very good question, I thought. I wonder if I can answer it.

"Because you did not ask Him for it. You asked the spirits instead. The spirits have no power to grant anything. If God had intervened, you would have thought it was the spirits who were answering you and you would have continued to believe in their power and to live in slavery to them."

Once more there was a prolonged consultation among the members of the delegation, more earnest than the previous ones but without the heat of emotion this time. Finally, when all discussion had ceased, their spokesman returned to face me.

"Very well," he announced, "we will not offer sacrifice to spirits anymore if God will give us rain. We have all agreed to it. What more must we do?"

"You must ask Him for rain yourselves," I replied.

The elder understood me perfectly. "You want us to pray," he said, "but we do not know how."

"To pray is simply to talk to God. You can talk to Him anywhere and at any time, for He is everywhere," I assured them. "He is also in that house." I indicated the chapel. "You can go there and talk to Him, if you like."

As I made this little speech, I watched the perplexed expressions on the faces before me. A glimmer of fear flickered in more than one pair of eyes. Their spokesman gave voice to this.

"But we don't know how. We have never talked to Him before. He is too big."

That again, I thought. Then I decided to reply with a question.

"Can a father be too big to listen to his own children when they are in need? Even the greatest chief will do that. God too is a Father, the Father of all. You can trust Him to listen to you and to answer you. Just tell Him what you came to tell me, about your people and the danger that they might starve if you don't get rain soon for your crops. But most important of all, tell Him you are willing now to listen to Him and to follow His wishes. That will please Him more than anything else."

When I had finished, the elder looked at me in silence for a moment. Then he looked slowly over his shoulder at the now silent delegation. After a long and thoughtful interval of mute communication with its members, he turned back to me.

"Will you come with us?" he asked.

"We'll go together," I replied.

I led the way into the chapel, followed by the twenty-five or thirty Daffiamans. All maintained an exemplary silence as they crowded in behind me. There were several unsuccessful attempts to imitate my genuflection and even to make the sign of the cross when I made mine.

"How shall we pray?" I asked them after I had got them to remove their hats and kneel on the packed-dirt floor.

The elder responded in their name. "Whatever you tell us to do, we will do it. But perhaps it would be best if you prayed in our name. You are a man of God and know His ways."

"Very well," I replied. I knelt before the altar and concentrated with all my being. Then slowly I began to address aloud the All-Powerful, Eternal, Majestic God, Creator of the universe, Tamer of spirits, and Protector of His children. I called upon Him to hear the prayers of these particular children of His who had come from Daffiama this day to honor Him and to beg His forgiveness for having doubted His power and mistakenly placed their trust in mere spirits who were powerless to help them. They now knew, I said, that they had done wrong and promised never to offer sacrifices to spirits again.

Pausing, I turned to the attentive congregation behind me.

"Do you agree?" I asked them.

Yes, they agreed.

I resumed praying.

"Almighty God and Father of all. We adore You as the only Being worthy of adoration. We want to serve You and You alone. We have come to understand that You want all men and women to know You and love You and serve You, and that You are angry when they are not free to do so if they wish. That is why we promise today that all in our village who wish to know You better and to pray with the Christians will be prevented no longer from doing so. We know we have displeased You greatly in this and we humbly beg Your forgiveness for having placed obstacles in their way in the past. We give our solemn word this day to refrain from ever offending You in this way again."

Once more I paused to check with the silent petitioners whose voice I had become.

"Do you all agree?"

Yes, they all agreed.

I continued to pray in their name, now thanking God for the gift of freedom. God was not a Master of slaves, I said, but the Father of a multitude of sons and daughters. We knew that a true father did not seek subservience from his children but love, and love cannot be commanded; it must be free or it is not love at all. He had taught us the value He Himself placed on freedom by creating all human beings free to serve Him or to reject Him. He would not coerce or buy anyone's love. Now we wanted to imitate His absolute regard for free will by honouring it at work in those around us. Because of this, and because we knew He expected it of us, we promised to stop trying to impose our wills on our children in the question of marriage. From now on, we the people of Daffiama solemnly promised God that the girls of our compounds would be free to choose their own husbands.

"Do you agree?"

There were a few pinched faces in the crowd and somewhat less enthusiasm this time in responding to my query, but all agreed to abide by the promise they had made, even though the wisdom of it clearly eluded some of them.

I went on to pray for another twenty minutes or so, voicing the pleas of the delegation for rain and expressing their firm faith in His desire and ability as Supreme Being to give it to them. Then I had them repeat the Our Father after me and we ended with another sign of the cross, which I explained to them briefly.

It was ten o'clock by the time we left the chapel and the delegation took its leave to begin the fifteen-mile trek home. When the swiftest walkers reached Daffiama four hours later, they were met by a soaking rain. Their immediate reaction was one of jubilation and the urge to retrace their steps to Jirapa to give thanks. But the rain was falling so heavily, they finally decided to wait until the next morning. Had they carried through with their original impulse, they would have been surprised to see that as soon as they left the boundaries of the village, all was as dry as before.

The rain that day, and for several days after that, fell only on Daffiama.

Early the next morning, a delegation comprising three of the elders was back at the mission, radiant and happy and very grateful. They had come, they said, to thank me.

"No, no, no!" I said. "Don't thank me. First of all because we all prayed together. But it is God you must thank. It was He to whom you spoke yesterday who answered your prayers and gave you the rain. Thank Him.

They did, and this time I didn't have to speak for them.

Word of what had happened at Daffiama soon spread to other similarly afflicted villages. Before long, delegations seeking rain were arriving from all over the Northwest and even from across the border in the French Sudan. The mission diary at Jirapa records a long list of such arrivals from early June until the middle of August. On one day alone, 18 July 1932, twenty separate delegations came to pray for rain. So generous was God with His answer in some cases that a new problem arose. On 22 October of that year, we were surprised when groups arrived from Nadoli, Daffiama, and Kaleo to pray for the rain to stop! The millet was in bloom then and any further rain would be detrimental to it. They too received the desired answer to their prayers.

One day in late October, as the millet stood white in the fields around Daffiama, a *malam* (local Muslim leader) appeared at the chief's compound and asked to see him. It was urgent, he said. When he was brought into the chief's presence, he told him a piece of news that startled him and made him dispatch messengers at once to summon all the elders to an emergency meeting.

By the time the last of those convoked had arrived, speculation about the reason for the sudden summons was running high. The chief would not prolong their suspense unnecessarily, however. When all had assembled, he called the malam and invited him to repeat the news he had brought him earlier.

The man stepped forward and began his recital. He had been walking home that day, he said, and had decided to cut through a millet field. As he was going along, stepping carefully through the high grass, he suddenly came upon a hole in the ground and noticed some movement around it and a noisy hum coming from inside. Going closer to investigate, he found the hole to be literally swarming with newly-hatched locusts. Instead of proceeding homeward, he had come immediately to alert the chief to the danger brewing.

The elders saw the seriousness of the situation at once. The presence of locusts in that hole was an alarm sounding or a knell tolling for the entire region. In thousands of such holes everywhere, similar swarms of locusts were preparing to take flight, perhaps at that very moment. And the tender millet and guinea corn would be entirely at their mercy. The prospect of hard times returned.

After the malam had withdrawn to return to his home, the chief threw the meeting open to suggestions on how to deal with the problem before them.

Some of the elders saw the hand of the spirits in the impending disaster; they (the spirits) were angered at the neglect they had suffered in Daffiama since the delegation had gone to Jirapa in search of rain. They were taking their vengeance now at the most crucial moment of the season. The only solution, they argued, was for every household to sacrifice a chicken to the spirits early the following morning so that the locusts would be prevented from destroying their crops.

Those of the elders who had prayed for rain in Jirapa four months earlier objected to this. One of them pointedly reminded the assembly of the undeniable failure of the spirits to bring rain despite countless sacrifices offered them each day for months. On the other hand, God had given them plenty of rain, and for all the farms of Daffiama without exception, and He had not needed their sacrifices to do it.

"Yes," replied the others, "but a lot of good your rain will have done us if the locusts devour the fruits of it. Perhaps your God did send the rains, but it is the spirits who now send the locusts. Unless we all sacrifice to them, their anger will not be appeased and we shall again find ourselves facing famine."

But the elders of the Jirapa experience, many of whom had now become catechumens, would hear nothing of such a solution. No, they said, they could not offer sacrifice to spirits. They had

given their word to God never to do so again, and they could not
go back on that solemn promise even in the face of locusts. God
had saved them once; He could do so again if they asked Him.

The chief, meanwhile, had been following the discussion closely,
now inclining toward the argument of one group and then of the
other. But his sentiments still favoured traditional ways over
innovations, and he found himself siding more and more with the
proponents of sacrifice. There was something he didn't like about
the attitude of the others. They seemed to set themselves apart
from everyone else now that they were praying with the Christians. He had a suspicion they no longer respected him as the
ultimate authority in Daffiama. That thought angered him sometimes, though he had tried not to show it for fear the rains might
stop if he did. But now the "miracle" of the rain and its importance
was overshadowed by this new and imminent threat to their well-
being which loomed ever larger in his mind.

Discussion among the elders continued unabated until the chief
raised his hand to signal that he had heard enough. He rose from
his seat and thanked them for coming at such short notice and
for advising him on the matter. After listening to all they had to
say, he had reached his decision.

"Go home at once and prepare," he ordered. "Early tomorrow
morning, the head of every compound in the village must offer
sacrifice to the spirits so that they will relent and spare our crops
from the locusts. The sacrifices will be repeated each morning
until the danger has passed."

There was an uneasy movement among some of the elders.
The chief noticed it and, in order to squelch any protest before
it could begin, he added:

"*All* heads of compounds, without exception. Under penalty
of imprisonment for those who disobey." (At that time, chiefs had
power to imprison their subjects.)

But if the threat of locusts could not move the elders who
prayed with the Christians to renege on their promise to God, it
was not likely the threat of prison would either. A spokesman for
the group stepped up to face the chief.

"You may put us in prison if you like, that is your right as chief of this village. But we are not making any sacrifices to spirits, neither tomorrow nor any day."

The chief glared in anger. The atmosphere grew tense. In the awkward silence that followed, many of those who belonged to neither camp reflected unhappily on the choices before them. Either one held disadvantages. If they refused to offer sacrifice, they would incur the chief's wrath with its unpleasant consequences. And if they did offer sacrifice to the spirits, who knew what price the God of the Christians would exact of them? His vengeful side had yet to be seen.

Meanwhile, the chief had managed to contain his fury and found his voice again.

"*All* heads of compounds," he repeated with dry authority, "without exception," and stomped out.

The news quickly spread from compound to compound and all through the village. Before nightfall the catechumens of the six different sections of Daffiama gathered together to pray and to discuss what they would do in the event the chief carried out his threat. About one thing they were all agreed: there would be no sacrificing to spirits on their part, come what might. Beyond that, they were unsure what to do. A messenger was chosen from among them to go to Jirapa at dawn to inform the missionaries and ask their advice.

Early the next morning the chief and a number of heads of compounds invoked the spirits and offered sacrifice to them. At the same time, those who had chosen to place their trust in God gathered in groups in their respective sections of the village for morning prayer. Both camps sought the same end, though one prayed in fear and the other in hope.

The messenger from Daffiama arrived at the mission around mid-morning. We listened to his report of the previous day's events and of the courageous stand of the Christian catechumens, tender plants (of the faith) like the flowering millet they were trying to save through God's intervention. Father Larochelle offered to go to the village and investigate the matter.

As he approached the outskirts of Daffiama around noon, he was surprised by the strange sight that greeted him. While some farms had been stripped bare of all growing things so that only stubble remained to indicate where crops had once stood, others had been left untouched and still lustily blooming.

He drove on to the chief's compound. There the chief himself came out to meet him, wearing an expression of pain and remorse on his face. Before Father Larochelle could ask him what had happened that morning, he began to speak. Gone was the self-assurance and authority of the previous day. In their stead, a subdued and chastened manner defined the man as he nearly choked on his chagrin.

"You cannot imagine the sorrow that is in my heart, Father," he said. "Some of us let *Sitana* (Satan) deceive us into making sacrifices this morning, and see how God has punished us. The locusts have eaten up the crops of all who sacrificed to the spirits and spared those of your people who refused to do so. I know now that God is indeed mightier than the spirits and that what you teach about Him must be true."

Father Larochelle went to verify what the grieving chief had just told him and found it to be so. Those who had trusted in God to protect them and had risked incurring the chief's ire still had their millet and corn standing in their fields unharmed, whereas all who had chosen to obey the chief had nothing to show for it but stubble and bitter memories to reap. The locusts had come out of the east like a dark rain cloud, which at first they were taken to be, at about nine o'clock that morning. By the time the cloud had got close enough to be identified for what it was, advance "scouts" were already landing at selected farms and beginning to devour every leaf and blade of grass in their path. The actual devastation, when the main force arrived, had taken place in a matter of minutes.

What happened that late October day in Daffiama was a painful lesson for some and a great grace for others. Prior to that, many who had become catechumens and were walking the fifteen miles to Jirapa each weekend to assist at Mass and receive instruction had been meeting with much opposition from their people at home. After this second manifestation by God of His power, confirming the first (that of the rain the previous June), the opposition began to fade. As for the catechumens themselves, they felt the presence of God among them, and following "God's way" now became the most important thing in their lives. They undertook to teach each other the prayers and texts of the catechism. On Sunday mornings, they would wake one another at four o'clock in order to arrive at Jirapa in time for Mass and instruction.[1]

The rain "events" did not all occur in 1932, despite what many have written or supposed. God went on showing His favour to those who prayed to Him for rain in the frequent periods of drought which afflicted and continue to afflict the North. In each instance the requisites were faith in His ability to do so and a willingness to serve Him and to be guided by Him.

One such occurrence took place around 1955. By that time, Chief Ganaa had died and had been replaced by Yelpoe I as Jirapa naa. The rainy season had begun well enough that year, with periodic showers to permit the farmers to work the soil and prepare the mounds to receive the seed. By the end of May, the young shoots had pushed their heads out of the ground in search of light and fruition. Then the rain suddenly stopped. For weeks not a cloud appeared on the horizon. The delicate plants began to wither and die while the farmers looked on, powerless to do anything about it.

In late June, the chiefs of Jirapa, Tizza, and Konzokola came on pilgrimage with their elders to the mission seeking relief from the drought. Our interview this time took place under a nim tree near the credit union office. Chief Yelpoe acted as spokesman for the group, explaining the problem to the head catechist, Charles Ganaa, who then repeated it to me. (When it came time for me to reply, the order was reversed: from me to Charles to the chief. All this repeating was unnecessary since the three of us were speaking the same language, Dagaare, and no communication problem existed. But it was the custom among the Dagaabas and other ethnic groups in the Northwest for chiefs to use intermediaries when speaking or being spoken to in their capacity as chiefs.)

Neither the chiefs who had gathered beneath the nim tree nor their elders were Christians, but they had come to pray to the Christian God because experience had proven that He listened better in times of distress than did the spirits. I showed approval of this attitude and commended them for placing their trust where it would not be deceived. But as I had done so many times before, I outlined God's terms for such assistance.

1. They must pray only to Him in the future, not to false intermediaries (spirits).

2. They must not forbid anyone to pray to Him or to go to the mission or to the village catechist to learn about Him.

3. They must not force their children to marry anyone against their will.

Of course there were other things God would eventually ask of them, but in the first stages of possible conversion these three conditions were considered essential.

One of the chiefs thought these were bargaining points and asked if God would be willing to settle for two out of three. (This was a fairly common misconception.) He did not say which of the three he found objectionable, though eventually we came to suspect it was the second. We heard a rumour later that his predecessor had laid a curse on anyone under his juridiction who embraced Christianity; as his successor, he was either unwilling or afraid to lift it.

I replied that it was all or nothing. Another chief brushed aside the suggestion of the first, saying: "Let us go into the church and tell God we accept all His conditions. It will be a small price to pay if He can save our crops." There was some reluctance to go along with this on the part of some, but finally the whole delegation stood and went into the church. I was asked to lead them in prayer and I did so for quite some time. When we had finished, they thanked me and went off, each to his own home.

That afternoon, no rain fell. Night approached and the sky remained stubbornly clear. The next day dawned limpid and bright with nary a cloud to relieve the monotonous blue.

Three days later, Charles Ganaa and I went to visit Konzokola village, five miles from Jirapa. The chief there, a sub-chief of the

Jirapa naa, had been one of the petitioners for rain earlier in the week. We greeted him at his compound before going about our affairs. He was a sincere and pleasant man, and, after returning our greeting warmly and offering us the customary calabash of pito to drink, he turned to what weighed heaviest on his mind.

"We still have had no rain," he reminded me.

"Well," I replied easily, "what did you expect? You did not agree to the conditions set down."

"Some of us didn't," he said, "but some of us did."

He looked away — sadly, I thought. Perhaps he was recalling the disagreement under the nim tree. Charles and I sipped our pito in silence and waited. After a few moments, the chief turned to us again and his face had brightened with what was apparently an inspiration.

"Couldn't we pray now... right here in the village? We could ask God again. I assure you that we are willing to accept all His conditions." He leaned forward eagerly in his chair, lending emphasis to his request.

"I would like nothing better," I told him. "Where do you suggest we pray?"

It was market day in Konzokola and the village was thronged. The chief sent messengers to the market place to invite the people to gather in an open field nearby where they would pray together to God to send them rain. When the chief, Charles, and I arrived at the spot, a large crowd had assembled and many of the people were already kneeling on the ground in anticipation of what was to take place. A fervent prayer went up from that open field in Konzokola that day "and God looked down with favour upon His people".

That very night Konzokola received a soaking, life-restoring rain, while the surrounding villages remained dry.

10

Obstacles

At the turn of the century, when the *zambogo* (raiders) Babatu and Samouri invaded northern Gold Coast, taking a number of slaves and whatever valuables they could find to their stronghold northwest of the present Ghana, British and French forces combined to overcome them. Boundaries were then drawn up giving Great Britain possession of all land south of the ninth parallel, from the Black Volta River on the west to a little beyond Bawku on the east. This meant that the Dagaabas were split into two groups, one on either side of the Black Volta frontier.

As Christianity began to attract those of northwest Gold Coast, it was only natural that they should share their enthusiasm with relatives and friends on the French-controlled side of the border. Soon individual Dagaabas began crossing over on weekends to make the long journey on foot to Jirapa. On 20 July 1932, a whole delegation arrived from the border village of Wessa (Ouessa) to pray for relief from the severe drought. Though there is no recorded proof in the Jirapa mission diary that their prayers obtained the desired effect, later developments would suggest that they did. A month later, on 23 August, great numbers arrived from the French side and asked to be inscribed in the list of prospective catechumens. Another great influx of them appeared at the mission on 19 October; and on 13 January 1933, five young men from Wessa presented themselves at the mission house and asked to be trained as catechists.

The Dagati chiefs in the French Sudan began to worry about the increasing traffic eastwards. Not all who left returned. And those who did return did so only once every two or three weeks, to attend to their farms, and then headed back to the mission. On the Gold Coast side, British colonial officials were alerted by the increased traffic on the roads and grew concerned about the periodic strains on Jirapa to absorb the migrants. When French colonial officials realized what was happening, they consulted the chiefs about the problem. What, they asked them, would be the most effective way to stop their Dagati subjects from going over to the Gold Coast? Simple, replied the chiefs. Just ask the French-speaking White Fathers in Bobo-Dioulasso and Wagadugu to open missions among the Dagaabas in French territory. Strangely enough, the suggestion was acted upon. Though French colonial officials at the time were not generally favourable to the expansion of the Catholic Church in their territory, they were still less favourable to the migration of tax-payers to British territory.

After some initial hesitation, the French commandant in charge of the region contacted Church authorities and requested a meeting with them for 22 February 1933 at Wessa. Representatives of the missionaries on both sides of the border were invited to study the problem and advise him on its solution.

On the day appointed, the White Father delegation arrived early in the morning as requested. It consisted of Bishop Joanny Thévenoud, vicar apostolic of Wagadugu; Monsignor Oscar Morin, prefect apostolic of Navrongo; Monsignor Césaire Esquerre, prefect apostolic of Bobo-Dioulasso; and Fathers Louis Durrieu, Marcel Paternot, Jean Lesourd, and I. The French commandant was awaiting us and, after introductions had been made, we got down to work immediately.

The meeting was a cordial one in which none of the old sources of contention arose. Our host outlined the situation and explained the need to have stable populations on both sides of the border in order to avoid "problems". He did not seem to be aware that the border itself was the problem. After he had finished his long exposition, he paused to invite our comments on the matter and any suggestions we might have to make for its solution.

No one in our group (comprised of five Frenchmen and two Canadians) made any suggestion of a solution to his problem. We all agreed, however, that it would not do to try to seal the border. Aside from the impracticality of such a move, it would be sure to be opposed by the British and eventually create more problems than it solved. The discussion went round in circles for some time, resolving nothing, until the commandant, trying to hide his disappointment, intervened to rescue it.

What followed was a curious experience for us who had been trying unsuccessfully for years to open a mission among the Dagaabas in the French Sudan. With an anticlerical government in power in Paris, the local authorities had always turned a deaf ear to our petitions. Now, as we sat there listening attentively, one of those same authorities began to almost plead with us to do just what we had wanted to do all along. Suddenly it sounded as if the glory of France and the good of the Church were about to embrace again after their long estrangement. We waited, expecting at any moment to hear him say: *"La France, fille-ainnée de l'Eglise!"* But he stopped just short of it.[1]

We showed no great enthusiasm for his scheme. One of us objected that funds were scarce just then and certainly not sufficient to open new missions, especially with all the restrictions the government placed on such projects. The restrictions could be lifted, countered the commandant. But then there was the question of personnel, said another. The society had many new commitments and few missionaries available to respond to them. The French authorities could not do much about that. No, the commandant agreed glumly, though he tried valiantly all the same to convince us that the area was rich in possibilities for the Church and that the harvest was indeed ripe.

We gradually allowed ourselves to be persuaded.

After that it was only a matter of choosing the locations. We had already decided among ourselves before the meeting that Dano and Dissin should be the sites. Most of the catechumens crossing the border into the Gold Coast came from those two villages. For some time Monsignor Esquerre had been hoping to open missions there, where the number of those under instruction already surpassed five thousand.[2]

As we headed homeward after a very good lunch hosted by a genial and satisfied commandant, we could not help feeling a trifle satisfied ourselves. It isn't often one has the opportunity to do a favour for the government.

***

On 15 May 1932, eleven student catechists had received the rosary in a special ceremony. Their training course was being accelerated both because of the urgent need of their services and because it was felt that their intensive preparation and daily proximity to the missionaries compensated for what it lacked in length. Subsequent courses would last a normal three-year period, and later, with the addition of English as a requirement, four years.

Meanwhile, the numbers arriving at the mission continued to increase. On weekends, between five thousand and ten thousand people from all over the Northwest descended on Jirapa, sleeping out in the open on three sides of the mission house, weather permitting. A few handfuls of groundnuts sufficed them for breakfast, lunch, and supper.

Sunday morning found the mission astir long before daybreak. The missionaries were normally the first to rise. Since we all wore beards, not much time was needed to perform our ablutions, and within a quarter of an hour we were on our way to the church in silence for morning prayer and meditation.

Our displacement did not go unnoticed, even at that early hour. By the time the "bell" (an automobile brake drum suspended from the roof by a piece of wire and dealt a series of resounding blows with an old pick) announced the approach of the six o'clock Mass, the church, barely able to accommodate four hundred people uncomfortably, somehow held more than five hundred! The High Mass at seven o'clock drew an even larger crowd, with the majority obliged to assist outdoors as best they could. Afterwards, before instructions could get underway, there began the long process of calling the roll. As numbers continued to grow, however, it became necessary to forego checking attendance. It was all we could do to manage the registration of newcomers before noon.

Father Larochelle and I were running hard and badly in need of reinforcements. In just two days (18-19 July 1932), more than a thousand new arrivals asked to be inscribed as Christian catechumens. As I was trying to register them, the crush about me became so great at one point that I was forced to scramble, none too gracefully, into a nearby tree. From my safe perch above the sea of heads, I continued to take names and add them to the seemingly endless list of prospective Christians.

But the apparent "success" of the mission in the Northwest did not go unopposed. Sitana, that patron advocate of ignorance and lies, was not going to loose his hold on the Dagaabas so easily. His great weapon was fear: fear of the spirits and fear of one's neighbour. Their belief that all misfortune was caused somehow by their enemies resulted in the constant need to protect themselves from witchcraft and even poison. Now Christianity had come along to dispel fear and replace it with an ethic of love.

The reaction of the Christian converts was one of profound relief at being freed from the constant fear of doing something to incur the wrath of the spirits. In their joy they would throw away all emblems of superstition — their jujus — and refuse to take part in animist rituals and sacrifices. But any mishap in the household or community was sure to be imputed to them. Missionaries and, later, catechumens would baptize children and adults in danger of death. When these died shortly after, the death was blamed on the baptism and/or the one who had administered it.

One catechumen from the village of Ginginkpwe, near Nandom, went around trying to persuade all his neighbours and friends to abandon their traditional rites and embrace Christianity too. On 26 July 1932, in a fit of zeal, he and several other catechumens seized the fetishes of the people and destroyed them. There was an uproar and the incident was reported to the chief. The accused were apprehended and taken to the DC in Lawra where they were judged and imprisoned for engaging in "subversive activities".

The very next day the same thing happened in the village of Baazing. A group of young catechumens brought pressure on the head of a compound to get him to destroy the fetishes. Again there was an outcry from the non-Christians and the matter was brought to the chief's attention. Baazing, like Ginginkpwe, fell under the jurisdiction of the DC of Lawra, so again the accused were taken before him for judgment. This time he was not so lenient. All were imprisoned for a few days, but the two catechist students among them were also flogged. The warning was clear.

But if the authorities thought to quench the zeal of the new converts by threatening them, they were soon disillusioned. Adversity and opposition have always fed religious zeal, not curbed it. The Dagati Christians were no exception. Didn't it mean they had the spirits on the run? They became more determined than ever, and they felt themselves invincible.

This attitude imbued even the very young who came in contact with Christianity in those days. If they were children of catechumens or of parents unopposed to the Ngwinsore, no problem resulted from their desire to follow Christ.But if they did meet with opposition in the family, being minors meant they had few resources available to them to overcome it. Some who lived close to the mission might try to assist at instruction classes secretly. Those who did not, and who could not easily absent themselves from home unnoticed, had no recourse but to bide their time and hope that God would send them the opportunity they longed for. Others, however, less patient than most, sometimes succeeded in creating their own opportunities. Such was the case of the five sons of the Sankana naa.[3]

When the second mission station in the Northwest was opened at Kaleo in 1932, it served to relieve some of the pressure on Jirapa. Henceforth the catechumens from Sankana had only four miles to walk to attend weekly instruction classes instead of twenty-five. Among those who began to frequent the new mission regularly were the chief's own children.

At first he did not seem to mind what was happening and no obstacle was placed in their way. But when he began to realize where it was all leading, and that they seemed to be serious in forsaking the ways of their ancestors to follow the new religion from the North, he became very angry and ordered them to cease their constant journeying to Kaleo. By this time the children had advanced far enough in their knowledge of the Christian faith to make it impossible for them to obey their father's order easily. The more they tried to skirt his authority, the angrier he grew and the stronger his threats of punishment became. Some of the children eventually bowed to his will out of fear. But nothing he could do seemed to deter the remaining five sons from pursuing their chosen course.

One Sunday morning, determined to thwart their plans to go
to Kaleo, he had his headmen lock them up in his own quarters.
These consisted of a double hut, the smaller part of which had a
door and a narrow window. It was in this part that the boys were
forcibly confined. But not for long. As soon as it seemed safe to
do so, they quietly pried open the window and managed to squeeze
through it despite its narrowness. Though now outside the hut,
they were still inside the walled compound and could not hope to
pass through its only gate without being seen by the chief and
his headmen who sat in front of it taking the morning sun. Neither
could they stay where they were. With the constant coming and
going of persons among the huts of the compound, someone was
apt to discover them at any moment. The eldest of the five, making
his way stealthily, came upon a momentarily deserted hut built
into the wall. Motioning to his brothers to follow quickly, he
entered it and began to remove a part of the grass-thatched roof
until an adequate opening had been made. Through this he sent
the next eldest boy who dropped to the ground outside the
compound and assisted the younger ones as they followed him
over the wall in turn.

Once free, the five brothers set off toward Kaleo as fast as the
slowest of them could run. They had not got far, however, before
someone spotted them escaping and gave the alarm. Leaping to
his feet, the chief shouted to the nearest headman to stop them
and bring them back. The latter quickly ran for his horse. When
they heard the shouts and glanced behind them, the brothers
caught sight of a figure on horseback galloping out of the compound
and heading in their direction. He, however, was not so quick to
see them as they dove under a bridge and hid themselves in the
water. When he had passed overhead, they emerged carefully
and followed him at a safe distance until they reached their usual
path to the mission which the horseman, continuing on the main
road, had missed. Too late for Mass that morning, they were at
least in time to assist at their instruction class. The headman,
meanwhile, not daring to go to the mission in search of them,
returned to Sankana gnashing his teeth.

When they arrived back home late that afternoon, it was to a
severe tongue-lashing and further dire threats from their father.
They were roundly punished for their disobedience and again
ordered to stay away from the Christians. This time the anger

of the chief was such that it left an impression on his young sons. They remained out of his favour all that week, so that when Sunday came there was still enough fear in them to make them hesitate to cross him again so soon. All but the youngest, that is. Rather than sit quietly and await a miracle of grace that would alter his father's negative attitude, he took his bow and two arrows and openly announced his intention to go to the mission as usual that morning.

His brothers stared at him. The chief could not believe his ears. He bellowed in fury at such boldness and ordered a headman to flog the boy on the spot and lock him up. The man, quick to obey, pulled up a fresh millet stalk nearby and began to whip him severely with it. But a youngster, especially a rebellious one, can be as slippery as a fish fighting for its life. Kicking and wiggling, the boy managed at last to free himself from the man's strong grasp. He ran forward a little, turned with his bow already armed, and let fly. The arrow might well have gone right through the headman had he not leaned forward at just the right moment. Instead, it pierced the goatskin on his back in two places, painfully grazing his skin as it did so. He screamed and made a desperate dash for the gate leading from the compound just as a second arrow whistled by, barely missing his shoulder. He was now so frightened, he could not wait to reach the gate but took the first opening he could find, which happened to be at the bottom of the wall. Falling on his stomach and ripping out the pegs that barred the opening, he tried frantically to crawl through it. The boy, his two arrows spent, seized his bow with both hands and began to bring it down repeatedly with all his might on the remaining parts of his escaping victim.

Meanwhile, the chief and all his headmen with him had been thoroughly taken aback by the extent of the youngest son's fury. Not waiting to see the fate of the unfortunate man howling with pain beneath the stinging blows of the bow, they fled the compound in generalized panic, every man for himself.

As soon as everyone has disappeared, the boys who had been afraid to cross their father rushed out and, in company with their brave "Benjamin", set off immediately for Kaleo. They all agreed on the way that they would never return to Sankana. If the missionaries could not take them in, they would look for somebody else with whom they could stay and who would give them work. All they really wanted was to be allowed to practise their religion freely.

The fathers at the mission listened attentively to their story and tried to dissuade them gently from leaving home. Their father was not a bad man, they said, merely a parent concerned for his sons and a chief concerned for traditional values in his village. Even this latter concern, they pointed out, had not moved him to stand in the way of others in Sankana, outside his own family circle, who wished to come to the mission to pray. Given time, he would relent with his family as well.

The boys were not convinced, however, and politely declined to return to their father's compound. But they were finally persuaded to do so when one of the priests offered to accompany them and plead their cause. Possibly because of this courtesy shown him by the missionaries and a new-found respect for the depth of his sons' determination to follow the Ngwinsore (not to mention a secret pride in the mettle his youngest one had shown that day), the chief heard the priest out and agreed to withdraw his opposition. Henceforth, peace would reign once more in his compound.

But though the case of the Sankana naa was settled amicably, antagonism continued in other quarters. The witch doctors, alarmed that their influence in the community and their lucrative livelihood were headed for ruin, increased their attacks on the adherents of the Ngwinsore. The elders were outraged when members of their compounds or of their extended family became "contaminated" and broke with tribal traditions, destroying their fetishes and refusing to take part in ritual sacrifices and vain observances. They reported to the chiefs that the white man's followers were fomenting revolution. The chiefs in turn reported this to administration officials.

Obviously we had hit a nerve that ran all the way down to Accra. On 30 September, the governor of the Gold Coast, accompanied by the DC, paid us a visit. It was not an unpleasant encounter — Governor Thomas was polite and affable — but the warning was unmistakeable. The catechists had to be curbed and our procedures revised.

"You don't realize the danger you are creating for the stability of the region, my dear fathers," he said, sitting on the mission house verandah and looking quite official. "I am sure you did not have this in mind when you conceived the idea of training assistants, but it is evolving in that direction. These young catechists of yours are becoming something of a problem."

We were aware of that. I had gone to Lawra for the trials of the catechumens the preceding July and had witnessed the floggings. But I certainly did not see that the stability of the region was in any jeopardy.

"How do you mean, Your Excellency?" I asked.

Governor Thomas nodded toward the DC. "Captain Armstrong tells me there have been several disruptive incidents in recent months involving, shall we say, 'over-zealous' converts to Christianity destroying private property of non-Christians. Those responsible, I am told, have been dealt with. But this has not put an end to the incidents. We cannot have that, you know. Your catechists have got to respect the rights of others."

Yes, we could agree that there had been a bit of over-zealousness there, and it would have to be reined in. We were already working on it.

"There is also the question of authority," he continued. "The chiefs are the recognized native authority in the villages and regions."

That was only partly true. In many ways the chief held less power than the tendaana. But the British administration did not recognize the latter and governed exclusively through the former.

"Your catechists are seriously eroding that authority, whether they are aware of it or not. A great number of people seem to regard them as the higher authority in their village. Many pay no attention to the chief anymore. Instead of going to him with their family problems and grievances, as they used to do, they now go to the catechist. This is surely very destabilizing," the governor said.

On that I could not agree and I said so.

"Excuse me, Governor, but there must be some misunderstanding here somewhere. Respect for legitimate authority, whether civil or religious, has always been a fundamental principle of our teaching. The student catechists are encouraged to show respect at all times to the chiefs. They are responsible for teaching the Commandments of God to the people, and you know as well as I do what the Fourth Commandment says."

The governor flashed a frightened look in my direction, as if he feared I might ask him to recite it.

"It centers on respect and obedience due to one's parents and, therefore, to all legitimate authority, in all that is not sinful," I continued.

"Quite so," agreed the governor.

"So you see, sir, it is just not true to say that the catechists pose a threat to the authority of the chiefs or to any legitimate authority for that matter."

The two officials reflected on that for a moment before the governor replied.

"I am sure you understand it that way, Father. And perhaps your young catechists do too. But the chiefs and the people do not. In their eyes, the catechists are setting themselves up as rivals to the chiefs, who are losing the loyalty of a significant segment of their people to these Christian 'usurpers'. It may not be true, as you maintain, but your methods and those of the catechists contradict this."

It was true that a kind of social revolution was taking place in the Northwest, but not, I argued, at the cost of the chiefs' prerogatives and legitimate authority. Whenever we missionaries went to a village, we first paid a courtesy visit to the chief in his compound. Certainly that should serve as an example to the Christian catechumens, if they needed one. And in all matters falling within their competence or jurisdiction, we were always careful to consult them before undertaking any initiative. However, if a chief tried to overstep his authority by interfering with God's right of free access to the hearts of His people, or by trying to force his subjects to offer sacrifice to spirits against their will, what were the Christians to do then? Betray their consciences? Could a system of government rooted in the Magna Carta, as Britain's was, turn a blind eye when individual rights were trampled upon in one of its territories?

The governor was already looking at his watch, anxious to be away. It was Captain Armstrong who answered for him.

"It seems to me, Father McCoy, that the animists have rights too. Your people must respect those rights as much as they desire theirs to be respected. Don't your agree?"

"Of course I do, Captain," I replied. "Every person deserves respect even when one disagrees with them. But that's just the point. There are rights and there are *rights*. And those that touch a person's conscience deeply, I believe, must normally take precedence over those of the authorities to maintain traditions, especially when those traditions fail to respect the legitimate right of persons to practise freely the religion of their choice. Am I wrong in this belief? Would King George be pleased to know that in these British-administered territories only the Christians are deprived of their right to worship God unmolested?"

The DC was now looking at his watch too.

"At any rate," I said, winding down my defense, "you may assure the chiefs that their authority is in no danger from the catechists. Not only because of the Fourth Commandment either. There are plenty of good reasons why they should sleep soundly in their beds and not imagine plots against them where there are none. As a matter of fact, the most basic one came from the mouth of the Saviour Himself as He stood before Pilate. It is in the Gospel of John. I'm sure you know it as well as I do."

But the governor was suddenly on his feet, taking his leave. Duty called as usual, he explained, offering his hand in farewell. The DC repeated the gesture of his superior, then descended the verandah steps quickly to hold the door of the car open for him. A few moments later, the officials were off in a cloud of dust.

I wondered if it was something I had said.

That was not the end of the matter by any means. Two days later we received a visit from the DC of Wa, Captain Ardron, a particularly antagonistic individual who made no effort to mask his dislike of Catholics and missionaries. His complaint against our catechists was that they were inciting the people to refuse to work for the chiefs and to boycott traditional funerals in their villages.

I explained to him carefully that the first accusation was inexact. Neither we nor the catechists begrudged the chiefs the use of their own subjects for occasional work when this was legal. Unfortunately, much of it was not. The only real conflict we had with the chiefs on this subject involved their road overseers who seemed to enjoy disrupting Sunday religious services to force Christian catechumens to do road work instead. (And this, I did not bother to add, was really a conflict with the DCs who held the chiefs accountable for the state of the roads in their territories and permitted them to press their people into service without compensation, even though it was against the law to do so.)

As for the traditional funeral rituals, we did not forbid the Christian catechumens to take part in them, only to participate in sacrifices if these were offered. It was true that in the beginning we had opposed the making of sacrifices during the funerals of Christians, whether baptized or catechumens. But later on, this restriction was relaxed to allay some of the opposition to the baptism of catechumens. We felt it was more important for a person to be baptized than it was to prevent certain traditional funeral rites from being performed. These latter could at least be tolerated since they had no effect on the deceased one way or the other.

But Captain Ardron also had a complaint to lodge against us directly. It had been reported that we were using forced labour to build on mission property. The use of such labour, legal or not, was a prerogative of the chiefs.

"I am sorry you have been misinformed, Captain," I told him, "but we have never used forced labour here and never will."

"Then I take it the mission pays the workers building those catechist lodgings?" he asked, convinced that it did not.

"In a manner of speaking, yes," I replied. "What your informants took to be forced labour is *really* voluntary labour in this case. The people want resident catechists in their villages so that they will not always have to walk to Jirapa for religious instruction. We are donating our time and efforts to train those catechists, and the people, who have no money, are donating what they do have — time and labour — to provide housing for them and their families while they undergo their training. They are working willingly and in their own interests. You may question them if you like."

This particular complaint would continue to surface for some time, and the DCs did nothing to counter it or to inform complainants of their error. Eventually, it would die a natural death.

The following day, the DC of Lawra returned to repeat the same accusations as those of his colleague from Wa. Clearly the authorities were bent on pursuing the catechist issue to the end. They were probably kicking themselves for ever having given permission for the training school to be opened.

Captain Armstrong received the same reply as had Captain Ardron the day before, except that I felt more at ease with this man. Although he was not a Catholic either, his attitude was not antagonistic or bigoted. But he was as much a DC as Ardron, and so we lived in two essentially different worlds. As time went on, he would fall more and more under the influence of the other man, causing our worlds to drift further and further apart.

I complained again about the chiefs' road overseers but got no satisfaction from him. It would take more than a conversation with him to remedy that situation. But we were already determined to go directly to the chief of Jirapa about it.[4]

When the DC had repeated the governor's warning again and I had rejected it again, he left.

A few days before these events, on 27 September, our first group of student catechists had embarked upon the final phase of their journey toward baptism. I would instruct them myself over the next three months, as anxious as they to see them reach their goal. That moment came on Christmas Eve 1932.

The catechumens began to arrive from every direction on 22 December. Few of them had much experience of Christmas as yet, but all of them knew the wonderful story of a virgin named

Mary and the marvellous small treasure she had given birth to that first Christmas Eve in Bethlehem. Though it was not a weekend, and thus not a normal day for catechetical instruction, many had set aside their work and come from as far as fifty miles away to assist at the first "normal" baptismal ceremony in the Northwest. They did not know what to expect. For many it would be the first time they would see anyone survive baptism. Until then we had only baptized people on their deathbeds.

Since we wanted the ceremony to be visible to everyone, it could not be held in the tiny chapel of the mission. (A proper church would not be built at Jirapa until 1934.) We decided to set up a portable altar on the second-floor verandah of the mission house. From there the baptismal liturgy and the Midnight Mass would be clearly visible to the crowd gathered down below.

In the afternoon, Father Jean-Baptiste Durand arrived from the new mission at Kaleo together with Brother Basilide who had been assigned there to build the first mission house. Kaleo had been opened officially on 8 December with as much material as we could spare from Jirapa mission. The rest of the missionary contingent that night consisted of Fathers Robert Lavallée and Stanislas Leblanc (two young Canadians who had arrived the previous month), Father Larochelle, Brother Evarist Kingseller from England, and myself.

At last the moment came to begin the ceremony. We seven filed out onto the upper verandah preceded by the baptismal candidates. It was a cool, dry night with a temperature in the mid-seventies (about 24 degrees centigrade), comfortable for those like ourselves who were adequately dressed for it but chilly for the majority of the lightly-clad assistants. By the warm light of several strategically-placed kerosene lanterns, the ceremony got underway with a simple explanation to the crowd of what was about to take place. Below in the courtyard, the lights from several more lanterns borne by the people danced in the darkness, illuminating ebony heads and lending an atmosphere of intimacy to the scene despite the numbers assisting.

As their names were called, the candidates stepped forward one by one. There were twelve that night. Eleven of them were catechists and their wives. The twelfth was not, strictly speaking, a candidate since he had received baptism earlier. During his catechumenate he had fallen gravely ill and we had judged it prudent to baptize him then and there, giving him the name Dominic. He had recovered from his illness and had gone on to finish his catechetical instruction. In his case, the ceremony of baptism would merely be completed this night.

The twelve, with their baptismal names given first, were:

John Kyefondeme
Joseph Gbare
James Nyangwane
Teresa, wife of James Nyangwane
Remi Kabiri
Anna, wife of Remi Kabiri
Yacobi Kpiende
Michael Kpienbare
Paulo Nora
Oscar Gokyi
Peter Dery
Dominic Gbang

Father Larochelle baptized the two women while I baptized the men. It was a very satisfying moment for us as we traced the sign of the cross on each of their heads with the water of life. We had come to know these young people well and to appreciate their qualities. It was only natural that we should feel something like parental pride in them this night.

When the ceremony had ended, and while we were busy clearing away the baptismal paraphernalia and preparing for the Midnight Mass to follow, Father Durand came out onto the verandah to sing "Silent Night" in his beautiful and powerful tenor voice. Until this moment, the great attraction of Father Durand had been his magnificent beard. It was a voluminous, cascading appendage that began just below his eyes and flowed down uninterruptedly over his mouth and chin onto his chest. The Dagaabas considered it one of the wonders of the world, if not *the* wonder. It was not uncommon for people to come long distances on foot just to view it. They would then return home to tell all their neighbours about the white man who had no mouth, just a beard as long as their arm. One Dagati man told me: "Father, if I had that beard, I'd be a rich man. I'd go around the whole world showing it off for money!" He could not understand why the fortunate possessor of that potential gold mine continued to ignore its commercial possibilities. But this night the fortunate one's stock would rise even higher.

As he stepped into the lantern light of the verandah, a murmur of excitement passed through the crowd. Neighbour nudged neighbour, newcomers jockeyed for position to get a better view of the phenomenon, while small children pressed closer to their mothers. The object of all this interest stood gazing down at them calmly as if assessing the degree of possibility of there being anyone in all that mass of humanity who would be able to make sense of what he was about to do. When quiet had returned and all attention was riveted on him, he shifted his gaze heavenward, opened his invisible mouth, and began to sing.

As the first pure notes of the traditional Western carol lifted into the still and starry night above Jirapa, a sudden wail of fright rose from somewhere in the crowd. Grown men bolted, women screamed, babies began to cry. There were groans and shouts as terrified observers, unprepared for the spectacle of a mouthless wizard emitting alien sounds at them from a high place, fled in panic, overturning lanterns and trampling one another underfoot. The great majority stood their ground, but of those who fled that night, many did so never to return.

Meanwhile, totally unperturbed, as if he stood alone on the planet surrounded by a silence of angels, Father Durand continued to fill the African midnight with his song of adoration of the new-born Saviour.

It was a memorable third Christmas among the Dagaabas.

Now that we had a handful of trained catechists, we could begin to assign them to villages as the catechumens had asked us to do. This would reduce some of the pressure on the mission and on the limited resources of Jirapa.

The commissioning of a resident catechist was done formally. If possible, the ceremony was presided over by the highest ecclesiastical authority of the region (bishop, vicar apostolic, or prefect apostolic) or his representative, in the presence of the mission staff and of the people. Each catechist when called would come forward, read his promise aloud, and sign it. In it he promised before God and those assembled to live an exemplary Christian life and to dedicate himself to the work of catechist for the purpose of helping others to know God and to live truly Christian lives. Relying on divine grace and the power of prayer to help him achieve this and remain faithful to his promise, he looked to God alone for his reward.[5]

Married catechists were assigned to villages — often, though not always, their own. In the beginning they were sent out in pairs. Unmarried ones remained attached to the mission until they took a wife.

When there was no priest available to say Mass in his village, the catechist would take charge of the Sunday service himself. This consisted first of all in leading the congregation in morning prayer and the recitation of the prayers of the Mass. (Even before the Second Vatican Council, the Mass was translated into the vernacular and memorized, so that when the long overdue reform of the liturgy took place after the Council, our Catholics were already accustomed to active participation.) The Kyrie, Gloria, Credo, etc., were learned in Latin and in English. Singing also played an important part in worship right from the beginning. Father Durand had translated hymn texts into Dagaare and adapted them to lively tunes easily learned and remembered. Finally, the rosary would be prayed together as well.

When the prayer service was over (or the Mass, on those Sundays when a priest was available), the roll call was taken before proceeding to the instruction phase. Regular attendance was a prerequisite for admission to another stage of the cate-chumenate. The subject of the instruction followed a monthly outline determined by the mission and distributed to all cate-chists. If possible, one instruction was prepared for the baptized and another for the catechumens. This was followed by a question and answer period. The whole package (prayer and instruction) took up the entire morning.

During the week, people came to the catechist with their prob-lems: family quarrels, disputes between neighbours, laxness of some members of the community in living up to their Christian ideals, etc. The early Dagati Christians were genuinely concerned for one another and for preserving the precious gift of faith they had received. Even though it had been given to each one of them individually, they saw it as a community gift in which all had an equal share and all shared responsibility for protecting and nurturing it. They were conscious of being the People of God. If they saw someone among them failing to live up to his or her Christian commitment, they would consult the catechist who would advise them what to do about it.

It was also the duty of the catechist to investigate proposed marriages to make sure both parties were free to marry, that neither one was being forced into marriage, or that parents had not been coerced into giving consent. It was not permitted to marry within the extended family.

The catechist visited the sick every day and went in search of "lost sheep" among them. If any of the seriously ill desired to be baptized, he would give them some basic instruction in the faith and prepare them to receive the sacrament before administering it.

He was responsible for preparing and conducting a weekly class for newcomers who were in the pre-catechumenate stage and for preparing Christians to receive their First Communion and Confirmation.

Each month the catechists assembled at the mission for a day of recollection during which they prayed together and reflected. This was followed by a meeting to discuss problems and report on their activities of the previous month. Before leaving the mission to return home the next day, they received their program for the coming month: the list of bible readings and catechetical lessons to be imparted. Both would be explained by the fathers and discussed with them until all their questions had been answered.

As the surrogate pastor of his flock in the priest's absence, there was little if any free time to care for his material needs and those of his family. In time, resident catechists were each provided with a small farm by the Christians of their villages and helped by them to maintain it. It provided no more than subsistence in most cases, but they had accepted poverty and dependence on Providence as part and parcel of their vocation to follow Christ.

With the resident catechist holding such a conspicuous position in the village, difficulties with the chiefs and headmen continued for some time. If the British colonial officials had seen fit to interfere on the side of the chiefs even before there were any catechists permanently installed in the villages, they were not likely to cease now that there were. Captain Ardron, the DC of Wa, still roamed abroad, if not like a roaring lion, at least like a man seeking someone to devour. Sometime later, when the catechist school had begun to field graduates every year, he appeared at Kaleo one day and forbade their installation in the Wa district.

Father Durand, who was now superior of Kaleo mission, was not intimidated by him. He listened quietly behind his beard until the DC had finished his litany of threats and complaints against the catechists and the missionaries. Then he replied in language any bureaucrat or military man would readily understand.

"Thank you, Captain. I shall have to take this up with my superior, the bishop. In the meantime, please put it in writing."

The DC never did so, of course. A written document might have found its way to Accra or even London, neither of which would have reacted kindly to a DC who represented His Majesty's government in the Gold Coast openly challenging the Roman Catholic Church on what was, for all practical purposes, its own terrain. It was one thing to caution but quite another to forbid.

A few years later, attempts were made to introduce politics into the controversy. Since Father McCoy was of Irish descent and a Catholic, it was reasoned, that lethal mixture could only produce anti-British sentiments. And if he was anti-British, he would be bent on putting obstacles in the way of indirect rule, as indeed he was doing with his resident catechist scheme. (I was flattered by the attention but slightly ashamed for my ancestors at being innocent of all accusations.)

Complaints were made to the bishop and he was asked to transfer me elsewhere. Bishop Morin refused, telling the government that I was only doing the job I had been sent there to do, and that if its administrators would only do their jobs as well, there would be no problem! He went on to ridicule the anti-British idea, reminding Accra that McCoy was a Canadian citizen and therefore a British subject.[6]

*
**

Another problem we had with the colonial government involved regular schools. Despite repeated efforts, we could not obtain authorization to open a primary school at Jirapa in the 1930s. Once, on a visit to Accra, I had encountered a friendly British official who told me the reason behind this refusal. There was no school as yet in the entire Northwest. Had there been an Anglican, Methodist, or any but a Catholic one already established there, permission would probably have been granted. The Colonial Office did not want all of the future leaders of the Northwest to be Catholics.

When permission was requested in 1931 to open the catechist training school, opposition was less because it was thought by officials in Accra that such a school would be innocuous enough, limited as it was to preparing missionaries' helpers to teach catechism and nothing more. Perhaps it was also felt that this would help to placate the Catholics for the earlier refusals. As additional insurance against any unpleasant surprises later on, it was stipulated that, aside from the catechism and strictly Church-related instruction, the curriculum was to be restricted to reading and writing. We added arithmetic, feeling its content would not easily excite suspicions of political subversion.

There was no age limit specified for students attending the catechist school. This made it possible from the start to recruit some intelligent younger boys whom we would later send on to boarding schools at Navrongo and Bolgatanga. Officially, they were all student catechists, but in reality the younger ones were students in an unauthorized, somewhat clandestine, regular school albeit of limited curriculum. Its locale was the old mission house. We had recruited a lay teacher from Navrongo, Denis Puntana, to teach them to read and write. Denis spoke Nankam, which is very closely related to Dagaare, so he had no trouble adapting himself.

Thus the catechist training school served as the initiator of adult and formal education in the Northwest. Among the first group of students to be sent to Navrongo to begin primary school in 1933 were Bartholomew Balaara, Matthias Banoeyeni, Gabriel Dapielee, Tenganabang, Puomaae, and Yelkyere. Few of them completed standard seven (form four) of the British system of education then in use.

Peter Dery never did return home to Zemopare to work as a catechist as his father had hoped and he himself had expected to do. God had other plans for him. In 1934 he was sent with the second group of students to Navrongo where he proved to be an excellent student. After completing the primary school program, he expressed the wish to study for the priesthood. He was accepted into the seminary and, on 11 February 1951, became the first Dagao in the Gold Coast to be ordained a priest.[7]

Peter Dery's was not the only religious vocation to come out of this unauthorized school. In 1935, Lawrence Kyemaalo, Hippllolyte Putiere, Evarist Kuuwulong, and Alfred Bayo were among the first group to be sent to Bolgatanga. All of these became priests eventually too.

The first qualified teachers in the Northwest also got their start there. Dedicated people like Bartholemew Balaara, Matthias Banoeyeni, Stanislaus Naa, Raphael Yennaa, Alfred Uriko, Gabriel Noa, and Maurice Zage enabled us to bring education to the Northwest much sooner than was expected.

The catechist training school continued at Jirapa until early 1944 when it was transferred to Kaleo. There hundreds more volunteers went on to prepare themselves over a four-year period for their apostolic mission in the Northwest. These catechists were the principal human reason the mission developed so rapidly and resulted in the conversion of so many Dagaabas. As the good right arm of the priests, they were a priceless asset in instructing through example first of all. They were responsible for animating Christian life and for maintaining the fervor of the catechumens and baptized Christians in the far-flung villages of this rural area. Enthusiasm and leadership were two of their outstanding qualities. Dedicated to helping their people become God's people, they were keen to learn and to understand all they could about Him so as to pass it on to them. For that reason, the Holy Spirit was with them and their mission prospered.

One of the pioneer catechists, John Kyefondeme, became head catechist of Jirapa. Early in his catechumenate, he had gone to his mother's village, Kalesegra, to spread the news of the arrival of the "men of God" and to urge the people not to risk being the only ones not to hear their message. As a result, some thirty villagers left for the mission the following Saturday evening. Their curiosity was rewarded and thereafter they, and others from Kalesegra, returned each weekend to learn of God and to pray with the missionaries. One of the original thirty, a small boy named Bayo, would be called later to the priesthood "to take the place of old Father Paquet", as he would say, the first missionary he had set eyes on that day in 1930.[8]

Martino Kyibineh, a Sissala, had to go through many hardships to become a Christian and a catechist, not the least being family opposition. He had lost his parents while still a boy and had gone to live with an uncle who did everything to prevent him from praying with the Christians. Despite this, Martino had started to follow religious instructions in Nandom in 1933. To punish him for his decision, the uncle refused to find him a wife or to pay the dowry. The young man was forced to leave home and go south in search of work to earn the dowry himself. After his baptism, he worked as catechist among his own people for a number of years. When a mission was opened among the Dagomba people in Tamale in 1946, and catechists were being sought for it, he was one of ten Dagaabas and Sissalas to volunteer. Robert Gurnbie and Remi Kabiri were others. God rewarded Martino's dedicated service by choosing one of his sons, Raphael, to be a priest among the Sissalas.

Robert Bongvla was introduced to Christ by Poreku. Later, he was selected to train as a catechist, eventually becoming one of the first to exercise that function on both sides of the border dividing the Dagaabas, in Nandom and Dano. Robert was one of those who frequently found themselves in court, the objects of the chiefs' displeasure because of what they taught and of misunderstanding about their intentions. He persevered nevertheless, retiring in 1975.[9]

Authorization could not be denied forever, and in 1937 the Department of Education in Accra finally granted permission to open a boys school in Nandom. Three years later, the first girls primary school was opened in Jirapa and placed in the capable hands of the Franciscan Missionaries of Mary who had arrived in May 1939. (In January 1949, this became a co-educational school.)

The education of girls was an innovation that few persons appreciated and many thought impossible. The girls themselves appreciated it though; to the point that they were in no hurry to return home when holiday time came. Students were selected from the three existing missions: Jirapa, Kaleo, and Nandom. In accordance with the education policy of the time, subjects were taught in Dagaare, with spoken English permitted for only half an hour each day.

Little by little, policies and the men implementing them changed. Mission schools gradually began opening wherever funds and staff could be made available. These gave impetus to Church growth and provided the basis for the spiritual, material, cultural, and socio-economic wealth the Northwest later came to know.

Equal He Created Them

Some of the colonial administrators were not only opposed to the methods of evangelization being used by the missionaries, they were opposed more basically to the introduction of Christianity among the people at all. (These officials were themselves Christians, supposedly.) There was an element of snobbishness involved. Christianity, they argued, was too demanding and sophisticated for simple "natives". It would be far better and far easier for them to become Muslims. The nub of the question, of course, was polygamy.

Governor Thomas put it in an unforgettable way one day as we conversed about the progress of the mission. What, he wanted to know, was the biggest problem the people had to face in deciding to become Christians?

"Giving up their extra wives," I answered.

"Really," he said with a shake of his head, "I don't see why you torment these poor people by imposing monogamy on them. After all, Solomon was a good Christian and he had many wives."

The early missionaries had to deal with the mentality of the people in overcoming such obstacles to conversion. For the Dagaabas and surrounding peoples, polygamy was above all a question of status. It was natural that a rich man have several wives, just as in the American West a wealthy rancher might have a thousand head of cattle to mark his status. When the people referred to a person as having three or four wives, it was immediately understood that he was a "big" man. One could not be important in Dagati society and possess only one wife. This was reflected in the household of the first Jirapa naa, who had fifty!

Insistence on monogamy accounted for the fact that very few chiefs became Christians. It was unheard of at the time that a chief have less than two wives. Some of them who were genuinely interested in becoming Christians, but lacked the courage to face life and society with only one spouse, used to lament to us on occasion that it was too bad we hadn't arrived on the scene sooner, "before we got so involved".

The early catechumens were not required to send off their surplus wives immediately. They needed all the help they could get to do so, and only an intimate knowledge of God and the gradual action of His grace in them could bring them eventually to make the decision required.

If the decision was a difficult one for the man to reach, it was often as difficult for the wives, whether renounced or retained, to accept. When a man sent away a wife or wives, it was frequently the younger and more able-bodied of them. The older one might object to being left suddenly with all the household chores to do, especially if she was past middle-age and the work was particularly onerous. Sometimes, for instance, the nearest source of water was miles from the compound, and it was the woman's task to fetch it each day. If she had grown-up children, she might try to convince her husband to choose one of his younger wives instead. Then she would move in with her children, but still within the same compound since the children always belonged to the husband, even when their mother ceased being his wife. In that case, a separation would be built in the compound and the ex-wife would have her own entrance to it. If all the members of the compound farmed together, its head would supply her food.

Though there was never any danger that renounced wives without grown children would be abandoned to their fate (for custom dictated then that they return to their parents, with the possibility of being given in marriage again), the big problem for them involved minor children. These would have to be left behind with their father when the ex-wife left the compound. If the youngest was still a baby, she was usually allowed to keep it with her until it was three or four years old, at which time she had to return it to the father or, if he had died in the meantime, to his family.

Some of the first catechumens pleaded with us to allow them more than one wife. I remember quite vividly one Sunday toward the end of 1931 when the first group of candidates to complete their pre-catechumenate course were about to receive the rosary, signifying their entry into the catechumenate proper. In the instruction that morning I had reminded them that several things were required of them at this stage in their formation. Regular attendance was one and life witness was another. This latter included giving up the practice of making sacrifices to fetishes and spirits, rejecting witch doctors, and regularizing their marriage situations since Christians were permitted but one wife.

That afternoon a delegation of some twenty or thirty of these candidates, most of them middle-aged men, presented themselves at the mission house and asked to speak with me. Their spokesman, an eloquent man, began very diplomatically.

"Father," he said, "you know that we have taken hold of your hand and we do not intend to let go. If you lead us into the water, we will go into the water; if you lead us into the fire, we will go into the fire. But there is one thing we want to ask you."

Yes, I thought, there would have to be a "but" after such a smoke screen; it signalled the assault.

"This thing about one wife," he continued. "For us Dagaabas, it is not at all practical. I will tell you why, Father. If you have only one wife and she should get sick or have a baby, who will prepare the food and cook for you, or sow the seed in planting time, or help with the harvest when it is ready? It will be a big problem, I tell you."

The others lent their unanimous support to this self-evident truth.

"So we want to ask you to let us have two wives," he said in a tone that implied the expectation that I could certainly agree to such a reasonable and really very minor adjustment in my original per capita allotment if I wanted to. But just in case I didn't want to, he hastened to add:

"No more than two though. We know that more is not always better. A lot of trouble can come of it. So we are willing to settle for two, Father."

I had no doubt they were sincere, but there was nothing I could do to accommodate them in the matter.

"I'm sorry," I replied, speaking slowly and enunciating carefully so that there would be no misunderstanding. "I am not God. I did not make the law. God did, and I believe He knew what He was doing when He did so. He knows it is not easy for you to accept it, but at least try to believe this: that He loves you and only wants what is best for you. As for me, I am merely His messenger. He has sent me to tell you about Him and to make known to you the plan He has for your happiness, even in this life. But I have no power to change any of His laws."

Glumness greeted my words, but the spokesman — certainly the most optimistic among them and, for that reason, a good choice for the task — was not ready to share it. If I could not be motivated to altruism, perhaps an appeal to selfish interests would work.

"If you let us have two wives," he said, "I assure you that many Dagati men and women will become Christians." It was a slight variation, without malice, on the temptation of Jesus in the desert (Matt. 4:9).

"I'm sorry but I can't do that," I repeated. "I am not God's agent to negotiate a compromise with you on this. His law is that a man shall have one wife and a woman one husband."

The argument shifted to my knowledge or, rather, lack of knowledge of their customs.

"Perhaps you do not understand, Father," they said, and then with utmost courtesy pressed their cause in a discussion that went on for two hours. When at last they saw that there was no hope of breaching my refusal to bargain, they went away sadly. About half their number never returned. Others, like the Galayiri brothers, had already begun to send away their extra wives. The rest, though undecided for the moment, elected to continue their course of instructions and to go on hoping, even though they were at least temporarily barred from being baptized.

One of these was Peter Ali, present chief of Sigri. He and his two wives had joined the pre-catechumenate together. They were model catechumens who did their best to live good Christian lives among their animist neighbours. Every Sunday the three of them and their children would walk the seven miles to church, even long after they had completed the instruction program. But Ali and his wives could not be baptized until he made up his mind which of them to keep. He agonized over it but without result. Ali truly loved them both. Meanwhile, the years passed and all their children had completed the four-year catechumenate and been baptized. Each morning and evening, as they had done from the beginning of their first contact with Christianity, Ali and his wives and children gathered together to pray. Then one day, after twenty-five years of conjugal life, one of the wives came to him and said: "Ali, I am leaving you. I have decided to return to my father's house. Now you and 'X' [the other wife] can be baptized. And so can I."

Related to polygamy, of course, was the woman's lack of freedom.

In the Northwest of the 1930s, the woman was essentially a housekeeper. She did not till the soil except perhaps a plot near the house where she grew some groundnuts and vegetables. She took part in the farming by sowing the seed at the opportune moment and later by cutting the tops off the millet and guinea corn. She would also pick the bambera beans and groundnuts. When harvest time came, it was her job to gather it in and carry it home. She brought food and drink to the men in the fields; and when they finished their work, she prepared a meal for them. Each day she had to go to the nearest source to fetch water for cooking, bathing, and laundering, and carry it home. Collecting wood for the cooking fire was another difficult and time-consuming chore due to its relative scarcity in the region. She ground the millet for the main meal of porridge using a homemade grinding mill composed of two granite stones.[1] The ingredients for the all-important sauce which gives the essentially tasteless porridge its flavour were either collected in the bush and carefully stored away, or bought when needed with money she herself earned by brewing and selling pito or with money her husband gave her for that purpose.

On the whole, family relationships among the Dagaabas were fairly cordial. That did not make it any less a man's world, however.

A girl or woman could not choose her own marriage partner. When the head of the clan or compound decided it was time for her to marry, she might not even be consulted. All discussion and bargaining went on behind her back, usually between the clan leader and a go-between *(ditina)* representing the would-be groom's family. Often the dowry had been paid before she had even become aware that negotiations were going on to seal her future.

Because a woman was dowried, she was the property of the man, just as purchased cattle were. However, there were situations where her father might call her back. For instance, if the husband did not go to farm for his father-in-law, as was the custom, or if he neglected to attend a funeral or an important celebration. If these things happened, the wife would return to her father's house. But the dowry was not returned to the husband's clan. Instead, it was set aside by the girl's father for his son or some other male member of the compound who would need it one day to purchase a wife.

In some families, however, there did exist an important ceremony of consent. Once the girl's family had agreed to the marriage, the prospective groom would go to his fiancée's home and present her with a number of cowrie shells. If she accepted them, it meant she accepted him; if she refused to accept them, it meant she rejected him. Sometimes, out of shyness, she might not come forward to take them directly from his hand, in which case he would throw them on the floor. If she stooped to pick them up, it indicated her willingness to marry him. In many cases, however, parental pressure brought to bear on the girl was so great that she had no choice but to bow to it.

Sometimes a girl was given in marriage to another compound because the family had relatives there. She would not be consulted, and often times her relatives would not tell her what was going on either. But it happened on occasion that the girl and her relatives met at instruction classes and they would inform her then.

Or if they did not want to do so directly, they would tell us about it and leave it in our hands. The man who wanted to marry her might be sixty or seventy years old and have anywhere from two to five wives already. If the girl was strongly opposed to the match, she would run away to an aunt or to some other relative, but sometimes there was no one and nowhere to run to.

Just as we had done in the case of women falsely accused of being witches, so we did now. We made it known far and wide that women being forced to marry against their will could take refuge at the mission until their problem was resolved. Maria, the former wife of a deceased chief, agreed to come and look after the girls and women who fled there.

At times we had as many as two to three dozen girls under old Maria's watchful eye. They would remain at the mission refuge for weeks or months, until their people came for them. But we would not allow any of them to be taken away until the head of the compound, in the presence of two trustworthy witnesses, signed a paper stating that the girl would be free once she left the mission. Before proceeding to the formal signing, however, we would try to find out through the catechist or some of the Christians in the compound or village whether the relatives really meant to allow the girl her freedom. Only when we were sufficiently sure of this would we have the paper drawn up and signed, and the girl would return with her relatives to her home. If later they tried to bring pressure to bear on her again, she would come back to the refuge.

Not all such cases were handled this way. One exception was that of a girl from Dapore.

At about 5:15 on the morning of 25 September 1935, as we were going to the church for meditation, we met a girl hurrying toward the mission. She was out of breath and perspiring profusely. It was Pogpla, one of our catechumens.[2] She had run away from home to escape an enforced marriage to a man who was not only a *mwinbapuorobo* (a non-believer) but who already had a wife. Her parents had intended to send her that very day to her future husband's place to begin living with him, but she had anticipated their move by taking to the bush during the night to seek refuge at the mission. After listening to her story, we took her to Maria and placed her in the old woman's care.[3]

We were trying at that time to put an end to this marriage custom altogether and not merely cripple it as we were doing with our introduction of the refuge. It seemed imperative therefore that native justice be induced to react against it at least once, to set a precedent. Accordingly, we brought the case (in Pogpla's name) to the attention of the chief of Kaleo who had authority over Dapore and was competent to judge such matters. Father Durand, as superior of Kaleo mission, would attend the hearing and plead Pogpla's cause himself. He knew the Kaleo chief and thought he would certainly judge in her favour.

At the hearing, however, Pogpla pleaded her own cause. She was a Christian catechumen, she claimed, who wished to be baptized when she completed her course of instruction. Therefore, she could not even think of marrying a man who already had a wife. Christians were forbidden to have more than one spouse. It was quite simple.

But the chiefs had got together earlier and decided among themselves that they could not let girls make their own choice in such an important clan matter as marriage. The survival of the clan depended on it, and one did not put such things in the hands of women. When the time came for the chief of Kaleo to hand down his decision, it went against Pogpla.

Father Durand was surprised and angry. He rose to challenge the chief's verdict like Moses confronting the pharoah.

"You cannot force the girl to marry someone she does not want to marry! Slavery does not exist here!" he said firmly.

But the chief replied just as firmly; "We cannot allow women to make their own choice in this, otherwise we would lose all our wives." It was, in effect, a confession of the inherent weakness in the system.

"Well," Father Durand retorted, "that is what is going to happen eventually. And whether you like it or not, you are going to have to accept it."

But they did not agree, and Pogpla was forced to return home and marry the man she had rejected.

Another case which occurred that year involved a girl named Veronica.

Veronica was also a catechumen, though further advanced than Pogpla since she was preparing to be baptized. The chief of Eremon, who already had fourteen or fifteen wives, wanted to add her to his collection. As her family were nearly all animists, they had agreed to the marriage and accepted the dowry the chief offered for her hand. When she discovered what was happening, and that the date had been set for accompanying the bride to her husband's compound, she realized she had no time to waste. She certainly had no intention of marrying the man. After examining her options, she decided to run away to her grandmother's house in Lyssa. She would be safe there, at least for a little while. And it would give her time to think what her next move should be.

She had been at Lyssa a few weeks when one day a young member of the family, accompanied by several of his friends, arrived bearing an urgent message. Her mother had fallen seriously ill while visiting a neighbouring village and was asking for her. If she wanted to see her alive, she would have to hurry.

Veronica gathered up her few belongings and set off quickly with her escort. She did not know the exact location of the compound where her mother lay dying, so she had no choice but to follow the small boy who was leading the way with such assurance. They had walked about ten miles when something familiar began to strike her about the area and she suddenly realized that they were on the road to the chief's compound. It was a trap! And they had used a child to spring it on her, using her love for her mother as bait. Fighting back a first impulse to run, she continued along while searching anxiously for a means of escape that would give her a needed head start on the group.

It was the time of the year when the millet was high. Evening was coming on and a storm was brewing, with rain already beginning to fall. When those accompanying her started to run, looking for shelter from what promised to be a downpour, Veronica lagged behind, letting them get well ahead of her. Then, with no one immediately aware of it, she darted off the path into the millet field and continued running until she came to the catechist's house about a mile away. The Eremon catechist welcomed her in from the rain. But as soon as he learned who she was and what she was doing there, he knew it was just a question of time — probably a very short time — before someone from the chief's compound came looking for her. Acting quickly, he set off with her for the mission where she was given refuge with the other women in her situation.[4]

Early the next morning we had a delegation on our doorstep from the chief of Eremon, accompanied by two of his native authority police and two representatives of the Jirapa naa. They informed us that they were looking for the wife of the chief of Eremon.

"Which one?" I asked. With so many of them around his compound, it was not surprising he should misplace one from time to time.

They were not amused. These fellows meant business. So I stretched out to my full six feet and put on a face to match their own.

"There is no wife of the chief of Eremon here," I stated categorically.

"This girl we speak of has been promised to him and the dowry has been paid. We are sure she is here," they replied.

"What does she look like then?" I asked, determined to slow them down and blunt their arrogance by making them cool their heels a bit before the girl should have to face them.

They described Veronica, told me where she came from, who her parents were, etc. When I could think of nothing more to ask them, I had her brought in. She had been advised of their arrival from the very first moment.

She came in and faced them squarely. No wilting violet, Veronica! They hardly acknowledged her, continuing to address me as if she weren't even present. I put an end to that by telling them that if they had anything to say to or about the girl, they should speak to her directly.

"She speaks Dagaare as well as you do," I said.

One of them turned to her then and said, "Why did you run away from your husband?"

"I have no husband," Veronica shot back.

"You belong to the chief of Eremon now," the man persisted. "The dowry has been paid and your family has accepted it."

"I don't want to marry him," she replied defiantly. "I am not a goat or a sheep to be traded. I am a human being and a Christian."

One of the chief's more tactful representatives intervened. "You can continue to pray even after you are married to the chief," he said.

But Veronica would hear of no compromise. "Pray or not pray, I still don't want to marry him!" she insisted.

A great and noisy argument ensued, with Veronica absolutely refusing to yield her ground and matching the lot of them in determination. Suddenly one very tall fellow, well over six feet, made a move toward her as if to strike her and drag her away.

"Stop!" I shouted above the din. "Leave her alone! You are not going to touch her!"

The fellow's hand halted in mid-air. Then, slowly, he lowered it.

"Veronica has come here of her own free will and that is the only way she is ever going to leave. Do you all understand me?" I was wearing my most formidable glower by now. There was a moment's hesitation and then they reluctantly began to withdraw. For the moment, at least, there was nothing more they could do.

Later I heard that the chiefs of Jirapa and Eremon had got together afterwards to discuss the case and the day's developments. Among the things they held in common was the very vocal opinion that "these white men are going to ruin the country".

The next day I went to Lawra to consult the DC. He didn't look particularly happy to see me. That didn't surprise me since my visits very rarely subtracted from his problems. When I started to tell him about Veronica, he interrupted me.

"Oh, yes. I heard about that case," he said. (The chief of Eremon, just as determined to have Veronica as she was to disappoint him, had been to see his superior, the chief of Lawra, and the two had already spent hours filling the DC in on the story.) "Aren't you moving a trifle too fast in trying to get freedom for these women, Father? You know English women only got their franchise a few years ago."

"It is not a question here of franchise," I replied, "but of something much more basic: the right of a human being to be treated as such rather than as a slave. I thought you were supposed to be a defender of human liberty. You represent the British government here. Isn't one of your duties to see to it that people are permitted to exercise religious and civil liberties?"

He looked uncomfortable but he didn't answer. So I said: "If you want to, Captain Armstrong, you can take the girl, bind her hand and foot — for she won't consent to be moved any other way — and deliver her to the chief of Eremon yourself. But I am certainly not going to do it."

That at least got a reaction out of him.

"Oh, I don't think we could do that," he said.

After a little while, he began to weaken. He was a good person, as I have said before, but sometimes the demands of the office one holds overshadow the dictates of conscience. At last he agreed to call in the chief of Lawra and tell him the dowry should be returned because one could not force customary marriage on Christians. It was not yet total victory, but a decisive battle had been won.

When the Lawra naa informed his sub-schief that his cause was lost, the latter accepted it well enough. A love-sick swain he was not. But the dowry bothered him; he was keen to recover what he had paid for the promise of Veronica's hand in marriage. Her family, meanwhile, was not nearly so keen to return it since it was not the custom to do so. Normally, it would remain in the family to be used as dowry payment for one of Veronica's brothers or some other male member of the extended family when it came time for him to marry. She had an uncle, however, a student catechist in Jirapa, who intervened decisively with her parents. He and many other Christians who had followed the case of his niece were anxious to see the DC's decision obeyed to the letter. Custom or no custom, as long as the dowry had not been paid back, there was still the chance that the chief of Eremon might one day revive his claim to Veronica. The uncle insisted that her family return the dowry. If they refused, he would borrow the money and pay it back himself. Seeing that either way the custom would be violated, the family yielded. They settled accounts with the unsuccessful suitor and the case was closed.

So Veronica was free. Later she married a student catechist, Vincent Dasaa, and had a very happy marriage and a fine family.[5]

This case was truly a watershed in the history of Christianity in the Northwest. The Lawra naa was then president of the confederation of chiefs and therefore an influential man. He was automatically consulted by the other chiefs on problems related to marriage. After Veronica's successful bid for freedom, he saw to it that Christian girls were not forced to marry anyone against their will. The freedom of choice accorded them in marriage became a major step forward in women's liberation in the Northwest.

It took a long time to alleviate the situation, however. Several years later, Bishop Morin himself went to see the chief commissioner about it. The two had a long talk, the result of which was the promulgation throughout the Northwest of a law forbidding forced marriages of any kind.

Christian marriage helped immeasurably then to improve the status of the woman. But old customs die hard. Sometimes families continued to hold to the local tradition in which the girl went to live with her future husband immediately after the dowry had been paid by his family to hers. The marriage would take place at some later date to be agreed upon by all.

Because of the strength of this tradition and others, and also because of the distance separating most of the Christians of this vast rural parish from Jirapa,[6] we decided in 1936 to provide a hostel at the mission where engaged girls could live safely and follow a month-long marriage course at the same time. Their future husbands came three times a week to follow a course of instruction in Christian living and to bring their fiancées food, which the girls cooked and shared among themselves and sometimes with their young suitors. On the other days of the week, the girls were instructed in hygiene, child care, food preparation, housekeeping, and other domestic subjects. A priest and the head catechist shared the religious instruction course, with the priest teaching it once a week and the catechist the rest of the time.

In the more than fifty years since it was introduced, the pre-marriage course has proven its worth many times over. Thousands of couples have benefitted from it. For the last twenty-five years, the head catechist of Jirapa, Charles Ganaa, himself responsible for having instructed more than fifteen hundred of these young couples, has been its director. He has done an excellent job, as did his predecessors: Philip Galenyoni, Yacobi Kpiende, and the first head catechist of Jirapa, John Kyefondeme.

There was another local tradition which worked in our favor once, or in favor of the stability of Christian marriage. The man who helped to set the precedent in this case was the same Lawra naa who had intervened, on the DC's request, with the chief of Eremon in the case of Veronica.

Oscar and Georgetta were both young Christians, married in the Church. Theirs was an apparently happy marriage, and within a year their first child was born. But then, sometime later, another man entered Georgetta's life and the two became infatuated with one another. One day she left Oscar and went to live with him. Neither the man's family nor Georgetta's was Christian, so they accepted the new arrangement. But in order to regularize it according to their customs, the man's family wanted to repay the dowry Oscar's family had paid to Georgetta's at the time of their marriage, while Georgetta's parents wanted the man's family to bring her dowry to them so that they could give it back to Oscar. But Oscar wanted his wife back. He knew that if he accepted the dowry, it would mean he agreed to the divorce.

He came to see me and we brought his case to the Lawra naa, Karbo. Oscar explained to the naa that he could not agree to his wife's leaving him. They were Christians, and divorce was not permitted in the case of Christian marriage. Georgetta had not been forced to marry him; she had done so freely, and they had lived together happily until this other man had come along. She had gone off with him, taking their child to whom she had no right according to Dagati tradition.[7]

The naa listened attentively to him, questioning his from time to time. He was genuinely interested in the welfare of his people and tried to apply justice in as fair a manner as possible. He advised Oscar to give food and money for the maintenance of the child, whether it was accepted or not. That would emphasize the fact that he rejected any idea of divorce. Meanwhile, he let it be known publicly that he found in Oscar's favour: that Georgetta was his lawful wife and no other's; that as theirs was a Christian marriage, it could never be broken; and, moreover, that any children born to Georgetta by her lover belonged to Oscar.

When Georgetta did have a child by the other man, Oscar gave food and money for its care as well. This infuriated the man. He began to pester the naa about the case, trying to convince him to change his ruling. But Chief Karbo would only say that since Oscar had not accepted the return of the dowry, and therefore did not agree to the divorce, all Georgetta's children belonged to him.

Things went on like this for quite some time. Then one day Georgetta began to have doubts about the wisdom of the course she had set for herself. Life had been good with Oscar. She could not deny that they had been happy. She had been recognized as his legitimate wife and had had status in the community. Now, with the impossibility of regularizing their situation, she and her new "husband" were experiencing a frustration that had corrosive effects on their relations. But worst of all, if she stayed with this man, she could never keep the children. They would always belong to Oscar, and he could come to claim them at any time with the full force of the law and tradition behind him. The more she thought about it, the more she saw that there was no future for her where she was. Finally, she decided to return to Oscar.

Oscar received her graciously when she showed up one day with her children and her belongings. They were shy with each other at first and did not know where or how to begin again. When Oscar suggested a visit to the mission, Georgetta agreed. They came and stayed several days during which they talked and prayed and spent some time in retreat. At the end of it, they renewed their marriage vows and returned home to live contentedly together to the present day. They had more children after that, one of whom (Alfredina) is a member of the current medical team at St. Joseph's Hospital in Jirapa. Oscar worked at the same hospital as gateman until his retirement in 1984.

There were other traditions dealing with male-female relations that resisted change even more stubbornly than those having to do with marriage. One of these persisted even among our Christians long after they were baptized. It was the practice of not permitting the women to eat with the men. New Christians found it very difficult to drop this tradition, so ingrained was it, despite our efforts to show them that their attitude was alien to the spirit of Christ who had lived and died for all, male and female alike. I remember saying this one day to a group of catechumens preparing for baptism. The response of the men was unanimous.

"Father," they told me quite seriously, "if we let our women join us for meals, they will become so proud we will not be able to control them anymore."

It was a man's world in other areas of life in the Northwest as well. Generally speaking, the male opinion of the female intelligence was very low. The men of the 1930s believed women were by nature unintelligent and meant to stay that way. Such things as tailoring, they thought, were certainly beyond their limited capabilities. Only a man was equipped to understand them.

When the Franciscan Missionaries of Mary arrived and opened a primary school for girls in 1940, people would come just to watch the pupils read and write, marvelling at the fact that girls could be taught to do things that until then they had thought only males capable of doing.

In 1959, the sisters opened Saint Francis Secondary School for Girls in Jirapa and found that the male mentality had not changed appreciably in twenty years! Opposition to secondary education for girls proved to be so strong at first that the bishop himself had to go from parish to parish trying to convince parents to send their daughters to school. Despite his efforts, only twelve showed up the first year. Gradually, however, opposition lessened as the girls showed what they could do if given the chance.

Even the student catechists were infected with this male chauvinist mentality. When I first proposed the idea of including some of their wives in the catechist training program, they tried to dissuade me, saying women were incapable of learning. They were made to eat their words quickly enough.

Today the status of women in the Northwest and all through the country has improved greatly from what it was in the early days of the mission, at least in regard to the recognition of women's rights and capabilities. Admittedly, it still has a very long way

EQUAL HE CREATED THEM 165

to go. The task of trying to change a mentality is as difficult, if not more so, as trying to change the direction of a river's flow. Nevertheless, gains have definitely been made. Ghanaian women have gone on to become sisters, nurses, teachers, technicians, writers, musicians, entrepreneurs, and to qualify for a host of other careers once thought to be beyond their reach intellectually. And most of that progress has been due to the pioneering efforts of the Christian missions.

12

The Healers

The healing ministry has always been closely associated with the Gospel ministry. Christ Himself saw to that by His example and by His directive to the twelve apostles as they were about to leave on their first mission. They were to preach the Kingdom of God *and* heal the sick (Matt. 10:7-8; Mark 6:13; Luke 9:2). Later, after His ascension into heaven, healing continued to be an important part of their ministry and that of their followers (Acts 3:1-8; 5:12-16).

The first year in Jirapa was mostly spent in doing just that: treating a variety of illnesses and diseases which, though mainly non-fatal ones, made their victims' lives a hell on earth. Yaws, dysentery, eye infections, tropical sores, malaria, and leprosy were just a few of the maladies afflicting our people. The nearest medical centre was in Lawra, twenty miles away, and there was no transportation other than leg-power to get them there. The opening of a small clinic at the mission was therefore a priority for us. We had come to serve the whole person, body as well as soul.

Soon after opening the clinic, with the help of the DC and the resident medical officer in Lawra, recognition of it was accorded by Accra, making it possible to receive medical supplies from the government through the Lawra medical centre. Thus began a close cooperation between mission and government health officials that continues to this day.

For ten years, while we tried to recruit women religious to come to Jirapa and help us, we functioned as part-time village health workers in the region. There was no one else to do the work and, because of its urgency, it could not be put aside. Finally, just before the outbreak of the Second World War, the Franciscan Missionaries of Mary agreed to come out and work on the mission. They were willing to take over the medical work we were doing and to help in whatever other areas of the apostolate they were needed.

The first contingent of sisters reached Jirapa on 14 May 1939, with the aptly named Mother Precursor in charge, accompanied by Sisters Wynnin, Caltry, Cannice, Blane, and Conrad — six sisters of almost as many nationalities: French, English, Canadian, Irish, and Scots. They were as eager to begin work as we were to see them arrive. After so many years of hoping and so many disappointments, we could hardly believe our good fortune.

Sister Caltry was a registered nurse, the first of such to work in the Northwest.[1] She soon saw that demands on the medical services offered were great and that until more nurses could be sent out, she would have to train some of the other sisters to help her.

Of equal importance was the language. The sisters began to learn it immediately so that within a short time they could dispense with interpreters when treating the people at the clinic. By the following July (1940), they were confident enough to open the first primary school for girls in the Northwest, conducted entirely in Dagaare. Sister Caltry herself became very proficient in the language, able to converse easily with her patients about their symptoms and so win their confidence and affection. Soon people, especially women, began to flock to her from all over the North.

On the sisters' arrival, a small mud hut with thatched roof had been built near their convent to serve as a dispensary. But gradually, more and more pregnant women began to show up every day. Something had to be done without delay to accommodate them, so it was decided to put up a makeshift labour room and maternity ward close to the convent. Although the arrangements were makeshift, the service rendered by the sisters was total. When the number of patients continued to increase, the original hut was replaced in 1941 by a long brick building to house the dispensary as well as casualty, children's, and maternity wards. This was the first stage in the evolution from mission clinic to hospital.

In the next few years, the congregation deepened its commitment to the people of the Northwest by sending more sisters, many of whom were registered nurses. Among them were Sisters Cyprian, Clementine, Antimond, Evremond, and Emilia. Later, Sister John joined them, to be followed by others as the work grew and the plea went out from Jirapa to "send help!".[2]

To those directly involved in the daily reception and care of patients at the mission clinic, the great need for a hospital in the Northwest cried to heaven. And heaven was attentive. For when the moment came to formally request it, the petition came from outside Jirapa. The doctors in Wa and the principal medical officer in Tamale, Doctor Pepper, had been impressed by the professionalism of the sisters in organizing and dispensing health care in relatively primitive conditions. Their adaptability to circumstances and ingenuity in coming up with practical solutions to frequently difficult problems, many of them caused by scarcity of funds, convinced the officials that they should be given a real hospital to work in. If they could do so much with so little, it seemed reasonable to expect them to do even more with proper facilities at their disposal. A formal request was drafted and dispatched to the Ministry of Health in Accra. It was an unusual request for the times and the place. Here were government doctors, among them a principal medical officer, urgently requesting the ministry to build a hospital at Jirapa to be run and staffed by the Catholic mission with the aid of a grant from the British colonial government!

As was to be expected, there was opposition among officials in Accra to the proposition that the government finance a hospital to be run by the Catholic Church. This had never been done before in the Gold Coast. For some it was an idea whose time had not yet come. For others it was like asking the queen's government to pay Peter's Pence. Some were fearful the proposed hospital would be run along confessional lines, with non-Catholics being turned away or given second-class treatment. Assurances were given by the mission that no discrimination, religious or other, had ever been practised in treating the sick who came to Jirapa nor would it ever be in the future. The only criterion necessary to qualify one for medical care was that the person be ill.

To counterbalance somewhat the opposition in the South, the Jirapa naa, Yelpoe I, and his people threw their total support behind the proposal. This, together with the forceful recommendations of the principal medical officer in Tamale and the doctors in the Northwest, did not fail to impress the authorities.

A more serious obstacle to be overcome before a hospital could be approved for Jirapa, however, was the scarcity of water there. In 1951-52, a team of geologists was sent up by the Water and Sewage Corporation of Kumasi to investigate. They spent some time surveying the area and then left abruptly, saying that they had found a solid bed of granite eight hundred feet deep beneath Jirapa which effectively prevented any kind of drilling. Something about their sudden departure and the fact that the mission had successfully dug several wells already without encountering granite made us suspicious. I decided to go down to Kumasi and talk with the general manager of the Water and Sewage Corporation.

In bustling, tropical Kumasi, far to the south, all was lush and green. What a contrast to the much poorer savanna of the Northern Territories. It was little wonder that no one from the South wanted to work there, or at least not for long, and that government functionaries tried to escape service in the North if at all possible. No wonder either that government policy toward the North was largely one of benign neglect. The addition of a good hospital would perhaps help to alleviate some of that neglect and lessen opposition toward development of badly-needed infrastructure in the region.

To my unexpected satisfaction, I found the general manager as suspicious of the geological report as I had been. Its conclusions had surprised him and he confessed himself to be "rather skeptical" about the seriousness of the team's work. My own suspicions centred on the DC in Wa. It was known that he wanted the new hospital to be located there at all costs. I suspected that he had instructed the geological team not to find water in Jirapa and

they had complied. When I added to this the proof of the successful digging of the mission wells, the general manager grew indig-
nant. He would send another team to Jirapa immediately, he
promised, but this time their instructions would be different.
Instead of sending them to see *if* they could find water in Jirapa,
they would be told to stay there until they did!

Not surprisingly, water was quickly found, and at one hundred
fifty feet instead of eight hundred or more.[3]

Meanwhile, a Public Works Department engineer from Tamale,
a Mr. Mullins, had been looking into the problem. He found that
it would be possible to increase the capacity of the dam at Kyaare
and also build a reservoir for the proposed hospital on the hill
where the rest house was located. This would serve as an alternative water supply, if need be. He also proposed building several
large concrete reservoirs on the hospital grounds to collect rain
water.[4]

The discovery of water, and the suggestions of Mr. Mullins for
alternative sources, cleared away the last obstacle to choosing
Jirapa as the site of the new hospital. In 1952 money was voted
for it by the government and an agreement drawn up by the
Ministry of Health and the Catholic mission designating it an
"agency hospital", the first of its kind in the country. This meant
that the land, buildings, and equipment were to be provided by
the government, while the mission guaranteed the administration, staff, and day-to-day running of the hospital. In other words,
it was our responsibility to recruit the necessary doctors, nurses,
and auxiliary staff, and to pay them according to government
standards. A small government grant and some medicine from
Ministry of Health stocks, as well as quite a lot of donated drugs
and medical supplies from overseas, helped to cover these
expenses.[5]

If the government had been having doubts about its part in
the hospital project, they were small when compared to the
dilemma facing the mission. To staff and run a 250-bed hospital
in an area that had not even a secondary school to supply raw
material for the future seemed more than a challenge; to some it
was madness. We had agreed to something we might eventually
have to abandon, they said. The Franciscan Missionaries of Mary
had been willing to send sisters to work on the mission at a variety

of tasks, including the mission clinic, but there had been no question of a hospital then. The response from their headquarters in Rome was a kind but firm no. They would continue in their present commitment to the mission, but they were unable to assume responsibility for the hospital.

In a way, history was repeating itself. Nearly a century earlier, our founder, Cardinal Charles Lavigerie, and Mother Mary of the Passion, foundress of the Franciscan Missionaries of Mary (FMM), had clashed and finally agreed to differ. The cardinal had wanted her to form the female counterpart of his male missionary society, and she had been favourable to the idea at first. But they were two strong personalities, and soon they found themselves in serious disagreement on how this was to be done, the kind of persons to be recruited, and the end-product desired. As a result, Mother Mary had bowed out of the project and gone on to found her own missionary congregation, while the cardinal had founded what was later to become the Missionary Sisters of Our Lady of Africa (MSOLA).

Now there was another difference of opinion between us, though not at so basic a level as that earlier one. Mother Marguerite, the superior general of the FMM, had refused my appeal for help in this particular instance. I could not blame her. The congregation was involved in a vast number of charitable works, and there was a limit to its possibilities to furnish qualified hospital personnel. But I had not forgot that one of the principal reasons Jirapa had been proposed as the site for the new hospital had been the sisters themselves. Without the guarantee of their full and continued participation in the project, its future would indeed be uncertain. It was worth insisting, even at the risk of making myself odious.

Perhaps Cardinal Lavigerie and Mother Mary of the Passion had settled their differences in heaven and agreed to agree, for the letter I wrote in reply to Mother Marguerite's refusal to send sisters for the hospital drew from her a relatively swift response by telegram reversing her previous decision: SENDING SISTERS TO START HOSPITAL IN JIRAPA, it read.

Now that that problem had been resolved, we turned our efforts toward finding doctors. This would not be so easy since here we would not be dealing with a superior general whose agreement it would only be necessary to obtain in order to assure the hospital a steady supply of personnel. In the case of doctors, we would have to recruit them one by one. Providence, however, had already begun to take things in hand.

Across the Atlantic Ocean in Washington, D.C., Doctor Linn Fenimore Cooper, great-grandson of North American novelist James Fenimore Cooper, was having an interview with Father Fred McGuire, then executive secretary of the Mission Secretariat of the National Catholic Welfare Conference. He had come to offer his skills as a specialist in internal medicine to the Catholic missions.

"I want to go where my medical skills are most needed," he told the priest. "I am not a Catholic, but most Protestant missions would want a man who is both doctor and clergyman. I do not feel capable of filling both positions."

In his capacity as executive secretary of the Mission Secretariat, Father McGuire was aware of our need for doctors in Jirapa. He put Doctor Cooper in contact with the Missionaries of Africa in Washington, and they referred him to me. I was on home leave in Canada at the time, so we were able to meet for an interview.

Every inch of the tall, lanky man with the wide smile and firm handshake exuded professionalism. Born in Albany, New York, in 1900 and raised on the family homestead in Cooperstown, site of the Baseball Hall of Fame, he had graduated from Yale University in 1921. From there he had gone on to establish a private medical practice in Washington until interest in tropical medicine had led him to do graduate work in that field at the University of Edinburgh. Later he had become medical director of the Washington Home for Incurables and professor at the Georgetown University School of Medicine until his enlistment in the air force in 1941. At the end of the Second World War, he had taught for two years at the Hsiang Ya Medical College in Changsha, China, but the arrival of communist forces had put an end to that.

I was impressed by his seriousness and lack of any romantic notions when discussing his desire to work in a medical mission situation. With time I would come to appreciate other qualities in him, particularly his ability to combine a Yankee candidness with an innate gentlemanliness.

Without my asking him, he volunteered certain private information about himself which he felt might disqualify him for consideration for a post in a hospital run by the Catholic mission.

"I was raised a Quaker," he told me, "but I am afraid it has been some time since I practised my religion. At present I hold to no particular denomination. In fact, I think I would have to go further and describe myself as an agnostic. Secondly, I am a divorced man, though I have not remarried and probably will not do so."

My reply to this was that neither of those facts, especially if he kept them more or less to himself, would have any effect on his usefulness to us as a doctor. A contract was drawn up and Linn Cooper became Jirapa Hospital's first resident physician.

Meanwhile, the cornerstone of the new hospital had been laid on 10 March 1953 by Mr. Burdon, chief commissioner from Tamale. Brother Basilide was again in charge of construction and had begun in April to dig the foundations with the help of local labour.

Doctor Cooper and I arrived at Jirapa on 1 November 1953, and the next morning he was already at work treating patients. For the time being, the existing clinic served as temporary hospital. If it was a trial to suddenly find himself working without modern equipment and other commodities he had been used to in America, he gave no sign of it. He had no complaints, certainly, about Mother Caltry or her staff of sister-nurses who were every bit as professional as he was.[6] Often times he would set up his consulting office out of doors, seated in a chair in the early morning sunshine or in a shady spot as the day wore on and the sun grew hotter. One sensed he was happy.

The contract he had signed had been for a year, and during all that time he gave of himself and of his talents unstintingly. Father McGuire had told him before he left for the Gold Coast that it would not be enough to practise medicine in a mission atmosphere; he would also have to give good example or at least avoid being, even unconsciously, a counter-witness to the work of the missionaries. So well had he taken this to heart that he had gone to the trouble of buying a Catholic missal and had learned how to use it before his departure for Africa. In Jirapa, he attended Mass regularly.

As his friendship with the missionaries grew, the subject of God and religion would occasionally crop up in his conversation with them. We had a number of such conversations in which it was clear to me that he was searching for the road home. He would try to reason things out; but in matters of faith, reason can only go so far. It inevitably reaches a chasm that only faith can bridge. Doctor Cooper could understand that well enough but he could not bring himself to make an act of faith. It seemed to lie just beyond his reach.

"You are constantly making acts of faith in your work," I told him one day as we sat chatting in the shade of the verandah. "You place faith in what your professors taught you in medical school, in what your ears tell you when you listen to a patient's chest with your stethoscope, in the effects of certain drugs on the body. If you read an article in a medical journal describing a new technique for the treatment of some disease, you are willing to try it. You trust what people tell you of their symptoms. These are acts of faith, too, though on a lesser scale. Why is it you are able to trust persons and things, whose fallibility is obvious, but not God who is much more reliable than they could ever be?"

"I would," he replied, "if I could only be sure He exists. You speak of a chasm, Father. I see it as a precipice with nothing but infinite, uninhabited space before me. To leap from it would be tantamount to suicide and therefore a kind of blasphemy against life and reason."

"But if we were sure He existed, there would be no need of faith," I said. "Theologians tell us that will be our state in heaven, when we see God face to face and as He really is. Right now we must make do with faith."

He wondered about that. "Why must it be so?" he asked.

I didn't really know but I mused on it for awhile and finally ventured an opinion.

"Perhaps it's because of the effect real certitude would have on this fragile human nature of ours," I said. "If we were absolutely sure God exists, and there were no curtain of faith separating us from Him, we might be rapt out of our existence. We might be drawn to Him irresistibly like a piece of metal to a powerful magnet. Our free will would be useless, violated, destroyed. But God will not have that because He has built His whole relationship with us and ours with Him on the principle of free will. And the only way He can guarantee our freedom to believe in Him or not, to love Him or reject Him, is to shroud His overwhelming attractiveness in a dense cloud of unknowing that only faith can in some dim way penetrate."

It was not a very satisfying answer, but Doctor Cooper would not be the one to tell me so.

He continued to assist at Mass, following the Latin prayers in his missal. We could only wonder if he was slowly making them his own and asking the God to whom they were addressed, if He existed, to give Him faith. He could not know that such was the daily prayer of all the sisters with whom he worked at the clinic-hospital and of the priests and brothers at the mission as well.

He fulfilled his year's contract and returned for a second tour of duty in 1955-56. After that, we lost contact with him for a while, until one day in 1959 when a letter arrived from the United States containing a clipping from the *Washington Post*. Doctor Cooper, it said, had signed a contract with the Mill Hill Fathers to work in Kanowit, Sarawak, in northern Borneo. But he had not forgot Africa. In January, while on one of his periodic returns to the consulting office he still maintained in the Georgetown section of Washington, D.C. ("to pick up his mail"), he had gone to see his good friend, Father Fred McGuire, to make him an offer the priest could not refuse.

"As you know," the physician told him, "I have developed the highest esteem for the work of Catholic missionaries in Africa. I think you should see the stations there first hand. I'll foot the bill."

Father McGuire, a Vincentian missionary who had worked in China for 18 years before going to Washington to head the Mission Secretariat, had never been to Africa. So off he went, while Doctor Cooper flew to Borneo.

On 14 November 1959, Brother Philip Nadeau answered the phone at the U.S. headquarters of the Missionaries of Africa in Washington. It was a Mrs. Dawson calling to inform the fathers that Doctor Linn Fenimore Cooper had died the previous day at

Kanowit of pneumonia and encephalitis. He was just 59. We had lost a good friend and a valued co-worker.

Sometime later, a letter arrived for me from Borneo. It was from the Catholic chaplain of the hospital at Kanowit. He was writing me, he said, at the request of the late Doctor Cooper who had wanted me to know that he had managed to make his leap before he died. He had asked to be baptized and the chaplain himself had administered the sacrament while Linn was still fully conscious. A new intercessor now watched over Jirapa.

*
* *

In 1951 Doctor Cheverton, principal medical officer at the Ministry of Health in Accra, had visited the mission to acquaint himself with the medical work being done there. He too had been impressed by what he found, and after visiting the middle school an idea had struck him. With all these qualified teachers and nurses available in one place, would it not be possible to start a training school either for nurses or midwives? This would serve to absorb some of the school leavers and get them interested in the health care of their own people.[7]

The idea struck a responsive chord among the sisters. The one chosen to transform it into reality, and to almost literally make something from nothing, was the newly-arrived Sister Cyprian. When the time came to move beyond the planning stage, a Miss Caulfield was sent up from Accra to thoroughly inspect conditions and verify needs. She returned to the Ministry of Health to recommend that permission be granted without delay for midwife training to begin at Jirapa under Sister Cyprian's direction. On 2 February 1952, the training school opened under a large tree, with a blackboard, some chalk, and one or two books.

Once the midwife training program began to run smoothly, Sister Cyprian saw the possibility of realizing the second part of Doctor Cheverton's idea. In 1953, even before the cornerstone of the new hospital had been laid, negotiations began with the Ministry of Health to set up a training program in Jirapa for nurses. Miss Marie White, a senior nursing tutor at Korle Bu Hospital in Accra, was sent to inspect and report her findings to the nurses board. In January 1954, permission was given to begin training qualified registered nurses (QRN) on a trial basis, again with

Sister Cyprian in charge. By the time Doctor Cooper's first contract with Jirapa Hospital ended, both training programs were in full swing.[8]

***
****

Doctor Cooper had not been a surgeon; he was an internist and something of an organizer. He had insisted from the start that the fledgling hospital set up archives and keep them in order. The second doctor to serve at Jirapa presented an almost total contrast to him in both style and interests.

Doctor Henry Archambault was first and foremost a surgeon. Institutional organization held no interest for him. He burned with a more than ordinary desire to reach out and heal, a desire that grew all the stronger as his own health began to deteriorate toward the end of his life. With such a man, paperwork of any kind could only hold the lowest priority. In fact, only one thing interested him less, and that was meeting "important" people. Thus when the new hospital was at last ready for occupancy, and the position of administrator was offered to him as a matter of course, he refused it out of hand.

"Quite definitely no!" he said. "I have been trained for medical work and that alone is my reason for being here. Period!"

Born in Barrie, Vermont, in 1913, Henry Archambault and his twin brother Rene came from a family of doctors. Their father, a graduate of McGill Medical School in Montreal, had set up practice in Vermont. Later, their elder brother Armand followed in his father's footsteps, practising general and internal medicine in Barrie. It came as no surprise to anyone when the twins decided in favour of the same profession and went off to Creighton University Medical School in Omaha, Nebraska.

Like most identical twins, Henry and Rene were close; they enjoyed being together and doing things together. After doing their internship in Philadelphia and a year of general practice in Vermont, Henry contracted tuberculosis and had to spend two years in Arizona undergoing treatment. Rene waited for his brother to recuperate before continuing with their plans to specialize in surgery at the University of Pennsylvania Medical School. After four years of residency there, Doctor Henry accepted a position at Providence Hospital in Detroit, while his brother went to Nankin Hospital in nearby Wayne, Michigan.

During his years of practice at Providence Hospital, Doctor Henry had dedicated a good deal of his time and energy to treating the poor, especially victims of drug and alcohol abuse, in the city's skid row. Though he had a strong spiritual life and always found time in his busy day for prayer, he was no moralizer or "bleeding heart". He was another Yankee, like Doctor Cooper, whose deep compassion for the sufferer knew no barriers of prejudice and expressed itself in practical rather than symbolic acts or mere words.

For some time Doctor Archambault had cherished the wish to work as a surgeon in the missions. When the moment came to realize that wish, it was again Father McGuire of the Mission Secretariat who intervened on our behalf. He knew that Doctor Cooper's contract would expire within the year and that Jirapa would then be needing a good physician again. When the letter reached him from Providence Hospital, it must have seemed doubly providential, therefore. He called Doctor Archambault and put him in contact with the Missionaries of Africa. It so happened that Bishop Bertrand, who had succeeded Bishop Morin as vicar apostolic of Navrongo, was in Canada at the time. Jirapa Hospital was within his vicariate, making him ultimately responsible for recruiting its doctors. Losing no time, he telephoned the doctor and set up a meeting with him at Providence Hospital.

The interview was a short one and, as it turned out, a satisfying one for both sides. Doctor Henry, knowing that the bishop was on a fund-raising tour for his poor vicariate, challenged him immediately on his priorities.

"What are you interested in most, Bishop: money or a doctor?"

"Both," came the instant reply.

"Well, I will make you an offer," the doctor persisted. "I am willing to send you five thousand dollars a year for the rest of my life or to work in your hospital for six months. Which would you honestly prefer?"

Bishop Bertrand did not hesitate. "I want a doctor," he said.

Doctor Archambault laughed in delight. "O.K., I'll go!" he said.

He went and stayed fifteen years. And the bishop got the money anyway.

Doctor Archambault's arrival at Jirapa on the evening of 22 October 1954 was memorable. The new hospital was still several months from completion and there were no facilities as yet for performing surgical operations. Almost before he had time to put his luggage down, let alone unpack it, an acute case of strangulated hernia presented itself at the mission clinic and he was asked by the sisters to take a look at it. The patient, Mr. Norbert Moglakpiere, was in great pain. One glance at him was sufficient for the physician to know that he would have to operate quickly. In the absence of proper facilities, the old maternity delivery room would have to do. There was no equipment either, so everything had to be improvised. The linen was sterilized in an old dustbin and the instruments in a stainless steel container, both of which were heated on a charcoal fire in the open. Light was provided by a kerosene lamp and a motorcycle lamp connected to a 1KV generator. Sister John assisted as nurse and anaesthetist while I held the motorcycle lamp and the patient's hand.

The operation went well, and the next day Doctor Archambault paid an early morning visit to this his first patient in Jirapa. Norbert lay very still in his bed, not daring to move a muscle for fear the pain of the previous day would return or the wound tear open and bleed. After examining him, the doctor told him to sit up. The sister translated this for him, but he refused to believe what he had heard. His eyes grew wide with fear and surprise. "No!" he said, beginning to tremble. But the strange new doctor insisted. Finally, he reluctantly allowed himself to be helped to a sitting position with his legs dangling over the side of the bed. He held his breath as long as he could and then let it seep out ever so slowly. For a long time he took shallow breaths, gradually relaxing. Just when he thought the worst was over and they would allow him to lie back in the position proper to any decent sick man, the doctor and the sister began pulling him to his feet! Were they throwing him out? He would surely fall, or the wound would break open and he would die. But the arms that supported him were strong and reassuring. He took a few steps about the room with the doctor and sister on either side of him. This seemed to please them, enough at least to win their permission to return to his bed. The same thing happened later in the day and again the following day. And on the third day he was up walking normally and ready to be discharged from the hospital.

This was something unheard of. Word spread rapidly that a new kind of doctor had arrived in Jirapa, a wonderworker who operates and gets patients up the same day and sends them home cured in three days.

Doctor "Shambo", as the people affectionately called him, was one of God's great gifts to Ghana. His reverence for life extended beyond the merely physical to the whole person — body, mind, and soul. In many instances his surgical skills seemed secondary to his ability to heal by love and concern for his patients. He had seen many cases during his practice in Detroit of persons whose physical illnesses were only symptoms of deeper psychological or spiritual problems. Even among the apparently healthy, he was often struck by the pitiable insufficiency of their soul growth in proportion to their physical development. The same could be said for his intellectual acquaintances who were so learned and clever in matters of the world and science, yet often so stunted in the spiritual part of their being. How strange to see these unevenly developed people, so far from being the whole persons they were capable of becoming and meant to become. For that reason, God was never absent from his mind when he treated his patients in Jirapa. He took a personal interest in each of them, visiting them twice daily and lifting their spirits with a few cheerful words in their own language. When he thought they needed it, he did not hesitate to speak to them of God's love for them and to encourage them to pray, to trust in Him, and to learn more about Him. The language barrier sometimes interfered, but in that case he would be concerned to find someone who could do it for him.

His influence did not stop at his patients. Those who worked with him, especially the graduate and student nurses and other members of the hospital staff, learned from his example a sense of dedication to duty and to the welfare of their patients that they could not have got from any book or classroom lecture. Though he would tolerate no carelessness or indifference on their part in the performance of their duties, he was also attentive to their needs. They knew that he was never too busy to listen to them, and that if he offered them a bit of advice from time to time, it was never as a busybody meddling in their affairs but as a brother genuinely concerned for their happiness and growth.

At Jirapa, Doctor Shambo had no "working hours". He was available at any and all times, even though Mother Caltry and I and others tried to convince him to be more prudent in measuring his strength. He listened with half an ear, aware that often there was little he could do about it. Unlike most of us in Europe and North Anerica who have effectively diminished our tolerance of pain by the over-availability of drugs to soothe it, the African still has a remarkably high pain threshold. The sick were often brought to Jirapa when it was already too late to save them or when the only recourse was an immediate surgical intervention. Many a night was spent performing desperate emergency operations. Doctor Shambo would not hesitate to scold family members for delaying to bring in a sick relative, just as he would rebuke sternly anyone he found doing something harmful to his or her own health.

He was, in what some would term the "old-fashioned" sense, a pious man. God came first. He was firmly convinced that nothing he could do with his considerable skills would have any ultimate value if it did not find its inspiration in God's tremendous love for His children. When he could not be found in the hospital, everyone knew that he was either taking his daily six-mile walk along the Bazu road, rosary in hand, or on his knees in the sisters' chapel. The Franciscan Missionaries of Mary had daily exposition of the Blessed Sacrament from 8 a.m. until 4 p.m. These visits were for him a replenishment and a natural extension of the Mass he served at and participated in each morning.

In material things, he was content with little. Only reluctantly did he ever spend anything on himself. He funnelled what he had to the poor, but always in a discreet way, demanding discretion in return. He had no pity to spare for the wasteful and spendthrift missionary, but when he found one in genuine need, he would give all he had earned to help him.

As soon as the hospital was completed and the Public Works Department inspectors had approved it, the move from the temporary hospital buildings began. Brother Aidan, who had taken over its construction when Brother Basilide had been called away to begin work on the new church at Ko, began the transfer of materials on 25 January 1955. The days of the clinic were over.[9]

With Doctor Archambault's categoric refusal to act as administrator, the burden fell to Mother Caltry. She added it to her many other duties both inside and outside the hospital, including those of matron (head of nurses), anaesthetist, and catechist. Later, Sister Clementine and Sister John would succeed her in the same post.[10]

When he learned in 1959 that Doctor Cooper had signed a contract to work in a mission hospital in Borneo, Doctor Archambault took it upon himself to recruit another doctor for Jirapa. He had known a dedicated nurse at Providence Hospital in Detroit who had gone on to study medicine. At this time she had just completed her medical degree course and was in residency in pediatrics. He wrote to her, telling her of the urgent need for a pediatrician at Jirapa. She was interested and volunteered to interrupt her studies for a year in order to lend a hand in Ghana.

When the people of Jirapa heard about it, they thought to themselves: here comes Doctor Shambo's future wife. But they were wrong again, just as they had been wrong with regard to the motives behind the arrival of the Franciscan Missionaries of Mary twenty years before.[11] Doctor Barbara Chapper had not come to Jirapa for love of Doctor Shambo, but for love of them.

She soon had the opportunity to prove it. Sick children were many, far more than she had yet seen at Providence Hospital, and she also had to share the burden of the adult patients with Doctor Archambault.

Though she only stayed a year, the benefits of her volunteer service to northern Ghana were to continue through her younger brother, Martin, then an engineer in their father's iron construction firm. The stories told by his sister on her return to Detroit awakened an interest in him that flowered into a missionary vocation. He was accepted by the White Fathers as a candidate for the brotherhood and posted to Wa diocese in 1968, where he remains to this day.

During his time in Jirapa, Doctor Archambault went home just twice, and then only because his health required it. The first time was in 1958, and the second was in December 1964 when doctors at the University of Michigan diagnosed him as suffering from tuberculosis of the larynx and multiple myeloma (a form of bone cancer). He was given only a month to live. His twin, Doctor Rene, refused to take the verdict of his peers as final and convinced his brother to go home to Wayne with him. There, at Nankin Hospital, he slowly and tenderly nursed him back to relative health by his own skills, supported by the prayers of thousands of people in northwest Ghana who had come to revere their beloved Doctor Shambo. Together they gained a temporary victory over the disease which went into remission. It was a long and painful illness, but all those who came in contact with him during that time agree that they never heard a word of complaint from his lips.

As soon as he was able to do so, he was back practising medicine again, helping his brother in the hospital until he felt strong enough to return to Jirapa. That moment came in September 1968. His arrival sparked great rejoicing and people came from near and far to greet him and to welcome him back. Uncharacteristically, he paused to enjoy it, even though briefly. But all too soon he was back to the old program of five or six major operations a day, six days a week, with frequent emergencies adding to the load. Out-patient consultations and the twice-daily visits to hospital patients took up most of the remainder of his time outside the operating room. When, on 1 April 1969, the doctor who had been loaned to Jirapa by the Presbyterian mission to do general medical work was called away to a hospital that had no doctor, Doctor Archambault was left alone to look after the 250-bed hospital.

In May, with his back beginning to trouble him again, he confided to someone that he suspected his multiple myeloma was active again. The hospital authorities advised him to return to the United States for a rest, but he refused on the grounds that he could not leave the hospital without a doctor.

Sensing that he did not have long to live, he now seemed intent on making the most of the time that remained to him. There was too little of it left to think of wasting it on himself. Crippled with the pain of collapsing vertebrae, his back becoming more and more bent, he continued to work as before, though sometimes he was so tired and weak that he had to have two nurses support him while he operated.

He might have gone on longer had not an attack of malaria intervened. Already considerably weakened by the progress of the myeloma, there was little resistance left to ward off a fresh enemy. On Sunday, 13 July 1969, the pain and weakness became so acute that even this valiant man finally had to bow to it.

During the next few days, his condition worsened. From his sickbed he maintained his concern for his patients, questioning the nurses about them and giving directives for their care. Several of the cases were serious, and he prayed fervently that God would send help quickly.

On Tuesday he received the sacrament of the sick, fully aware that the end was near and completely resigned to it. Word had begun to spread of Doctor Shambo's condition, and people began to gather by the hundreds outside the hospital to accompany him as far as they could on his last journey.

On Wednesday evening, his prayer was answered with the unexpected arrival of Doctor Rene. It was characteristic of Doctor Henry that, close as he was to his brother, he did not inform him of his illness himself. His excuse had been that he did not want to worry him. But he was also afraid Doctor Rene would try to take him back to the United States, and he was not prepared to accept that. Before leaving the hospital in Wayne in 1968, he had told a friend on the staff that he wanted to work in Africa until he died. Someone else had informed his brother; and God had seen to it that when his plane landed in Tamale, Father Songliedong happened to be there. The priest had borrowed a car and driven him to Jirapa immediately.

Doctor Henry was overjoyed to see his brother again; it was a grace he had not counted on. But he wasted no time on sentiment. They both knew the seriousness of the situation. Instead he called for his patients' charts and began to brief Doctor Rene on the most urgent cases awaiting his attention. There was none among them that could not wait until the following day. His brother assured him that he would begin operating the very first thing in the morning.

At 10:30 p.m. it was decided to let the patient rest. Doctor Rene and Father Songliedong retired to the next room where they would be within easy reach should the nurses keeping vigil over Doctor Henry need help during the night.

Sometime before dawn, Doctor Rene awoke. Tired as he was from the long and tedious journey, he had slept only fitfully through the night. He got up quietly, trying not to awaken the sleeping priest in the other bed, and went in to see his brother. Even before he reached the bed on which he lay, he knew the vigil was over. Doctor Henry had passed away peacefully in his sleep without disturbing anyone. It was 17 July 1969.

The news of Doctor Shambo's death brought forth an outpouring of popular grief and homage unprecedented in northern Ghana. More than just a doctor, the ordinary people he loved so well had lost a friend, a brother, a mentor. The good we had seen him perform in our midst, great as it was, was small in comparison to the good he had kept hidden from us and which now revealed itself as person after person came to tell us what Doctor Shambo had done for them.

Doctor Rene kept his word and began the operations he had promised to do even as people began to stream into Jirapa for the funeral of his brother. His personal grief would have to wait. Life took precedence over death, even at times like this.

The funeral was one Doctor Shambo would certainly not have approved of for himself. For a man who naturally shied away from personal publicity and the click of a camera shutter, it would not have pleased him to know that he was being treated in death as he had never permitted himself to be treated in life. But the people would have the last word, and they were not to be denied their final act of homage. It was they who made his funeral that of an important chief, the biggest ever experienced in the North. Father Lawrence Kyemaalo, one of the first Dagati priests, who had been assigned to Jirapa since 1952, had never seen anything like it. Two bishops and eighteen priests concelebrated the funeral Mass, and thousands of Ghanaians — coming from all directions and professing all shades of belief — joined together in the bond of shared loss. As Doctor Shambo had loved them all equally, so they would set aside their differences to bid him a common farewell. They came on foot, bicycle, bus, tractor, car, or lorry — by any means possible. By the time the funeral began in the late afternoon, there was not a square meter of unoccupied space in Jirapa.

One of the attractive features of African Christianity — when it has not become too Westernized — is its spontaneity. During the wake and funeral, the mourners repeatedly broke into extemporaneous funeral chants, just as they had done so many years before at the funeral of Bagile's brother. Then it had been to torment him for abandoning the ways of his ancestors to embrace the Ngwinsore. Now the tradition served to express both their sense of deep loss as well as their gratitude for a job well-done, a fight well-fought, by a great man whom everyone claimed as his own.

> Nurses, when did Shambo get sick? And why did you not inform us?
> Shambo, you did not tell us you were sick.
> Shambo, you took us by surprise.

As each refrain erupted from a lone voice in a different part of the enormous throng, it was taken up in chorus by those within hearing and repeated to the rhythm of drums in the background.

> All black people, you may mourn for he is gone.
> Orphans, neglected people, cry now for you are doomed.
> Shambo is a tree that shelters orphans.
> Shambo, shelter of orphans, what will they do now?
> Shambo, friend of the blind, the lame, the lepers.
> Shambo, relative of those who have no one, to whom will they go now?
> Shambo, mother and father of orphans and the poor, the orphans call in the bush in search of you.
> Shambo, "pearl of great price", they have been searching for you with lighted torches and no one can find you.
> Shambo, your children are weeping. Open your eyes and see us.

Anyone recalling Henry Archambault and his dislike of the cult of the personality, would have had to smile at this. What was going on here was indeed enough to make him open his eyes, sit up, and send the crowds home with a stern rebuke. It would not have surprised some had he stirred up a sudden dust storm or a drenching shower to send everyone scurrying.

> Shambo is a valuable pot that has been broken. There is not the potter who can make such a one again. And even if there were, who could afford its price?

It is Shambo who comes! No, it is his brother.
Shambo is dead! No stores to be opened in Jirapa.
You sick in hospital, he who goes round to see and attend you
     is dead! For whom do you wait?

Christians, Muslims, and animists vied with one another in expressing their praise and grief. These were genuine sentiments voiced by a people accustomed to seeing death in their midst, and yet this death held a special meaning for them. If it could help them to understand something of the God who inspired such love and selflessness, Doctor Shambo would have accomplished more in Jirapa than he could ever have dreamed possible.

Shambo is a brave man not to be compared with others.
Shambo has laboured unto death.
Shambo, helper of the poor, the poor are crying. Listen to
     them!

A Christian segment of the crowd began to make itself heard. The Ghanaian sisters were in among them, lending their voices to the refrains.

Shambo has gone to attend High Mass in heaven.
Shambo has gone to heaven to adore God face to face.
Shambo has gone to heaven to perform operations.

Would they allow him no rest then? Were there strangulated hernias to be attended to even in heaven? Doctor Henry would have been amused to hear it. Then the praise-singers lifted their voices to recall the well-known fact of his strong filial devotion to the humble Mother of God.

Shambo, in heaven sit near our Lady.
Mary, run to meet your child and take him in your arms.
Our Lady has come to take her child.

Doctor Shambo was laid to rest in a special plot at the entrance to the hospital. There he continues to be a part of its daily life: inspiring by the memory of his great humanity and his dedication to the total welfare of the people; witnessing, by the gift of his life to them, to the existence of values that forcefully contradict those prevalent in the world today; and assuring, by his resting place in the soil of the Northwest, God's continued special regard for that small corner of a great continent.[12]

*
**

If I have written here exclusively of Jirapa Hospital, it is because I was directly involved in it from the start. To the north, however, in Nandom, a smiliar project was developing almost simultaneously.

Nandom mission, founded in 1933, was the third mission in the Northwest. As had happened in Jirapa, the medical apostolate went hand in hand with the apostolate of the Word from the first moment of the missionaries' arrival there. Father Julien Chantereau, from Orléans, France, was chiefly responsible for this. When the Missionary Sisters of Our Lady of Africa (or the White Sisters, as they were more popularly known then) arrived some twenty years later, they took over his work and set up a dispensary and a maternity clinic in four huts behind the church. The personnel comprised two White Sisters: Annette Mercure and Monique Belanger; one member of the Ghanaian Sisters of Mary Immaculate, Sister Pia; and Elizabeth, a laywoman.

The set-up was poor, but a remarkable amount of good work was accomplished in it. In the first four months, more than two hundred babies were born in one of the huts set aside for that purpose.

The out-patients dispensary covered a vast area but was entirely without medical services. Eventually, the Nandom local council offered financial help to buy drugs so that the dispensary could be that in more than name. The seriously ill, meanwhile, were admitted to the huts. Patients with infectious diseases, such as smallpox, yaws, and meningitis, were treated in special camps set up away from the population. Those in need of a doctor's attention were transferred to Jirapa Hospital.

Construction of the present hospital was begun by the government in 1961 and completed by the mission in 1965. It was administered and staffed by the White Sisters (MSOLA) until 1975 when, under Sister Columban, they began a gradual transfer of responsibility to the Sisters of Mary Immaculate.[13]

Today the hospital serves a population of forty-five thousand people. The prolonged economic crisis in the country, which affects rural areas worst of all, has caused many problems for the continued operation of the hospital, especially in regard to drugs, equipment, spare-parts, and general maintenance. Nevertheless, it struggles on, trying to meet the needs of all the sick who come to it for help.

Humanly speaking, it was not easy to attract qualified medical personnel — doctors, nurses, technicians — to work in Jirapa or Nandom Hospitals. All we had to offer them was plenty of work under often very trying conditions due to diet, climate, language barrier, lack of proper equipment, and scarcity of medical supplies. Their motivation in coming had to be something other than material. Yet more than fifty expatriate doctors alone answered the call for help since Doctor Cooper's arrival in 1953. They were joined by a long list of expatriate nurses, laboratory technicians, physical therapists, mechanical engineers, and social workers. They came from Canada, England, France, Germany, India, Ireland, Italy, the Netherlands, the Philippines, Poland, Scotland, Spain, and the United States. Of those doctors from the United States, nearly all were recruited and screened by the Catholic Medical Mission Board in New York. Others came to us through personal contacts with missionaries or with doctors who had either served in Jirapa or Nandom or had heard about our need. Sometimes a letter arrived from a doctor somewhere in the world who had heard about us and wanted to offer his services directly. While they were with us, this medical personnel spared no efforts to bring the best health care possible not only to those who came to the hospitals, but to people in faraway villages as well. Mobile clinics became a regular sight on the dusty roads of the Northwest.[14]

Today the two hospitals have local nurses, laboratory technicians, radiographers, pharmacists, etc. What they lack most are local doctors. Several excellent and deeply motivated ones have served the area since the first arrived in 1976, but most of them for short terms of only one or two years. Doctor Edward Gyader, who became medical superintendent of Jirapa Hospital in 1979, after completing medical studies and qualifying as a surgeon in Italy, was an exception. He remained for six years, giving hope that others like him would follow his example.

One of the serious problems concerning professional people in Third World countries is the brain drain. Doctors are prominent among those who fail to return home once they have completed their studies abroad. Aside from humanitarian reasons or soli-

darity with one's people, there are few incentives to lure the
foreign-trained doctor home to a less economically developed
region. Besides the low wages and frequent lack of adequate
medical facilities, equipment, and drugs with which to carry on
his work, he often has to put up with prejudice among his own
people. Instead of being welcomed home as a valuable asset in
the battle against disease and infirmity in the country, petty jeal-
ousies surface in the form of misunderstandings, false accusations, lack of cooperation, etc. It is possible to overcome these,
of course, but no one should blame the doctor too harshly who
wonders if it is worth the struggle and decides to remain where
his skills are appreciated and rewarded.

The arrival of Doctor Adibo as regional medical officer marked
the beginning of a new era for the development of health care in
the whole Upper Region of Ghana. A man of vision, a dedicated
doctor and surgeon with much experience working in rural areas,
and an excellent administrator, he has demonstrated that his main
concern is the welfare of the patient. Through his efforts, a new
awareness is taking root, an awareness that perhaps takes us
back to the early days of the first health care attempted in the
Jirapa area, when the missionaries went about the villages
dispensing their little remedies and words of advice. No matter
how efficient and well-run the hospital may be, the basic problems
and causes of sickness will remain, inviting health workers to
move out among the people to deal with them. In this area of
primary health care, emphasized by Doctor Adibo, Jirapa Hospital has an important role to play.

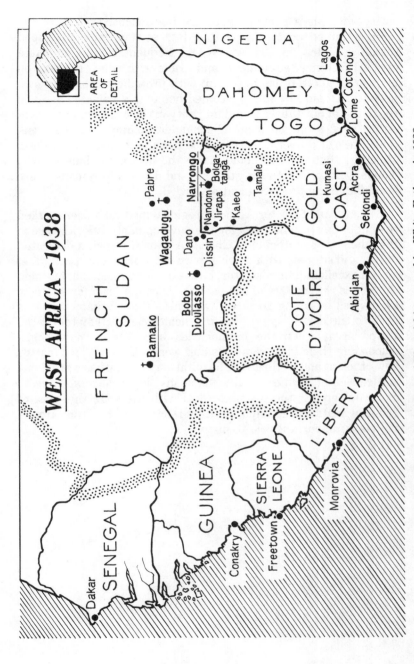

WEST AFRICA~1938

AREA OF DETAIL

NIGERIA

DAHOMEY

TOGO

Lagos
Cotonou
Lome

GOLD COAST

Kumasi
Accra
Sekondi

Tamale

Navrongo
Bolga- tanga
Nandom
Jirapa
Kaleo

Dano
Dissin

Pabre

Wagadugu

FRENCH SUDAN

Bobo Dioulasso

Bamako

COTE D'IVOIRE

Abidjan

LIBERIA

Monrovia

SIERRA LEONE

Freetown

GUINEA

Conakry

SENEGAL

Dakar

Dotted border encloses area of West Africa served by White Fathers in 1938.

13

Growth

Celibacy held no positive value in the eyes of the Dagaabas and Sissalas. It was alien to all they felt and understood to be "natural", and for that reason they found it incomprehensible. Before our arrival in 1929, they had neither heard of such a concept nor seen it put into practice. It was simply beyond their imagining.

When the first sisters arrived at Jirapa in 1939, therefore, even some of the Christians thought they were really the missionaries' wives come at last. We explained to them that such was not the case. But though they held a generally high opinion of us and of our capabilities, they were not willing to concede us the possibility of an exemption from the ordinary requirements of human nature as they knew them. One of these was the need to procreate. No amount of explanation on our part could convince them otherwise.

As a result, many people spent sleepless nights hidden behind trees and bushes, spying on the sisters' convent and the priests' house. So convinced were they that nocturnal communications between the two had to exist somehow, that many months of fruitless night-spying were necessary before the most skeptical among them were willing to accept celibacy as a possibility and that the missionaries were capable of abiding by it.

The first fruits of the sisters' presence in Jirapa were not slow in appearing. Within a year of their arrival, four as yet illiterate Dagati girls, moved by the Spirit, presented themselves at the mission one day with a boldness that surprised even them. They wanted to give their lives to God as the sisters had done.

Did they know what that entailed? they were asked.

Yes, they had some idea. It meant they must serve God first and put their trust in Him. Wherever He led them, they would follow and be glad of it. They would sacrifice anything for this, even the supreme earthly good of bearing children. The sisters, they said, had done this and were happy. That was what attracted them most. The sisters were mothers to all the Dagaabas instead of to just the children of one husband.

Of the other two vows that would be required of them eventually, poverty would present no serious problem. Obedience, as it very seldom does when untried, did not daunt them either.

After consultation with Bishop Morin, it was decided that the four — Rose, Sabina, Pia, and Juliana — would go to Pabre, near Wagadugu, in French Sudan. There the Missionary Sisters of Our Lady of Africa had founded an African congregation of sisters in 1927, to which Bishop Morin had already sent a number of girls from Navrongo who had been attracted to the same religious ideal. They would first be taught to read and write. Then the sisters would train them in the religious life with a view to their eventual return to begin a local congregation in the Navrongo vicariate.

I was not present in the Gold Coast at the time of this development. After eleven years of the good life in the missions, I was "serving time" in North America. I had gone to our motherhouse in Algiers at the end of 1936 to follow a three-month refresher course and a thirty-day Ignatian retreat, prior to taking my first home leave in Canada since coming to Africa as a newly-ordained priest. There the superior general had told me I would not be returning to the Gold Coast immediately. The society was interested in establishing itself in the United States and someone was needed to seek out a bishop willing to welcome it into his diocese. I was to have that honor. Like the instructions of the general manager of the Water and Sewage Corporation in Kumasi to his drilling team some fifteen years later, I was not simply to look for a diocese to receive us but to stay there until I found one! This did not seem to be a particularly difficult assignment viewed from Algiers. It was only when I began to canvas the bishops and listen to their excuses that I began to understand the true dimensions of the assignment I had undertaken. It was an entirely new kind of challenge, as demanding as that of opening a new mission in a new territory in Africa. As door after episcopal door was closed to us, I seriously wondered if the Holy Spirit had decided to remain behind in Dagao rather than accompany me home.[1]

Frustration followed frustration as one year passed into another and my quest got nowhere. Not all the bishops said no, of course; sometimes their diocesan consultors did. Meanwhile I was longing to return to Africa, to be a part again of what was happening there. Letters reached me occasionally, telling me of new developments, increasing my homesickness. A group of young men, inspired by the example of the life and dedication of Brother Basilide, had asked to live as he did, working and praying. Five or six of them were being trained in Kaleo by Father Durand. More girls had followed Rose, Sabina, Pia, and Juliana to Pabre in search of their ideal of living a consecrated life of prayer and service to God and neighbour. A primary school for girls had opened at Jirapa with the government's blessing. Nandom's Christian community was increasing at a rhythm similar to that of Jirapa. And there I sat, still trying to get my foot inside the door of some United States diocese.

Even the Japanese conspired against me. On 7 December 1941, the attack on Pearl Harbor in the Hawaiian Islands ushered the United States into what became the Second World War. All thought of the missions seemed to fade from the collective consciousness as the entire nation turned its efforts toward gearing up to stop the axis advance in Europe, Asia, and the Pacific. My own hopes of an early return to Africa died that fateful day.

But suddenly, when everything seemed to be going wrong and my hope of succeeding in the mission entrusted to me by the superior general lay in tatters, a ray of light pierced the gloom. Persuaded by some of his own priests, the bishop of Ogdensburg, New York, withdrew his initial refusal and accepted us into his diocese. We were permitted to settle in Alexandria Bay, on the Saint Lawrence River.

That was in 1942, when the fortunes of the allies were at low ebb. Since there was little chance of crossing the Atlantic in the circumstances, I had to bide my time until travel restrictions would be relaxed for the non-military. Meanwhile, I was instructed by my superiors in Algiers to find another bishop in another part of the country who would receive us into his diocese too. In 1944, with the allies closing the distance between themselves and the axis powers, we were permitted by the Baltimore-Washington archdiocese to acquire a property in Bethesda, Maryland.

At about the same time, in Nandom, the first community of local sisters was established. Its pioneers were Sisters Colette, Bernadette, Marie, and Diana, all of whom had been trained and professed at Pabre.[2]

Having accomplished my mission in the United States, the superiors released me for active duty in Africa again. Restrictions on travel across the Atlantic had eased with the defeat of Hitler's forces in Europe and North Africa, so that by July 1945 I was back in the Gold Coast.

It was a radically changed Gold Coast from the one I had left eight years earlier. Self-government and independence were in the air, thanks in part to increasing criticism of the colonial relationship by both the United States and Russia, though for different reasons. Franklin Roosevelt and Winston Churchill had signed the Atlantic Charter which, among other things, confirmed the "right of all people to choose the form of government under which they live" and pledged the signers to work toward the restoration of the sovereign rights and self-government of those "who have been forcibly deprived of them". During the war, the British had begun to introduce constitutional changes in some of their colonies which gave Africans slightly more participation in the political process. But by doing this, they had merely succeeded in whetting appetites for more political autonomy than they were willing to grant. Even Churchill denied that the sections of the Atlantic Charter quoted above applied to British colonies in Africa, thereby infuriating nationalists in these countries and fueling further criticism from the United States and Russia.

In northern Gold Coast, normally so isolated from the currents of life in the South, the fever of nationalism was present in a less virulent form than it was in Accra and Cape Coast, but it was present nonetheless. Workers returning from Kumasi and further south had brought it back north with them. Soon the young men who had served in the African units of the British army during the war, and were now being discharged and repatriated, would add to it.

Meanwhile, however, the work of the mission went on and I was glad to be a direct part of it again. Bishop Morin had informed me that I would not be returning to Jirapa right away. He was in need of a general bursar for the vicariate, so I was assigned to Navrongo again, my first mission post in the Gold Coast on my arrival from Canada in 1925.

"Can you drive a lorry and repair it?" he asked me at our first meeting after my return that July.

"I can drive a car," I answered, "but I have never had anything to do with lorries."

"Well, you will learn," said the bishop, settling the matter.

It would certainly be in my interests to do so since the nearest garage was at Kumasi, 356 miles away over bad roads.

"Brother Ludovic can perhaps help you here if anything goes seriously wrong with the lorry," he went on, "but he is very busy building a school and will not have much free time. Of course, when on the road, you are entirely on your own." He smiled sweetly at me.

"Of course," I replied, returning the smile for no good reason.

I soon found out he was right.

Shortly after taking over my new assignment, the bishop decided the time had come to begin training our future Sisters of Mary Immaculate (SMI) on their own native soil. He had hoped to build their headquarters, postulate, and novitiate in Navrongo, but the vicariate treasury (never very robust) was practically exhausted, and funding appeals to Rome and elsewhere had been unsuccessful. Instead, he fell back on the surplus of good will and the spirit of adventure still very much a part of life in the missionary Church under his jurisdiction. The Missionary Sisters of Our Lady of Africa (MSOLA), who had agreed to administer the new congregation and see to the training of its aspirants until it could become autonomous, now offered the postulancy and novitiate a temporary home with them in Navrongo. Classroom facilities would be available from the nearby parish school. Sisters Pia and Juliana, the first Dagati girls to be professed, and four MSOLA composed the staff.

At the beginning of December, Bishop Morin accompanied me to Pabre to pick up our postulants and novices and transport them home. It was a festive occasion, not only because it was the feast of the Immaculate Conception of Mary and the homecoming of the SMI, but the discipline of the convent at Pabre had not diminished the spontaneity and good humour of the twenty-five young religious who now filled the back of the five-ton lorry. As we drove south toward Navrongo, we had the pleasant accompaniment of innocent laughter and song between the occasional recitation of the rosary.

It had been an uneventful drive up, but now the additional weight combined with the poor condition of the road and the low quality of the tires to produce two flats. The jolly caravan ground to a halt. We were miles from anything or anyone, and I had no spares. Except for a government vehicle now and then, traffic was practically non-existent on the road. Unless I could repair the two flat tires, we would have to roll on the rims or start walking.

The sisters wandered away in groups to look for shade, which was not too plentiful in that sparsely wooded area, but the bishop stayed bravely perspiring at my side. If he remembered what he had said to me in our interview of the previous July, he was tactful enough not to repeat it now. In the interim, I had learned a lot about lorries; but when it came to repairing tires, expertise was not enough. With the poor equipment we had then, one relied on miracles or nothing.

It was no fun working in the blazing sun to get cheap glue to hold cheap patches to cheap tires. Time after time they failed to hold, and down went the tire. After four hours of trying, and a barrage of rosaries laid down by the sisters to hold my frustrations at bay and my tongue from expressing them, the patches seemed to adhere at last and we embarked on our journey once more. With care and prayer and a slightly more subdued atmosphere among the passengers, we were finally able to reach Navrongo with our precious cargo.

Rome approved the young congregation in April 1946. In 1952, a convent was built in Kaleo and the SMI began work there. Other parishes were soon asking for their help, and foundations succeeded one another as quickly as the sisters could be trained to staff them.

By the early fifties it was evident that the majority of the SMI vocations were coming from Dagao and that the postulate and novitiate had outgrown the possibilities of the MSOLA in Navrongo to absorb them. Rome, in the meantime, had made a building grant to the vicariate for that purpose. With these three strong reasons behind him, Bishop Bertrand, who had replaced an ailing Bishop Morin, decided the new SMI complex should be built as close to the centre of Dagati territory as possible. The new parish of Daffiama was chosen, and Brother Lorenzo got to work on the buildings. Sisters Gabriel de l'Annonciation, Edmond Campion, and Christoph, of the Missionary Sisters of Our Lady of Africa, agreed to accompany the novitiate to Daffiama.[3]

At the end of 1954, the transfer was made from Navrongo even though the buildings were not yet finished. The postulants and novices pitched in to help Brother Lorenzo and his masons in whatever way they could, mostly by carrying sand and stones. Before long, everything was ready and the regular novitiate schedule could be observed.

Illiterate girls continued to be accepted for some time. On entering the pre-postulate at Nandom and later at Ko, they followed a literacy course which lasted two or three years. In 1959 the MSOLA were asked to collaborate in the program at Ko. Sisters Louise Myriam and Theresa of the Child Jesus took charge of classes for aspirants, while Sister Jean de la Lande began a sewing workroom with the help of Sister Priscilla of the SMI and a laywoman named Modesta.[4] As primary and middle school education became the norm all over the country, the pre-postulate disappeared and completion of middle school became the requirement for all religious candidates.[5]

With numbers increasing steadily and communities of sisters blossoming all over the North in answer to the needs of the three new dioceses that had been carved out of the Navrongo vicariate — Tamale, Navrongo, and Wa — it was felt that the congregation had reached sufficient maturity to govern itself.[6] A general chapter was convened in August 1970 at the SMI headquarters in Daffiama. There the congregation's first superior general, Sister Emiliana Lokore (a Dagati girl from the Nandom area) and her general council were elected. From that moment on, all responsibility for administration and formation passed from the hands of the MSOLA to them.

At the time of the jubilee celebrations in Wa diocese in 1979, marking the fiftieth anniversary of the evangelization of the Northwest, the Sisters of Mary Immaculate had 148 professed members spread among eighteen convents in the three northern dioceses of Ghana. In 1975 they had replaced the MSOLA as administrators and nursing staff of the hospital in Nandom. Their work in the field of evangelization continues to occupy a major portion of their time and to produce remarkable results.

Efforts to launch an African congregation of brothers at Jirapa in the early forties had not been successful. Despite an abundance of good will, the young men who had requested the opportunity to train as brothers gradually came to recognize, one by one, that they were not called to that particular vocation after all.

For the remainder of the decade, no further efforts were made along those lines. The principal reason for this was the prior necessity to establish a native clergy so that the Church in the Northwest could eventually govern itself. In this the Missionaries of Africa were being faithful to the instructions of their founder, Cardinal Lavigerie.

In February 1946, thanks to a generous gift from Monsignor Victor Primeau, a good friend and benefactor from the United States, the first seminary in northern Gold Coast was opened in Navrongo by Father J. Alfred Richard of Rhode Island. It began with five major seminarians who until then had been studying at the regional major seminary of Amisano in the South. One of these was Peter Dery.

"I remember very well when Father Richard came to us," Father Dery recalled in an article written some years later. "It was in the middle of January.... The seminarians and their professors were homeless. We lived in a secondary school. The noise made it impossible to study or even to hear the professor at times. How often we would smile when Father Richard scratched his head in despair. Occasionally he had to call off the spiritual reading for he couldn't be heard above the noise."

Navrongo was not the ideal location for such an institution, and within two months Saint Victor's Seminary (as it was called, in honor of its benefactor) moved to Wiagha mission, a much quieter spot but not without its own inconveniences, as staff and students soon found.

"There we had the greatest time of our lives," Father Dery wrote. "We lived on top of each other in the old dilapidated mission house.... The walls were wobbly. Bats were everywhere and with the usual results. The roof was in such disrepair that the first wind sent the iron sheets all over the place. The sheets we were unable to nail down because of the rotting timbers were weighed down with stones. The professors who occupied the second floor were worse off than we were. One downpour proved that the roof was less cover than a basket would have been.

"If there was anything lacking in those days, it was certainly space. There were three rooms allotted to the major seminarians. In these rooms we studied, held classes and spiritual reading. There also we ate our meals and took recreation. I often wonder how we stuck it out without complaint.

"Our troubles were nothing compared to Father Richard's. He was rector of the two seminaries, minor and major, superior of the mission, a contractor (he had started the new house), and vicar general of the diocese. He would run from the classroom to the construction site and back to the classroom again. And he was striving to learn a new language, for we were no longer in Dagati country. The local people used to say to us: *Your superior fada be good man oh*, or, *Your 'big man' no fear work at all, at all. E fada and moda born 'im proper.*"[7]

Saint Victor's continued to function as both minor and major seminary until 1953 when the major seminary moved to specially constructed quarters at its present location in Tamale.

Already by 1950 it was felt that the number of seminarians from the North was sufficient to warrant cautious optimism for the future, enough at least to convince the missionaries to again seek candidates for a local religious brotherhood.

Mr. Edward Dagme was sent from Jirapa to Kaleo in January 1951 to open the training centre for what would become the Congregation of the Brothers of Saint Joseph. He was soon joined by Father Maurice Carrier, who was almost literally plucked from the roof of the parish house he was then constructing in Daffiama and deposited in Kaleo. Brother Lorenzo took the tools from his hands and completed the roof, while he sped to the brothers training centre to become teacher in carpentry, masonry, and mechanics, as well as superior of the community. Twelve young aspirants had presented themselves, of whom seven would persevere to receive the religious habit of the brothers on 19 March 1953.[8]

The congregation's aim was to spread the Gospel of Jesus Christ through a life of prayer, manual work, and catechetical instruction. Candidates were trained in all three and required to dedicate themselves totally to the service of God and His people by taking solemn vows to observe evangelical poverty, chastity, and obedience.

The first Brother of Saint Joseph to be professed, on 19 March 1958, was Anthony Yirtare from Nadoli. He was followed a year later by Lawrence Kanlonno. Ever so slowly the infant congregation began to grow and put down roots in the fertile spiritual soil of what was now — by virtue of its political independence from Great Britain on 6 March 1957 — the new sovereign nation of Ghana.

It was about this time that Rome decided to give northern Ghana its first native-born bishop. The first step was taken on 3 November 1959 when 11,547 square kilometers of the already existing diocese of Tamale were removed to create the new diocese of Wa. On the following 16 March, the former shepherd boy of Zemopare, once destined by his witch doctor uncle for a far different profession, was chosen to be chief spiritual shepherd of his people. Fourteen priests from Third World countries were elected bishops that day, nine of them from Africa. The joint episcopal ordination would take place on 8 May 1960 in Saint Peter's Basilica, with Pope John XXIII himself officiating as ordaining bishop.

Young Peter Dery had come a long way since that memorable night thirty years earlier when I had found his brother and him huddled together against the rain beneath a ga tree in the mission yard, thoroughly soaked but happy. His simple answer to my query about the reason for their being there — "We have come to learn about God" — echoed in my mind the day the news of his election reached us. He had been too shy then to tell me the rest of the reason he was there: his dream of becoming a catechist and carrying the Good News back to his village so that his people would not have to journey so far each week to hear it. God had had something else in mind for him, however, and others had carried the message of salvation to Zemopare.

After his ordination to the priesthood in 1951, Peter Dery had served as assistant general manager of schools in Tamale diocese until 1957 when the Canadian Knights of Columbus gave him a scholarship to Saint Francis Xavier University in Antigonish, Nova Scotia, to study the organization of credit unions and cooperatives. Another scholarship the following year, this time from Auxiliary Bishop John J. Boardman of Brooklyn, New York, enabled him to enroll in the catechetical program at famed Lumen Vitae Institute at the University of Louvain in Belgium. On his return to Ghana in 1959, he was named vicar general of the diocese and parish priest. When Rome began looking for someone to head the new diocese of Wa, it was fitting that the choice should fall upon the son of Poreku, the outstanding apostle of Christ in northwest Ghana.

Two of Bishop Dery's goals in Wa diocese were to develop an active lay apostolate and to cultivate priestly and religious vocations among youth. When the Missionaries of Africa began casting about for a religious congregation to take over responsibility for the training of the Brothers of Saint Joseph, Bishop Dery managed to convince the Brothers of the Immaculate Conception (FIC) from Huybergen, the Netherlands, to accept the challenge. Their one condition, after sending a delegation to Jirapa to examine the situation at first-hand, was that the Ghanaian congregation be integrated into their own. This was agreed to and the first community of Brothers of the Immaculate Conception arrived in the diocese to begin work in September 1965. The Brothers of Saint Joseph merged with them, the first of these making their promise of loyalty as members of the Netherlands-based congregation in 1966.[9]

During their first years in Ghana, the brothers were occupied almost exclusively with the training of young men for the religious life. But by 1968 they had begun to enter the educational field in answer to some manifest needs of the people in the area. Nandom Secondary School was the first result. The Franciscan Missionaries of Mary had opened a secondary school for girls in Jirapa in 1959. But aside from the junior seminary in Wa, nothing similar existed for boys in the Northwest.

The school actually opened in Kaleo, with a single stream under the direction of Brother Bosco, though it was destined from the start for Nandom where Brother John had begun construction of the buildings. The move to Nandom took place in 1972 and the school simultaneously entered the national system of public education while yet remaining a distinctively Catholic institution. Students of all religious denominations are accepted so long as they respect the Christian principles upon which the school is founded and according to which it operates.

In recent years the brothers have put more emphasis on Christian leadership training in the school without neglecting the academic side. A Christian Community Building program was introduced to encourage students to take more responsibility in christianizing their community and environment.

Other needs in the diocese inspired the brothers to develop technical training for middle school leavers who otherwise would encounter few opportunities to further their education and find gainful employment. Until that time, the people of the North (farmers for the most part) had no opportunity to develop skills for lack of technical training facilities. Whenever skilled work was needed, one had to look outside the region to find it. It was in order to put a stop to this and to the migration of young men from the North during the dry season, in search of income for themselves and their families, that the Nandom Practical Vocational Centre was inaugurated in 1972. A course in rural building was offered which combined practical experience with sound technical knowledge. Later, a second course — rural engineering — was introduced to train students in diesel mechanics and blacksmithing. Both trades are linked to produce more rounded tradesmen, able not only to use agricultural implements correctly but to maintain them as well.

Each course lasts four years, with the first year spent in school while the remaining three include one term in school each year and the other in supervised on-the-job training.

Government approval was given the centre in 1977, and full recognition of the teaching program came in March 1978 when the first trainees obtained their National Craftsmanship Certificate in Rural Building.

In January 1973 a carpentry school specializing in furniture-making was opened by the brothers in Kaleo. Besides practical training, the four-year program includes courses in English, mathematics, bookkeeping, civics, religion, and the basics of carpentry.

The brothers, who were founded in the Netherlands in 1954 to work among youth, are also engaged in Ghana in elementary school education and in various Catholic youth organizations.

The mishap on the way back from Pabre with the lorryload of future Sisters of Mary Immaculate, in December 1945, was nothing unusual in those days. Far worse things than flat tires frequently occurred on the road, and much time and effort were spent trying to repair a lorry for which spare parts were not readily or easily available. As bursar of the vicariate, with responsibility for the material upkeep of all the missions, I was very interested therefore when the U.S. Army bases in Accra and Takoradi began liquidating their surplus materials at the end of the war. The bargains, especially in vehicles and good tires made of real rubber, were too good and too tempting to ignore, even with the limited funds at our command. I was in a good position to have first choice on most items since I had brought back to Ghana all the money I had collected during my stay in the United States, and the Americans were then demanding payment in U.S. funds. Not many others there had such currency at the time. I bought a few lorries and some spare tires for them at very reasonable prices. Then I set about training young local lads to drive and repair them.

A great deal of calculating and soul-searching preceded this major purchase. The diocesan budget in those days allowed only fifty cents a day per missionary for food and upkeep. With about five thousand dollars a year in grants from Rome (the Propagation of the Faith and the Holy Childhood Association) and donations from our missionaries in Canada and the United States, I had to provide for the building and maintenance of seven developing central missions and the schools of the diocese, including the catechist school now in Kaleo. Teachers' salaries were not then paid by the government. Our full-time catechists had to be helped to meet their material needs as well. Each year the burden on the diocese increased while income remained more or less stationary. Only the good spirit and ingenuity of the missionaries — priests, sisters, and brothers — in stretching the meagre funds available and sharing the gifts they received from their friends and relatives in their home countries enabled us to keep going in those rapidly developing missions. The local people also did their part, often refusing remuneration for their work on behalf of the mission or by making gifts of food at opportune moments.

In 1946 Bishop Morin decided he could no longer delay establishing a Christian presence in the fast-growing capital of northern Gold Coast. I was sent with his blessing to Tamale on 15 September to open the first mission among the predominately Muslim population. My arrival there was far different from that in Jirapa seventeen years earlier. No welcoming committee awaited me, nor was the government representative there to lend support. Bishop Morin had informed the chief commissioner personally of his intent to move into Tamale and the latter had not hidden his disapproval. As far as the British colonial government was concerned, Tamale was strictly a Muslim preserve.

Looking for a place to stay, I took temporary possession of the rest house, a big round hut like all the rest houses in the North. In a few days I was joined by Father Paul Haskew, an Englishman, and Father John McNulty, a Scot. Together we set about learning Dagbane, a language similar to Dagaare but quite different, and contacting the Dagomba people of the area. There would be no movement into the Church here as there had been in Jirapa. God, after all, was not unknown to the Dagombas in quite the same way He had been to the Dagaabas. And Islam maintained a much stronger hold on its adherents than the fetish priests or witch doctors of Dagao had been capable of exercising. The Christian presence would grow among the Dagombas, but by individual rather than group conversion.

In May 1948 I was assigned once more to Jirapa. It was a real homecoming for me. One of the first things I was asked by the Christians upon my return was: "When will we have our church?" I had started a building fund among them for that purpose in 1936. If there was to be a proper church in Jirapa, it was imperative that it come from the people themselves and that it be the fruit of their own labour and sacrifice. They had responded generously, contributing with regularity whatever they could manage to accumulate and save. As the money came in, I used it to have laterite stones dressed by the masons Brother Basilide had trained. The finished stones were then carried by the people to the site of their future church.

At the end of that year I was sent to North America, and the project went into temporary suspension. I returned twelve years later to find most of the stones still there, though some had been "borrowed" for other projects in the meantime. Of the money collected over that time, only two hundred dollars in cash remained. That too, of course, had been "borrowed" for other necessities.

The eight thousand Christians at Jirapa still wanted their church, and they wanted it badly enough to be willing to volunteer all the unskilled labour necessary and as much of the costs of cement, wood, roofing sheets, and skilled labour as they could manage. God had been infinitely good to them. They in turn would prove their love by giving Him their sweat and hunger to build Him a house among them.

The cornerstone was laid on 8 December 1948, but it was six years before the church was finally finished. Whenever funds ran out, construction ceased until more were forthcoming. No high-powered methods of fund-raising were used. The only spur was the people's own desire to have a church.

All went smoothly until it came time to install the trusses used to support the roof. Made of very heavy timbers and entirely constructed on the ground first, these had to be hauled up by means of ropes and raw manpower. There were no cranes available then, nor was there sufficient wood or metal to make scaffolding and thus build the trusses in place.

When it came time to lift the first one, many eager hands seized the ropes and began to pull and strain in unison. The heavy framework righted itself and slowly inched its way upward between the walls of the sanctuary. Workmen stood positioned at the top of the walls waiting to receive it and guide it into place. Just as it had very nearly reached them, the main rope snapped, sending those who had been pulling on it with all their might hurtling backwards on top of one another in surprise and confusion. Fortunately, the truss merely slid down a few feet and lodged between the walls. No one was injured, but panic had ensued. When a new rope was brought, no one would return to man it. Someone wanted to saw the trusses into sections and lift them into place piece by piece. I would not hear of it, of course, but neither would they be coaxed out of their fear of taking up the ropes again. Thinking quickly, I walked over to the girls middle school and called the students out of class to help me. Girls in the Gold Coast were used to hard work, so there was no hesitation on their part. They followed me to the church en masse, grabbed the ropes the men had abandoned, and prepared to pull at my command. Meanwhile I climbed up onto the walls with one or two others to help guide the truss into place.

When the men saw "mere" girls stepping in almost gaily to replace them, their reaction was immediate. Love might not be able to cast out fear in this particular instance, but pride could and did. The men returned to the ropes, albeit somewhat sheepishly, and the trusses were properly installed without further incident.

This was also the time when the first seeds were being sown in Jirapa of something that would eventually bear fruit throughout Africa.

One day in 1953, John McNulty found himself on trek to Sabuli, site of one of the outstations served by the central mission at Jirapa. He had been appointed to our community the previous November and had just passed his language exam in Dagaare. The local catechist in charge there was George Tenga.

Shortly after arriving and washing away the usual accumulation of dust from the trip, John began preparations to hear confessions while George filled him in on events in Sabuli, the progress of the catechumens, marriages and baptisms to be performed, various problems he had encountered in carrying out his duties, etc. As George talked, the priest detected an undercurrent of sadness in his voice and manner.

"What is it, George?" he asked him. "Is anything the matter?"

The catechist looked at him and lowered his gaze, speaking with resignation. He had just lost his life savings, ten pounds in all, not to thieves but to a voracious band of white ants. To protect the money, he had taken the precaution of placing it in an empty Players cigarette tin before burying it. When he had gone to dig it up, he had found the tin badly corroded and the bills almost completely eaten up.

John asked to see the tin with its remaining contents. Only a faint trace of the notes was left, enough to indicate they had indeed been there once. Though he could not offer much hope to George, he asked permission to take the tin with him.

Back in Jirapa, he wrote to the manager of the bank in Accra to explain what had happened. Very soon, a note arrived from the manager asking that the tin and its contents be sent down to him. Father McNulty complied immediately and received in exchange, by return post, ten brand new one pound notes. The delight of George Tenga when they were placed in his hands can only be imagined.

This incident got the priest thinking. How many more people in the area were doing just like George, burying their hard-earned savings in the ground and reaping the same heartbreak at digging them up again? Chances were they numbered in the hundreds. The more he thought about it, the more convinced he became that something could and should be done to correct the problem. But what? Talking it over with the others in the White Father community at Jirapa, the consensus was that some sort of cooperative was needed in which the people could be taught to put their savings to good use and help others as well as themselves. But finding the proper formula for this was not so simple.

The problem continued to preoccupy John during his home leave in Scotland in 1954. Grasping at a straw, he finally wrote to the Catholic Social Guild in Oxford, England, explaining the problem and outlining some ideas for solving it. Did they have any suggestions on how to implement them?

Within the week a reply came from Father Paul Crane, SJ, of the Guild. The man who could certainly help, he said, was Monsignor MacKinnon at Saint Francis Xavier University in Antigonish, Nova Scotia.

"MacKinnon" and "Nova Scotia". The names were like a heavenly omen for my Scots colleague. He quickly wrote off to the monsignor as Father Crane had suggested. Again the reply was swift. It contained a sizeable packet of information on the Antigonish Movement and credit unions, which John immediately seized upon and began studying. As he got further into it, his enthusiasm increased. This was exactly what he had been looking for!

When he returned to Jirapa in January 1955, he presented us with all he had discovered about credit unions, answering our questions in a way that indicated he had not only absorbed the literature Monsignor MacKinnon had sent him, but he had also thought deeply about how to apply it to the concrete situation in Jirapa. His enthusiasm proved contagious, and we all agreed that credit unions should be introduced into the diocese. Would the bishop agree? There was always the possibility he would not. Credit unions were then something entirely new and untried.

When Father McNulty approached him on the subject, Bishop Champagne reacted rather skeptically though not unkindly. He did not like to stifle initiative if he could help it.

"Have you ever run a credit union?" he asked the priest.

John admitted he hadn't, and that his knowledge of how one should be run came only from reading about them. "But," he went on, "that doesn't mean I can't do it. I am like the Scotsman invited to a wedding celebration at which the pianist fails to appear. The host comes to him in desperation and asks if he can play the piano. 'I don't know,' the Scot answers, 'I've never tried.' You ask me, Bishop, if I can run a credit union. All I can reply is: I don't know, I've never tried. But I'm willing to try."

The bishop had a sense of humour and he appreciated it in others. Though somewhat reluctantly, he nevertheless gave his permission to begin setting up what would be (although we didn't know it at the time) the first credit union on the African continent.

Father McNulty's method of laying the foundations for this new venture was to create an awareness among the people of their need for something like a credit union *before* proceeding to set it up. This was achieved through regularly held meetings over an eight month period to study and discuss the structure, operation, and benefits of credit unions as outlined in the Antigonish materials. Adherence to this method of preparation was to mark the difference between success and failure of the credit unions subsequently set up in various parts of the country.[10]

As more and more people began to ask: "When are we going to start a credit union here?", the time was judged ripe to do so. It was September 1955. By the end of the first month of its existence, there were seventy members with a share capital of thirty-eight pounds. When he left Jirapa in 1961, there were over five hundred members with a total capital of more than seven thousand pounds.

General meetings were held every six weeks to familiarize members with credit union principles and to instruct them in voting procedures, how to voice complaints, etc. The meetings were always well-attended and avidly followed. As the weeks passed, suggestions began to be heard from the members. One of the first came from a woman who suggested that some of the share capital be invested in a grinding mill. Her proposal was well-received and the mill was built by communal labour. By early 1957 it had more than repaid the initial investment.

Another suggestion by the members resulted in the establishment of purchasing cooperatives (called "buying clubs") to enable the people to buy household necessities such as soap, sugar, salt, kerosene, cloth, and bicycle parts in bulk. This was an important source of savings since the petty traders, on whom the people depended for their supplies, charged exorbitant prices for their wares. Bicycle spokes, for instance, cost five pence each and kerosene cost ten pence a bottle. Through the purchasing cooperatives, bicycle spokes could be had at two for a penny and kerosene cost only four pence per bottle.

The standard of life in and around Jirapa began to reflect the presence and good-functioning of the credit union.

Bulk buying soon extended to other areas of necessity. In the regular meetings of credit union members, the question of improved housing came up frequently. Why not buy building materials in bulk as well, someone suggested. Soon trucks were delivering roofing sheets, timber, cement, and other construction items to the Jirapa Credit Union. As a result, many were able to improve their homes or build better ones. The traditional mud and thatch huts gave way to dwellings that were, if not always as esthetically pleasing, more hygienic and secure.

All this time Father McNulty had been trying to interest some overseas agency or organization in sponsoring a local person to study in Antigonish. Funding bodies were not so plentiful in 1955 as they are today. Finally, Monsignor MacKinnon persuaded the Canadian Knights of Columbus to offer a scholarship. But there was a string attached to it: the Knights had stipulated that the recipient had to be a priest. Monsignor MacKinnon hoped the recipient would be Father McNulty himself, and Bishop Champagne encouraged him to accept it. But he himself felt strongly that it should go toward the training of a local person instead. If it had to be a priest, then why not send Peter Dery? Why not indeed, said the bishop, and the matter was agreed.

Father Dery left for Antigonish in September 1957, returning two years later to champion and promote the credit union movement throughout the country. After he became bishop of Wa in 1960, he managed to convince Misereor of West Germany and, later, Raiffeisen of the Netherlands to provide funds for a credit union training program in the North. Father Marcelin Lévesque was placed in charge of it and some U.S. Peace Corps Volunteers were assigned by their agency to help him.

The credit union idea was a good thing that could not help but grow and multiply. Those at Jirapa who had been introduced to it would not rest until they had shared it with others, so that it began to spread somewhat in the way the Gospel message had done twenty-five years earlier. Many of the people who had engaged actively in the primary evangelization of their brothers and sisters now saw the credit union as a natural social outgrowth of the New Testament and became enthusiastic supporters and propagandists of the idea.

At a general meeting in early 1956, the members decided to do something to publicize credit unions throughout the region so that their benefits might be enjoyed more widely. The first Credit Union Day would be proclaimed and held at Jirapa in October, on Mission Sunday. Invitations went out to all the neighbouring missions and beyond.

The people worked hard at preparing the occasion, organizing everything from lectures and discussions to refreshments and entertainment. The biggest ovation of the day went to Philomena Kyilma for her talk on "The Role of Women in the Credit Union". It marked the first time a woman had addressed such a large public gathering in which most of the participants were men.

But the event that perhaps carried the most impact was a play, conceived and produced by local members, entitled simply: *The Jirapa Credit Union Story*. It is a safe generalization to say, I believe, that Africans everywhere grasp ideas more readily from seeing them dramatized than they do from listening to them in a sermon or a lecture or from reading them in a book. They are often masters of the art and certainly have no peers when it comes to improvising on a theme at short notice before a live audience.

The Jirapa Credit Union Story effectively summarized all the important materials dealt with in the various lectures and discussions earlier in the day — and it did so in lively fashion and with welcome comic relief. Ideas that had remained only partially digested before, now became clear to the audience. When it came time for them to return to their villages, they would carry with them the seeds of the credit union movement planted in their minds. The results of this became increasingly evident in subsequent months as one credit union after another began to appear in places like Nandom, Ko, Kaleo, and Daffiama.

It was only a question of time before the idea would spread beyond the frontiers of Ghana to other parts of the continent. Father McNulty had written an article for *The Month* (London) in October 1960 entitled: "Credit Unions in Northern Ghana: the Church goes to the People". It was reprinted in part in the thesis of a Mill Hill Missionary working in East Africa. Both these publications helped to launch credit unions in that part of Africa. The decade of the sixties saw the movement take root in Tanzania, Mauritius, Lesotho, Malawi, Cameroon, Kenya, Togo, the Seychelles, Upper Volta (Burkina Faso), Zaire, and Nigeria. In all of these, missionaries and Church leaders played an important pioneering role in introducing them and encouraging their growth.

Events moved along at a rapid pace until, in January 1968, a conference on the "Mobilization of Local Savings" was convoked in Lesotho, From the fruitful discussions at this international gathering came the decision to establish national credit union organizations in individual African countries and an umbrella association at continental level. The immediate practical outcome was the founding that April of the Ghana National Credit Union Association in Tamale. Father J. McKillip,SVD, was elected its first national chairman, with Bartholomew Quainoo as southern organizer and Charles Dongyire as northern organizer. The following September witnessed the establishment of the umbrella organization with its headquarters in Nairobi. Baptized the *Africa Cooperative Savings and Credit Association (ACOSCA)*, its purposes, according to the first constitution and by-laws, were:

1. To assist the organization and promotion of cooperative savings and credit societies.
2. To assist said societies in their operational and technical problems.
3. To assist in obtaining legal recognition of such societies.
4. To assist in the establishment of national associations of cooperative savings and credit societies.
5. To coordinate the activities of these societies in African countries and offshore islands.
6. To promote collaboration between cooperative savings and credit societies and other sectors of the cooperative movement.

The original charter was signed by delegates from thirteen countries: Cameroon, Ethiopia, Ghana, Kenya, Lesotho, Liberia, Malawi, Mauritania, Nigeria, Sierra Leone, Uganda, Tanzania, and Zambia. Others would join as time passed and the benefits of the cooperative savings and credit idea emerged as a powerful means of economic liberation for the ordinary person through the mobilization of savings and a wise use of credit. By the end of the first decade of its existence, countries affiliated with ACOSCA numbered twenty-one.

In August 1978, the association celebrated its tenth anniversary by convoking an education conference in Nairobi. One of those invited to attend was our own Father McNulty, the canny Scot who had seen in George Tenga's plight not only a challenge but a moral responsibility to find a long-term solution. Now the moment had come to acknowledge his achievement across the breadth of Africa.

On Wednesday afternoon, 23 August, Jirapa and indeed all Ghana was honored in his person as he was presented with a special Certificate of Appreciation that read as follows:

The Board of Directors and Delegates of the Africa Cooperative Savings and Credit Association (ACOSCA), recognizing the valiant efforts and enormous sacrifices of our pioneer in the initiation and organization of the first Savings and Credit Cooperative Societies in the African nation of Ghana, on the historic occasion of the Tenth Anniversary Conference of Delegates in Nairobi, Kenya, 22 August 1978, expresses ACOSCA's deep appreciation to Rev. JOHN McNULTY for your deep concern for the social and economic development of mankind and pays tribute to your inspiring contribution to security, peace, and happiness in Africa.

As Father McNulty would say later, credit unions are not the only answer to the social and economic problems of the people in Africa. But they do have a great role to play nevertheless and have already brought the hope of an improved material existence to many. Where patience has been exercised and care taken to found solid, viable savings and credit societies at grassroots level, men and women everywhere in Africa have come together to create opportunity where there was none before. In the process, they have built up mutual trust among themselves and concern for common causes which, in turn, has had a beneficial effect on their own self-esteem.

If someone is wondering what this has to do with the history of the Christian faith in northwest Ghana, let me assure you that it has a great deal to do with it. All through this book I have been at pains to emphasize the holistic nature of our mission among the Dagaabas and Sissalas. Helping to improve material conditions always goes hand in hand with preaching the Gospel of Jesus Christ. In fact, until people's stomachs have been filled, their bodies clothed, their troubles listened to sympathetically, their tears shared, it is often useless and even disrespectful to try to fill and clothe their souls. Saint Francis of Assisi, himself no stranger to physical hunger, advised his brothers not to presume to preach to the hungry. Saint James went further, not hesitating to condemn the so-called faith of those who, seeing the ill-clad and hungry before them, would content themselves with a pious prayer on their behalf without realizing that they were meant by God to be a practical part of His answer to that prayer as well.[11]

The credit union movement could be seen as one of many signs of God's practical providence at work among His children. If they were so frequently part of the problem of their own and others' existence, they could be part of the solution as well. And the beauty of this solution was that it enabled people to help themselves, as opposed to those that perhaps answered their material needs better but left them as dependent on others afterwards as they had been originally.

14

Birofo

It was 10:30 in the morning on the first Friday of March 1957. I had just finished conducting a holy hour in Saint Joseph's Church when Sister Sabina, a young Ghanaian member of the Franciscan Missionaries of Mary, came to me with a message.

"Excuse me, Father," she began, "but there are two men outside who are very anxious to speak with you."

"Oh?" I said. "Who are they? Did they say?"

Sister Sabina's bright eyes sparkled in the morning sunlight streaming through the sacristy windows. As she smiled in anticipation of her answer, they seemed to dance on the two edges of her upturned mouth.

"No, they didn't. But they did tell me where they are from and why they want to see you." She caught her breath. "They're from Birofo, Father! And they want to become Christians!"

I put down the surplice I had just taken off and returned her smile with one of my own. This was news!

Birofo is a village some twelve miles west of Jirapa on the banks of the Black Volta River which forms the boundary between Ghana and Burkina Faso. It is also the name of an ethnic group closely allied to the Dagaabas and whose language is Dagaare with some variations. The Birofos were a very special people:

energetic, enterprising, good farmers, and — because they had been ruled with an iron hand for many years by a former police officer — very disciplined and orderly. Old Chief Gandaa was a powerful fetish priest whom people came from far and wide to consult. His influence was great, and fear of him extended beyond the limits of Birofo. If his people had not yet accepted the call of God and followed their Dagati cousins into the Church, it was only because they were afraid of him. As far as religion was concerned, he believed that what was good enough for him was certainly good enough for his people too. But he had died now and the Birofos were beginning to awaken slowly as from a long sleep.

I went out to meet my visitors and found two vigourous young men in their late twenties waiting a bit nervously at the door. They introduced themselves a Dery and Bayo. Despite the relative proximity of their village, they had never been to Jirapa before and had not known whom to contact on their arrival. Seeing Sister Sabina supervising the children's recreation on the school playground, they had approached her for help.

I invited the two into the parish office and put them at their ease with small talk about Birofo and its surroundings, about which I knew quite a lot after nearly thirty years acquaintance with the area. Then they got to the point of their visit.

"We want to become Christians, Father, but we don't know how to go about it. Our friends told us to come here and we would be told what to do."

"And who are these friends of yours?" I asked.

They mentioned two young Dagati Christians from Nandom, whose names I did not recognize, and went on to tell me the rest of the story without further prompting.

Dery and Bayo had gone to Obuasi, in the South, to work in the most productive gold mine in Ghana. There men came together from all parts of the northern and central regions of the country to earn a little extra money during the long dry season. The labourers were lodged by the company on the very grounds of the mine. And so it was that Dery and Bayo found themselves with the two young Dagati Christians from Nandom as roommates.

The Dagati pair had arrived sometime earlier and were already acquainted with the system in operation at the mine, as well as the pecking order in the social intercourse of the men outside working hours. They were kind and helpful in orienting the Birofos and sharing their leisure time with them. Soon the four became good friends.

The two Christians remained different from their Birofo friends, however, though without ever seeming exclusive. They said their prayers together each morning and evening, and often recited the catechism texts aloud to one another in an effort to preserve them fresh in their memory. It was all done in a natural manner, much as they would expect their Birofo roommates to share with them any news of their families that might reach them.

As the bonds of friendship grew stronger, the reticence of the Birofos to approach their friends on the subject of religion slowly disappeared. Little by little, they allowed their curiosity to be aroused by what the Dagati men believed and put into practice. It was not long before the quartet found itself passing most of its free time talking about Jesus Christ and His teaching. Just as in the beginning of His ministry on earth, hearts were again being set afire by contact with His message.

Some months and many long discussions later, Dery and Bayo came to the conclusion that had brought them to Jirapa for the first time in their lives. After sharing their decision with their Nandom friends, the four spent some time mulling over the best way to go about carrying it out. It was important, said the two Dagaabas, that all be done above board and in the open. Their conversion to Christ should be a testimony that all Birofo would understand and that no one with an open mind could misinterpret. Therefore it would be best to return home and start from there with the full knowledge of the people.

As soon as their contract at the mine came to an end, the two took the road to Birofo. They went with light hearts; and before they knew it, the village lay before them. Each went to his family compound to greet and be greeted by his loved ones and to savour the sights and smells and feel of being home again. Then they called their families together and told them of what had happened to them at the mine, of their friendship with the two Christians from Nandom who had been so helpful to them, and of how they had discovered Jesus Christ through them. They ended with their decision to go to Jirapa the next day and find out how they could become Christians themselves.

Both families registered their surprise, but neither group tried to interfere or to dissuade the would-be Christians. Perhaps it was because the Nandom duo had been so helpful to their kin in strange surroundings — the two Birofos had mentioned many concrete examples of their friends' generous behaviour toward them, which had brought appreciative comments from their audiences during the narrative — or perhaps it was a natural reaction, after years of strict discipline under Chief Gandaa, to lean now toward greater tolerance of non-conformity. Whatever the reason, no one objected to the decision of the two young men to pursue their announced objective. One of the elders summed up the general feeling of both families by saying: "This is your decision to make, not ours. Though I for one do not plan to follow you in this, you are certainly old enough to know your own minds and to choose your own way."

Now the two sat before me, virtually on the edge of their seats, telling me all this and of their determination to break with Sitana and all fetish worship to become Christians.

I called in our head catechist at that time, Charles Ganaa, and between us we examined them on what they already knew of their new faith. Their Nandom friends had been good teachers, for Dery and Bayo were already fairly well-advanced in their understanding of basic Christian doctrine. We gave them their first formal instruction and sent them on their way, two very happy fellows who had had the great good fortune to find the priceless pearl and were prepared to sacrifice all else to possess it forever.

Charles and I had been favourably impressed. We marvelled at the ability of God's Spirit to continually surprise and confound. In His own time and in His own way, but always unexpectedly, He managed to outmaneuver all obstacles to reach His goal. Even the quickest-witted could not foresee His moves. The most we could do, we agreed, was to live "in expectation of surprise" as we went on working in our own fumbling ways toward what we hoped was the same goal. Wasn't that, after all, what faith was all about?

In the case of the Birofos, as it happened, the surprises had only just begun.

Sometime after our first interview with Dery and Bayo, the head of a large compound in Birofo called his entire household together to make an unprecedented announcement in that village. The family members were unbelieving at first when they heard their clan leader, Bayuo, order them to fetch from their homes all fetishes and jujus, and all that could be construed as being connected with spirit worship, so that he could have the personal pleasure of burying them in a large hole he had dug in his courtyard. They eyed the hole with fear and noticed that it was already partially filled with rubbish.

The reason he gave them for this shocking decision had nothing to do directly with Christianity — as yet, neither Bayuo nor anyone else in his compound had had anything to do with Dery, Bayo, or the mission — and because of that, perhaps, it carried more weight with his family. He reminded them of all the harmful events that had befallen them despite their cult of the spirits, as well as the capricious nature of their interventions in the life of the compound. Nothing but harm had come to them through the spirits and he was thoroughly "fed up" with their evil and arbitrary ways. They were no more concerned about the welfare of their subjects than they were capable of recognizing the difference between a deliberate transgression and an accidental one. Making slaves of the impressionable was all that interested them. Well, here was one compound where their tyranny had come to an end!

"Bring out those damned playthings of the evil ones," he shouted, "and I shall give them a fitting burial in this rubbish hole! We shall never again be slaves to them! Bring them here, all of them, NOW!"

Bayuo was an impressive man both physically and morally. A decorated veteran of the war in Burma some years earlier, he was respected and trusted by his people for his leadership qualities as well as the heroic aura that still clung to him from his military days in a faraway land. They obeyed his command, accepting his reasoning — some of them because they shared it, others because they were more immediately afraid of contradicting him than they were of any possible retaliatory measures on the part of the spirits — and began to haul out from their respective houses *ggiel* stones from entrance shrines, *tengane* earth, *kontoma* statues, and everything else associated with fetish worship. The collection made an impressive heap at the bottom of the trench. Then Bayuo himself began to throw dirt and refuse on top of the jujus, until slowly one or two other members of his stunned household joined in. Once the burial had been completed and the earth packed down, he gave them a solemn warning never to dig them up again or seek to replace them with others.

"Or you will have to deal with a force worse than that of any mere spirit!"

That was clearly meant to be the end of it. But Bayuo had erred in one thing: he had failed to provide a substitute power to fill the vacuum created by his unceremonious dethronement of the spirits. Even an atheist must believe in something, be it only himself — sometimes the most tyrannical of gods.

Bayuo and his household were like that. They were rudderless without a mystery more substantial than themselves to believe in. He suspected that some in his extended family had secretly returned to the old slavery, something he was not prepared to do. He had meant what he said about the spirits and would never retract it. But an element in his life was lacking. Could a man be a whole man with nothing but the things of this world to occupy his existence? Bayuo felt deep within himself that he could not. He began to search in earnest for the One he had, in effect, already found.

The search eventually led him to Dery and Bayo. By this time the two no longer covered the twenty-two mile round-trip to Jirapa by themselves each Sunday. Four other Birofo men, one woman (Dery's mother), and two school boys had joined them as catechumens.

Bayuo questioned them closely on what they had learned about God on their weekly trips to the mission. What he heard amazed him; it was so alien to anything he had ever heard before. Could it be true that the All-Powerful had once been a child like those he saw running and playing in his compound every day? He was plainly skeptical. With power went the will to dominate and to bully. It was inevitable. What kind of a God would willingly place Himself in the power of His own creatures, to be totally dependent on them as a newborn infant must be? It was preposterous, it was madness. Yet it might just be true. Who was he to say that God had not indulged a caprice once upon a time. The spirits made a habit of it, but their caprices were nearly always of a harmful kind, while this one of God — becoming a little child — was harmless, it seemed to him, and even mysteriously beautiful. Even a soldier's heart could be touched by it.

But Bayuo needed more assurance. An innocent indulgence today might lead to a more destructive one tomorrow. What proof was there that this God of the white men was deserving of more trust than the spirits had been? Perhaps the proof lay in the reason He had had for acting as He did, if reason there was.

"Did the white men tell you *why* God became a little child?" he asked. "Was he mad?"

Dery and Bayo eyed him, slightly startled by his choice of word. Was Bayuo trying to bait them? A brief moment passed during which they decided that the ex-soldier was certainly sincere. There was as much guile in him as one might expect to find in a mango.

"The missionaries say that God loves us. Not only us, but everyone; every man, woman, and child in Ghana and outside Ghana. He loves those who love Him, but He also loves those who do not and even those who hate Him. This He has always done and always will do. And that, they say, is why God did it: He became a child, like any other human child, to be able to live in our world as we do, so that we might learn to let Him love us and to love Him in return, and from that to learn how to love each other."

Bayo paused a moment to allow the man to ask anonther question if he chose. When none came, he continued.

"Was He mad to do that? I don't know. But I do know that people always lose their minds a little when they fall in love. We get over it soon enough. But it seems God still hasn't recovered. I suppose that if you are the Great, Almighty, Eternal God, you are bound to love in a great, almighty, and eternal way... and there is no getting over it then."

In the silence that followed, only the rain could be heard. It was the first of the season, falling on earth so parched that within an hour of stopping, hardly a trace would be left of it. Without witnesses, it would be difficult to prove to anyone that it had indeed rained in Birofo that day.

The three men sat lost in thought. Bayuo did not notice the rain. He had begun to feel something warm in the region beneath his heart, something he had never felt there before. A soldier was not trained to feel but to think, and ideally to *out*think the adversary. But there was no logic, as he knew it, in what he had just heard from the mouths of the two Christians, no logic at all. He was at a loss. Then why did he feel the way he did: so light-hearted suddenly, so contented, so strangely alive? He could almost feel another life beginning to stir within him.

When at last the silence was broken, it was Bayuo asking Dery and Bayo if he might join them on their next trip to Jirapa.

Thereafter, the little group of catechumens from Birofo increased in number Sunday after Sunday. In an effort to spare them some unnecessary walking, I had recommended that they go to Konyukoan for their instructions. The village was seven miles closer to Birofo and had a capable resident catechist. But for some reason, they preferred to come to the mission, and they were welcome to do so. The stream continued to flow between Birofo and Jirapa for many years, until finally the village received its own resident catechist. Most of the original catechumens from the late fifties persevered in their four-year catechumenate and were baptized. Today the Christian faith in Birofo is in its third generation.

But the surprises were not over yet.

Among the early catechumens had been several of the sons of the late Chief Gandaa. But one of the most promising, Tissup, had declined to join them. Though he frequently attended Mass at Jirapa in the years he was stationed there as agricultural offi-cer, he had always hung back from committing himself further and enrolling in the catechumenate program.

A few years after the baptism of the first catechumens from Birofo, Tissup was chosen by the Ministry of Agriculture in Accra as one of several employees to follow courses at the University

Pope John XXIII embraces the newly-ordained Bishop Dery during the episcopal ordination ceremony in St. Peter's Basilica, Rome, 8 May 1960.

Ordination of Peter Dery to the priesthood (11 February 1951). On the right, Bishop Bertrand of Navrongo.

Bishop-elect Peter Dery in the Generalate of the Missionaries of Africa (Rome) on the eve of his episcopal ordination in 1960. With him are a member of the Ghanaian Sisters of Mary Immaculate and Father John McNulty, originator of the credit union movement in Africa.

Father J. Alfred Richard (l.) and Father (now Msgr.) Lawrence Kyemaalo (r.) on the occasion of Bishop Dery's installation as bishop of Wa in 1960.

L. to r.: Fathers Gordon Fournier and Remigius McCoy, Doctor Linn Cooper, and Father Eugene Coutu, at Jirapa in 1954.

Doctor Cooper receiving patients al fresco (Jirapa 1954).

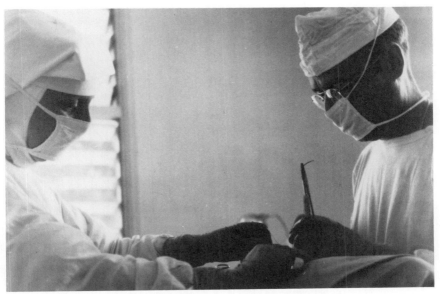

Doctor Archambault in the operating room at Jirapa Hospital, assisted by Sister Clementine, FMM.

Doctor Henry Archambault
("Doctor Shambo")

Doctor Shambo's resting place,
before the hospital compound at
Jirapa.

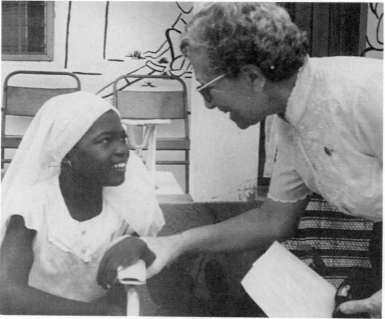

Sister Nazarena Porporato, FMM (r.), and a patient, Noella Pharoah,
at the opening of the new physical therapy unit at Jirapa Hospital.
Sister Porporato, a nurse, is in charge of the unit. (Photo by Dewart,
3 April 1987)

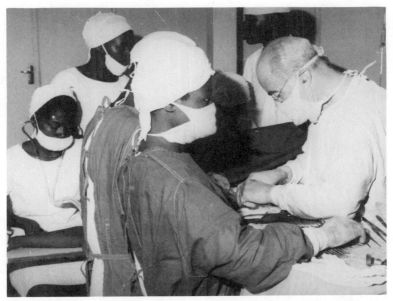

Doctor Dermid Bingham in the operating room at Jirapa Hospital (1973) assisted by a staff of qualified nurses trained on the spot.

View of the central passageway linking wards and units of Jirapa Hospital. In the centre, a patient being wheeled to the operating room at the end of the passage. (Photo by J.C. Dewart, 10 June 1987)

Fiftieth anniversary of the arrival of the first missionaries in NW Ghana (1979). L. to r.: Father McCoy, Brother John (Aidan) Ryan, Archbishop Dery, Brother Basilide Koot, and Bishop Bertrand.

Head catechist, Charles Ganaa, and three young women following marriage preparation courses at the parish in Jirapa. (Photo by Dewart, 7 May 1987)

Father Arthur Paquet, one of the first three missionaries to settle in Jirapa in 1929. (Photo by Sally Foster, 1967)

Rt. Rev. Gregory E. Kpiebaya, bishop of Wa diocese.

Sisters of Mary Immaculate from Bole greet the village catechist and his family at Seripe. The sisters visit Seripe at regular intervals to care for the sick. (Photos "Vivante Univers")

Father Joseph Larochelle on the 50th anniversary
of his ordination to the priesthood (1980).

Archbishop Peter P. Dery today.

Mr. Oscar Gokyi (l.) and Archbishop Dery (c.), the only remaining members of the first baptismal class in NW Ghana (Christmas Eve 1932), with Father McCoy, the man who baptized them. (Jirapa, 13 July 1985)

Father McCoy prays over newly-ordained Alphonsus Bakyil, first Ghanaian member of the Missionaries of Africa. (Jirapa, 13 July 1985)

Father Bakyil bestows a first priestly blessing on Father McCoy
following the ordination ceremony. (Jirapa, 13 July 1985)

Saint Francis Secondary School, inaugurated by the FMM in 1959.
(Photo by Dewart. Jirapa, 10 June 1987)

Father McCoy and Joan Cameron Dewart with a group of local
children in front of St. Joseph Church, Jirapa. (Photo by Dewart,
January 1987)

Interior of Saint Joseph Church, Jirapa. (Photo by Dewart, 1987)

of California's Berkeley campus. The news reached me in Chicago where I was then on my second tour of duty in the United States, this time trying to fire up interest among young men in becoming missionaries for Christ in Africa. I was proud of Tissup and happy for Birofo. It was the kind of honor that would lift the self-esteem of the entire village. Chances were it would be a positive experience for him, though that was more a wish than a firm conviction on my part. Times were heady then, with a dynamic young president in the White House and idealism riding high again in the national consciousness. But there was also the race issue, gathering momentum daily despite powerful forces bent on obstructing it by any means, legal or otherwise, and the appearance of early warning signs of the national trauma to come as the country began its gradual slide into the morass of Vietnam. University campuses across the United States were alive as never before with political and social issues.

One day in late 1962, after spending the morning trying to light a bonfire under a group of Catholic high school boys, I returned home to find a letter with a California postmark awaiting me. It was from Tissup. He was installed at the great university and attending classes in agriculture. There were no complaints or hints of serious homesickness in his letter; he seemed to be adjusting well and enjoying the temporary emancipation from family constraints. But whereas the average young college student, on his own for the first time and keen to exercise his new-found freedom, often seems to do no more than exchange one set of constraints for another, Tissup had his sights trained on the ultimate freedom — the freedom of the children of God. He wanted to become a Christian.

Praise God! I thought. While so many African Christians seemed to lose their faith on contact with American and European values, Tissup had defied the odds and found his at Berkeley!

I sat down at once and wrote two letters: one to Tissup advising him to contact the Newman Club chaplain on campus, whose name and address I included in the letter, and the other to the chaplain himself. Soon after receipt of my letters, the two arranged to meet. Instruction classes were set up, and the following year Tissup was baptized in the Newman Club chapel.

Evidently the Holy Spirit and His chaplain at the University of California had found good soil for the Word of God in this son of Chief Gandaa, for when he returned to his work in the Department of Agriculture (this time in Tamale), he was chosen within a short time to be leader of the Christian community in Tamale parish. Today, a quarter of a century later, he is Chief Tissup of Birofo and manager of the Agricultural Development Bank of Lawra. But he still remains an active Christian leader in the community.

At the time of his departure for America, Tissup was already married and quite happy in his choice of spouse. The couple raised a lovely family of healthy youngsters, all of whom were baptized in the Catholic Church. But his wife refused to be baptized and has maintained her refusal to the present day. She feels that her husband, an educated man, should have a wife equally well-educated. Aware of Church laws governing Christian marriage, she knows that so long as she remains unbaptized and willing to step aside, it would be relatively easy for Tissup to marry again in the Church should he find the right woman. But every time she has approached him on the subject, his answer has been the same.

"No, I do not want anyone but you. I chose you, once for all, and you accepted me. Do you regret that now?"

Oh no, there are no regrets, she assures him. But how strange he should turn things around that way when she is really trying to spare him regrets. Poor Tissup, she thinks. What can she do to make him realize how much happier he would be with someone more on his own level, better equipped to further his career and to share a part of his life she cannot hope to share? He seems not even to care about such considerations when she brings them up.

"How could we ever think of separating now?" he asks her. "Our lives are so deeply interwoven, they are one life shared. You have been all I could ask for in a wife and all our children could need in a mother, and I hope I have been a good husband and a good father, too. We are happy together. Is there anything else that really matters?"

She knows there is, of course. He would like to see her accept Jesus Christ and be baptized as he and their children are. But

he has tried to make her understand that he does not want this
for himself but for her, and that therefore she must not do it for
him. If ever she comes to such a decision, it must be in her own
time and for the proper motives of faith. In this he speaks from
the experience of his own pilgrimage.

As for their love, he tells her, that stands apart from all else.
He loves her for herself, just as she is. And nothing — not even
baptism — could ever change that.

I suspect Tissup's prayer will be answered one of these days,
as mine was in his regard so many years ago.

15

Yesterday... Was Yesterday

Northwest Ghana is, in many ways, far different today from what it was when we arrived there to set up the first mission station in 1929. For one thing, Christianity is no longer a totally foreign element in the region but a vital part of daily life for a large percentage of its 400,000 inhabitants. In what is now Wa diocese, Catholics alone number a little more than 100,000. Some ninety-four per cent of these are Dagaabas.

Why the Dagaabas embraced the Christian message in such numbers while other ethnic groups did not, remains a subject of conjecture. I have hinted at several possible reasons for this in the foregoing text: Their naturally religious background and incorporeal concept of God which, together with a rather high moral code and a value system similar to that of Christianity, made it relatively easy for them to accept the Ngwinsore; their gradual dissatisfaction with the fruits of spirit worship; the relative tolerance of personal choice and alternative lifestyles among the Dagaabas, abetted by a remarkably unservile attitude toward their chiefs.

Others have suggested that we just happened to arrive in the right place at the right moment with the right message, and that the response might well have been different had the message been presented earlier or later. Unfortunately, no one will ever know.

Still others, among them the present bishop of Wa, think it was due in large part to the Dagaabas' desire to assure their own physical and spiritual welfare.

"Through the *rain events,*" Bishop Gregory Kpiebaya says, "they experienced the living presence of the Christian God and His concern for persons in their most desperate situations. They quickly came to the conclusion that it must be in this God that they would find their security and well-being, the things they most sought after in life. To me then, one of the motives behind the Dagaabas' massive response to the missionaries' preaching was their hope and assurance of finding salvation in the Christian faith."[1]

No single human cause can explain it, of course. Just as in the functioning of a healthy human body, all is simple and infinitely complex at the same time, so it is where divine grace is concerned. Only God can know if and in what measure some or all of these various causes, interacting and interweaving, contributed to the "miracle". It *was* grace in any event, regardless of what components God used to bring it about.

The Dagaabas apart, there are several other ethnic groups in the Northwest that remain to be properly exposed to the Good News of Jesus Christ. The Sissalas are among these, despite some modest results obtained by the missionaries over the years, as are the Walas, the Lowillis, and the Lobis. Christianity has still to get a foothold in many areas of the North.

Part of the reason for this lies in a certain flagging of zeal and perseverance in missionary efforts where some villages were concerned. We were inclined over the years to spend more time on and devote more attention to villages that had shown interest in Christianity from the start rather than on those in which interest was late in coming and resistance marked. We were not lazy by any means. The friendly villages provided more than enough work to occupy us; in fact it was often impossible for the available personnel to cope with it all. But they also became at times a temptation and an excuse to neglect the more difficult areas and the exercise of our more basic charism which is to blaze new trails and push back the frontiers of faith. This goes by the name of "primary evangelization". There are many opportunities for such work in northern Ghana today.

With the growth of urban areas, a new problem has surfaced for the Church in the appearance of "neo-pagans". These are often members of the educated class (from primary school level to that of the university-educated) who have undergone a religious crisis resulting in loss of faith. The cause of this can often be attributed to the internal upheaval experienced by those emerging from a traditional cultural setting (the close-knit village atmosphere with its relatively clear-cut value system) to a modern one (the city where greater numbers and lack of roots make for anonymity and where moral values are less sharply defined). This is not a problem peculiar to Africa, of course. All urban areas all over the world, but especially in the industrialized nations, are afflicted by the phenomenon. Africa is only the latest of these to experience it. At its basis, as in many human and societal ills, is insecurity. Though the problem is much more pronounced in the larger cities and towns of the South, the North too has its share of neopagans calling for attention.

Over the years, the missionaries have been joined in their apostolic work by an increasing number of local men and women. The catechists were the first to collaborate in spreading the Gospel in the Northwest. Later, vocations to the priesthood, sisterhood, and brotherhood increased the size and scope of this local collaboration. What had once been religious communities of expatriates alone, gradually became mixed communities of expatriates and Ghanaians. Then, as the local Church continued to receive priestly vocations and became self-ministering and (to a large extent) self-supporting, the balance began to shift. The missionary presence, except in certain specialized areas of the apostolate such as seminary training, spiritual animation centres, inter-religious dialogue, and some social services, began to diminish. This was a kind of programmed obsolescence whose origin lay not so much in a conscious decision on the part of missionary institutes to withdraw at a given moment, as from the very nature of the missionary vocation itself. It is by now a trite statement, but no less true for being so, that missionaries exist to work themselves out of a job.[2] Cardinal Lavigerie put it another way when he said that in the final analysis, Africa would be brought to Christ by the Africans themselves.

Today, as a result, only six of the sixty-six priests in the diocese of Wa are expatriates. Nearly all fifteen parishes or "resident stations", as well as all diocesan administrative posts and commissions, are held by Ghanaian personnel, either clerics or lay persons. The Sisters of Mary Immaculate are fully autonomous now and African vocations to the Brothers of the Immaculate Conception (FIC) are encouraging.

Does this increase in African personnel and reduction of the expatriate missionary presence add up to what is called the *africanization* of the Church in northwest Ghana? Not necessarily. External changes, even those of adapting the liturgy to the mentality of the people or introducing African elements into theology, are not enough by themselves to ensure the inter-penetration of culture and faith.

Bishop Kpiebaya sees the africanization process taking place at a deeper level. "Africanization," he says, "is to be gauged not merely by external changes, but above all by the quality of Christian life exhibited by the African Christians. How, as an African, do I live the Gospel in an African situation? The Gospel demands faith in God and loving service of the neighbour from all Christ's followers whether they are Europeans or Africans. The question is, how do I live my faith and practise this evangelical charity in the context of underdevelopment, ignorance, poverty, tribalism, etc., which are the concrete problems of Africa?

"When we talk of africanization, therefore, we must think first in terms of incarnating the demands of the Gospel in African societies rather than of africanizing church structures. Surely Christ's message is not meant to destroy what is good in people's cultures, but neither is it meant to preserve cultures as they are. Becoming a Christian does not simply mean acting in a more loving way within the accepted structures of a given society. Any society or culture which embraces Christianity has to be transformed into a new society, a new culture, penetrated with those outstanding qualities of Christ which are love, sincerity, justice, peace, forgiveness; in short, a striving for God's Kingdom."[3]

For this reason, when he was appointed in 1975 to succeed Bishop Peter Dery in Wa, he chose as his priority for the diocese the formation of small Christian communities. His predecessor, who was and (as archbishop of Tamale) remains the great apostle of the laity in northern Ghana, had prepared the way for this. When he became the first bishop of Wa in 1960, he had chosen specialized Catholic Action among young people in the villages as his focal point. Bishop Gregory was able to build upon this foundation to deepen and strengthen the awareness of his people of their faith and of its implications for them in their daily lives.

The time may have passed when it was necessary to shoot one's way to catechism or suffer indignity, prejudice, opposition, even flogging and/or imprisonment for one's faith in the Ngwinsore. But that is not to say there is no challenge or peril for modern Ghanaian Christians. If anything, there is more. It is easier in some ways to struggle for a thing than to preserve it once it has been gained. To preserve an ideal or a way of life, one must keep it actively alive. Religion is not a commodity to be quick-frozen and maintained as it was at any given moment in the past. Nor is it to be left on the shelf where it will certainly spoil. One must live it, engage it, stretch it, apply it daily. Few people anywhere do this naturally. We are, in the majority, "clingers", holding on for dear life to what is familiar to us simply because it is familiar. Only when our faith in God is stronger than our fears can we break free of them and walk on our own two feet as responsible adult sons and daughters of God. Only then can we begin to make a difference in the world about us, the kind of difference that will slowly transform society in the way Bishop Kpiebaya describes.

I am one of those increasingly numerous people who believe that the future of the Church in the twenty-first century, and perhaps beyond, lies with Africa and other areas of the Third and Fourth Worlds. In order for this prediction to come true, however, mere statistics will not be enough; the quality of Christian life will be the deciding factor. But fear robs life of quality and makes slaves of its victims. So does routine. The only answer to that is to react against our inertia and fears, whatever their source.

The early Christians in northwest Ghana did just that. They heard a distant music and were not afraid to dance to it, even though it was new and in many ways strange to them. They brought others to hear it, too. And though the music was the same for all, each perceived it according to his or her capabilities or needs, and reacted to it by devising his or her own steps to it. Some missionaries, who knew none but American or European steps, tried for a while to teach these to the people and to discourage them from "improvising", but they were only ever partially successful in this. Eventually they came to see that they too could learn new steps to the music and that their appreciation of it was enriched thereby.

The music is still there for all to hear who care to listen, sounding as new today as it did then. And the same young Piper of God, His eternally youthful Spirit, continues to skip on ahead, always ahead, leading us out of ourselves, if we will but allow it, and deeper into the mystery of God where the centre of our being lies.

I shudder sometimes when I see how timid Christians are, not so much in the way they profess their faith before the world (which they should always do without showing disrespect for other faiths or for those who profess them), but in their lack of faith in God's ability to meet the challenge of change. Change is a law of mortal life, put there by God Himself in the very act of creation. As long as time exists, there will be change. Some people try to pit God against it, but this is to make Him the ally of stagnation. While we should not deny the value of the past but strive to learn from it, neither should we make it the mold into which the present is forced. Yesterday is not today in this created universe, nor could it ever be. Only God — not our idea of Him — is eternal and unchanging.

That, I think, is the challenge facing the Christians of Ghana today: to be *creative* in living their faith in Jesus Christ. To take that faith for granted is surely to lose it. It takes more than a little water poured on the head to the accompaniment of a religious formula to make a Christian. It takes a quiet determination, renewed daily, to accept one's life as a battleground of good and evil where what one knows, or at least perceives, to be right before God continually confronts one's own inclinations to circumvent if not actually oppose it. Some of the most heroic encounters can occur there with only God as witness to them.

The creative element will come in the way Ghanaian Catholics, as loyal and mature sons and daughters of the Church, shoulder responsibility for helping to create a more just and caring society based on Christian values. It is outside the sanctuary that the Church of Ghana is obliged above all to be Ghanaian with the Ghanaians. She has a mission to foster honesty in one's dealings with God and one's fellow human beings; courage in denouncing evil and corruption at all levels while showing compassion for its victims (among whom are to be found the guilty themselves); respect for legitimate authority even when one must, for its own and the common good, criticize what are perceived to be serious failures in fulfilling its role of service; respect for the fragile ecology of the country which, as the patrimony of all Ghana's citizens, it is the sacred responsibility of all to safeguard for future generations; respect, too, for civil liberties and human rights, without which no one, not even those who violate them, can claim to be truly free, etc. The list is not exhaustive.

Much remains to be done, therefore, but it is work best left to the local Church itself with its special understanding of its own people and its abilities to make the message of Christ at once fully Christian and fully Ghanaian. At the same time, a missionary presence in the diocese — in any diocese anywhere in the world — remains important if only to insure that it will not end up contemplating its own navel and lose its awareness of the greater Church of which it is a part and in whose life it is called to participate actively.

Epilogue

by Rene Dionne*

The baked-brick church stands in the African sunshine like a great hen gathering its brood beneath its wings. From every direction, near and far, people flock into its shelter until it is packed to capacity; and still they come, crowding in good-humouredly at the prospect of joy.

Across the way, on the verandah of the parish house (which serves as vesting area for the clergy today), a crowd of clerics, two of them bishops, and a young ordinand with his proud parents await the signal to begin the procession to the church. Unlike the preceeding fifty-seven young men ordained for the Wa diocese since its foundation in 1960, this one wears the habit of a White Father. For the first time in history, the Church in Ghana is giving one of her sons to the missionary society that has given so many of its sons to her.

Near the bishops, just passing an alb over his snow-white head and thrusting his arms into its sleeves, stands another reason for the day's festivities. Remigius McCoy is marking sixty years as a missionary priest, forty of them spent in Ghana but all of them devoted to her and especially to her people directly or indi-

---

* Based in part on an eye-witness report of this event by Sister Marie Therese Chambers, FMM.

rectly. The diocese of Wa is celebrating the event officially this 13 July 1985.

At last the procession begins to form and make its way toward the church, with Father McCoy taking his place among the more than fifty priests (diocesan and missionary) lined up behind the cross-bearer and acolytes. After them come the young man, Alphonsus Bakyil, and his parents, followed by Archbishop Peter P. Dery of Tamale and the ordaining prelate, Bishop Gregory Kpiebaya of Wa.

The jubilant atmosphere inside the church, now channelled into a spirited entrance song communally and exuberantly sung, rushes to meet and envelope the long double line of clerics and altar boys as it reaches the main doors and slowly begins to make its way down the central aisle. Even Nature seems caught up in the occasion: the flowers decorating the sanctuary have not wilted for once.

At the altar Bishop Gregory pauses to set the tone of the celebration with a few remarks to the congregation.

"What we are really celebrating here today," he tells them, "is God's love for the Dagaabas. We are among those fortunate people of the world whom He has chosen to bless again and again. Christianity came to us nearly fifty-six years ago, but little more than twenty of those had passed before the first Dagati priest in Ghana was ordained. And less than nine years later — only three short decades since the arrival of the first missionaries — the first diocese in the Northwest was established with a Dagati bishop at its head. Great things were happening in our small corner of the Lord's vineyard.

"The truth is: God's love is so mysterious and so wonderfully conceived. When we are able to catch even a fleeting glimpse of its workings, it can make us dizzy with delight. For instance, how was it that of all the possible places Father McCoy's superiors could have sent him, they chose Jirapa? And how is it that of all the parishes of northern Ghana in which the Missionaries of Africa have served, it is from Jirapa that God has raised up the first Ghanaian vocation to the priesthood in that society? The first place in the Northwest to receive the Word of God now sends forth the first missionary priest of the Northwest to carry that

Word beyond the frontiers of Ghana. This day the Church in Jirapa and the Church of Wa diocese have truly come of age! Just as Alphonsus can say, with Mary: 'My soul magnifies the Lord!', so Father McCoy can echo the words of Simeon: 'Now, Master, let Your servant go in peace, for my eyes have seen the salvation of the Dagaabas'. From the local Church he and his companions planted and struggled for, the Lord has raised up bishops, priests, sisters, brothers, catechists, and a dynamic and dedicated laity. But today, crowning all that for him and opening up a new era for the Church of northwest Ghana, he is privileged to witness one of his own spiritual sons, one of us, receive a commission to carry God's Good News to another people across the continent in Malawi. Praise the Lord for the trust He has placed in us!"

The liturgy continues. Meanwhile, Alphonsus stands calmly between his parents — he awaiting his call to come forward, they their moment to withdraw.

When the time arrives for the traditional laying on of hands in the ritual of ordination, silence fills the church, broken only by the occasional brief wail of a hungry infant (quickly pacified with its mother's breast). Following the bishops, the priests proceed one by one to lay their hands on the head of the newly-ordained Father Bakyil. The founder of Jirapa parish moves along with the rest slowly and quietly, awaiting his turn before the kneeling figure in the center of the sanctuary. When it comes, he places his gnarled hands reverently on the young priest's head and applies just enough pressure to convince them both of the reality of the situation.

For Albert Bakyil and his wife, it is an unforgettable moment. One day Father McCoy had asked Albert, a catechist in Jirapa until his retirement, how he felt about his son becoming a missionary and going off to work in a distant land. Albert had replied that it seemed only fitting that those who have received something freely should also share it freely with others. God had sent the missionaries many thousands of miles from their homes and families to bring the Good News to the Dagaabas. The time had evidently come for Him to send the Dagaabas in their turn to faraway lands with the same message. But it is only now as he watches his old friend silently pray over his son that the importance of the historic moment strikes him.

Afterwards, amid the happy, animated chatter of the crowd spilling out of the church, Father McCoy poses with the few remaining members of the first group to be baptized in the Northwest on that unforgettable Christmas Eve in 1932. There are only two of them left now: Archbishop Dery and Mr. Oscar Gokyi.

The archbishop has a personal tribute to pay his father in the faith. He begins by thanking him for a long list of "favours": for helping his father Poreku through the first difficult years of his efforts to follow the Ngwinsore despite opposition from family, neighbours, and chiefs, as well as complications caused by colonial authorities; for helping him, the son of Poreku, to escape a future of fetishism and ignorance, and making it possible for him to know Jesus Christ; for giving him the opportunity to learn to read and write, to become interested in the world outside Zemopare and to be able to communicate with its people, appreciate other cultures, and to enjoy so many other blessings.

"If anyone has a right to sing the praises of Cardinal Lavigerie," he says, eyes dancing and arms upraised to emphasize his words, "I am the one! More than many another, I have profitted from his missionary vision regarding Africa.

"Father McCoy, worthy son of Cardinal Lavigerie, we praise God in you. We extol His wonderful gifts and His marvellous work in you. Planted in the house of the Lord, you are still flourishing in His courts. You are now a senior citizen but still full of sap nevertheless, still green, still bearing fruit, so that you may proclaim that God is great and that you are His mighty tree.

"Thank you from the bottom of our hearts for being who you are and what you are. And, above all, thank you for the quality of the love you have always shown us — that of a wise father whose only desire is to see his sons and daughters grow healthy and strong and able to guide their own destinies with the help of God. Far from being a possessive or dominating love, yours has been a liberating and life-giving love from the very start.

"In return, we have no gift to give you other than ourselves. But that one we give you willingly, and we proclaim it sincerely, joyfully, gratefully: WE ARE OUR GIFT TO YOU!"

Warm applause sweeps the crowd, seconding the archbishop's words. When at last it dies down, the old missionary steps forward to speak. Like Saint John the Apostle who, legend has it, grew old in his exile on Patmos repeating the same message of God's love over and over again to whoever would listen, so Father McCoy's remarks have ceased long ago to contain anything new. They are merely the distillation of a lifetime of faith and trust in God, reduced to one essential guideline: "God's love for us is steadfast, never wavering. So must ours be for Him." Remembering days of greater fervour, perhaps, he invites all those listening to him to live their faith in depth and to recall that that faith is essentially the same today as it was sixty years ago.

"The Commandments of God have not changed. The first Dagati Christians were people who witnessed to their faith in God amidst great difficulties of every kind. There is still the need for that kind of total commitment to Christ today. Though of another kind, the difficulties to be faced remain great. But just as He was present to the first Christians to see them through the hard times, so He is present today to see you safely through them. Face them bravely and hold on tight!"

More applause, more photos, and then everyone begins to move cheerfully across to Saint Francis Secondary School where lunch is served. Man does not live by words alone....

An almost monastic silence descends on the parish compound now as human life moves indoors or into the meagre shade of buildings. The high-riding sun bakes the dusty earth and lulls the senses. Only the ever-present bundaa *seem to welcome its heat as they bask in it, unmoving as statues, storing up warmth for the night to come.[1] Now can be heard the busy murmur and drone of insects among the trees and shrubbery. They, and an occasional hot breeze stirring the dust, are the only visible signs of movement.*

But just beyond the range of corporeal vision, the incorporeal remain. They too have shared the day's festivities. The life of the "dead" does not consist merely in being present in the minds of the living. Life, after all, in whatever mode or plane it is lived, is one and, because of that, is as eternal as its Author. And what better right has anyone to be here than those whose brief span on earth was spent weaving the strands of their lives together to produce the pattern revealed by God this day?

The eye of the casual observer may see no more than a deserted landscape, but the steady eye of faith discerns a host of presences: Bishop Morin, Father Paquet, Brother Basilide, Maria of Tebano (she who "stole" her way into the flock of Christ to become one of its most effective unofficial shepherds); John Kyefondeme and his brothers; Anglieremwin and Joseph Gbare, Poreku and the Nandom naa; and lest anyone presume to place limits on the mercy of God, Poreku's brother, Ngmankurinaa (washed in the blood, not of an ineffectual chicken, but of the Lamb).

As one's "eyes" accustom themselves to the light, other presences begin to detach themselves from the mass: Doctor Cooper is there with Doctor Shambo, and Mother Caltry, Doctor Ackiebo, and Brother Aidan as well; Bishop Bertrand and Bishop Champagne, Father Coutu and Brother Ludovic, Captain Armstrong and, yes, Captain Ardron, too; Chief Ganaa, who had welcomed the first Christian missionaries to his territory and received a blessing for it ("Whoever welcomes God's messenger because he is God's messenger, will share in his reward" — Matt. 10:41); Father Durand of the angelic voice and the patriarchal beard (who never made a penny on either of them), Governor Thomas (better-informed now regarding Solomon's Christianity), and countless others, more numerous than the stars; some shining brighter than others, but all proclaiming by their presence on this wonderful day that not only have great things happened here in the past, but great things are happening, for great things always happen when God enters human history.

Chronology

1899-1901

Wars of the Zabog people devastate northern Gold Coast. Many people flee never to return.

1906

March: First Catholic mission station in northern Gold Coast opens at Navaro (Navrongo).

1908

June: Seven Kassenas enroll in Christian catechumenate at Navrongo.

September: Kassena catechumens now number eighty.

1913

Baptism of first six adult Kassenas to complete catechetical program.

1925

28 June: Remigius McCoy ordained to the priesthood in Carthage, Tunisia.

1926

11 January: Prefecture apostolic of Navrongo established by Rome.

| April: | Father McCoy opens first school in Navrongo with enrollment of eighty-five boys. |
| 14 April: | Father (later Msgr.) Oscar Morin, M.Afr., appointed prefect apostolic of Navrongo. |

1929

29 November:	Friday. Fathers McCoy and Paquet set out from Navrongo to found first mission station in northwest Gold Coast, at Jirapa, among the Dagaabas.
30 November:	Saturday. Feast of St. Andrew the Apostle. Mass celebrated for first time in Dagati territory, at district commissioner's house in Lawra. Arrival at Jirapa later in day.
1 December:	Sunday. Site for new mission chosen at Jirapa.
12 December:	Thursday. Cornerstone of future mission house laid (Jirapa).
13 December:	Friday. Missionaries move from rest house to huts of temporary compound built by people.
25 December:	Wednesday. "A very quiet Christmas" among the Dagaabas.
28 December:	Saturday. Brother Basilide leaves Navrongo for Jirapa. His arrival completes mission staff.
30 December:	Monday. Brother Basilide takes over construction of new mission.

1930

| 19 March: | Completion and blessing of mud-brick and thatch mission house and chapel. Father McCoy makes his first public speech in Dagaare. |
| 28 March: | Doctor Seth-Smith arrives from Lawra with medical supplies for |

	mission clinic and trains Fathers McCoy and Paquet to diagnose illnesses common to region and treat them.
August:	Kyefondeme and Yelesigra become first Dagaabas to enroll in Christian catechumenate.
October:	Poreku of Zemopare enrolls in catechumenate program.
Christmas:	The first Christmas for the Dagaabas. Over a dozen catechumens receive medal of Blessed Virgin Mary, signifying start of catechetical training.

1931

6 January:	A row with Jirapa naa over unreported cases of chickenpox in his compound.
July:	Father Paquet, suffering from diphtheria, evacuated to government hospital at Zuarungu. Father Coutu sent to replace him temporarily.
9 September:	Incident of "witches" in Gbare village.
4 October:	Catechumens: 420 enrolled.
11 October:	Catechumens: 640 enrolled.
18 October:	Catechumens: 750 enrolled.
23 October:	Catechumens: 400 enrolled.
7 November:	Father Joseph Larochelle arrives at Jirapa to join staff.
16 November:	Catechist training program inaugurated by Father McCoy.
Fall:	First Dagaare catechism appears, printed at Missionaries of Africa Press, Maison Carrée, Algiers (Algeria).
	First group of Dagati boys sent to school in Navrongo.
13 December:	Catechumens: 660 enrolled.

20 December:	Catechumens: 600 enrolled. Catechumens to date: 7,000 + .
	Trouble with chiefs of Guo, Zemopare, and Tuopare regarding mandatory road work.

1932

January:	Catechist school under construction.
February:	"Sunday Every Day" instituted by mission for surrounding villages.
11-12 March:	Father McCoy on trek to Nadoli, Daffiama, Buree, and Sabuli. Enrolls 1,000 + catechumens.
21 March:	Father McCoy on trek. Numbers of those asking to be inscribed as catechumens too great to be handled. Only names of old and sick recorded. Others must present themselves at Jirapa to be inscribed and follow instructions in faith.
26 March:	Student catechists begin to give instruction in villages: Nadoli, Buree, Daffiama.
5 April:	Only Bartholomew Balaara and Matthias Banoeyeni return to school in Navrongo. Others in original group remain behind.
12 April:	Roof of permanent mission (brick house) completed.
15 April:	New catechist school being roofed by 200-300 volunteers.
20 April:	Monsignor Morin blesses new mission house.
15 May:	Eleven student catechists receive rosary marking new stage in their training.
21 May:	Student catechists number thirty.
27 May:	Clandestine adult education school opens at Jirapa.

5 June:	Elders of Daffiama come to mission seeking rain. Father McCoy leads them in prayer. Rain falls on Daffiama around 4 p.m.
29 June:	Delegations from Lyssa and Baazing come to mission to pray for rain.
5 July:	Delegation of elders from Buree comes to mission to pray for rain.
11 July:	Father McCoy on trek to Nadoli, Kyerepong, and Nator. Father Larochelle goes to Issa at request of inhabitants.
13 July:	Thanksgiving offered for rain.
15 July:	Delegations seeking rain arrive from Kokolugu and Ginginkpwe. Delegations come from Nandom Piri and Zabpo to offer thanks to God for rain received.
18 July:	Some twenty delegations, from North and South, come to mission seeking rain for their parched lands.
19 July:	In two days, more than 1,000 newcomers ask to be enrolled as catechumens.
20 July:	People from Wessa (on border with French Sudan) come to pray for rain.
23 July:	Jirapa naa brings his elders to mission and urges them to pray for rain rather than offer sacrifices to spirits.
26 July:	Incident at Ginginkpwe where group of catechumens destroy fetishes of people of their compound. Accused brought before district commissioner (DC) in Lawra for judgment and are imprisoned. Similar incident in Baazing.
27 July:	Dapla and Kabiri, two student catechists from Baazing, are imprisoned and flogged in connection with incident of previous day.

28 July: Five young men condemned to
                      imprisonment for their zeal in
                      destroying fetishes of others.

30 July: Chief of Ullo sends gift of a sheep to
                      mission and asks the missionaries to
                      visit his village.

1 August: After delegation from Kyere prays
                      for rain at mission, village receives
                      showers three times in one week.

7 August: First attempt made to evangelize
                      Lawra. Chief favourable.

11 August: Delegations from Nator and
                      Ginginkpwe come seeking rain.

14 August: Twenty-one catechists and school
                      children receive rosary in ceremony.

15 August: Newcomers will no longer be enrolled
                      as catechumens until after they qual-
                      ify to receive medal of Blessed Virgin
                      Mary (i.e., after three to six months
                      of preliminary instruction and
                      prayer).

18 August: People from the North come to offer
                      thanks for rain. Twenty-one hens
                      received.

23 August: People from Nandom and French
                      Sudan come in great numbers to
                      "pray with the Christians".

September: Medals distributed every day to
                      groups from villages (as assigned).

9 September: Medals distributed to many from
                      French Sudan.

10 September: Monday. Five hundred medals
                      distributed in villages whose
                      "Sunday" is today.

14 September: Trouble with chiefs of Fiang and
                      Tuopare concerning Sunday rest for
                      Christian catechumens. Catechists
                      insulted by people.

27 September:	First group of Dagati catechumens begins final preparations for baptism. Three month course will culminate in reception of sacrament at Christmas.
30 September:	Governor of Gold Coast visits mission in company of DC. Cautions missionaries that their procedures seem to pose threat to authority of chiefs. Father McCoy rejects accusation.
2 October:	Captain Ardron (DC of Wa) complains that catechists are inciting people to refuse to work for chiefs and to oppose traditional rites in village funerals of Christian catechumens.
3 October:	Captain Armstrong (DC of Lawra) returns to mission to underline Governor's warning of previous 30 September. Father McCoy counters by complaining that Christian converts are not allowed freedom for Sunday worship.
17 October:	Father McCoy meets with Jirapa naa and elders to seek solution to problem of respect for Sunday worship of Christians. Some progress made.
19 October:	Large numbers of catechumens coming from French Sudan to Jirapa each weekend.
22 October:	Delegations from Nadoli, Daffiama, and Kaleo come to mission to pray that rains stop! The millet is in bloom and in danger of being spoiled by too much rain.
23 October:	Young men arrive from Sankana (Takpo) and ask to be admitted to catechist training program.
1 November:	Arrival of Fathers Stanislas Leblanc and Robert Lavallée.

25 November:	Complaints heard again that mission uses forced labour to build catechist housing. Government official turns up unexpectedly to inspect. Catechists themselves refute accusation.
4 December:	Some forty porters carry provisions from Jirapa to Kaleo for foundation of new mission there.
5 December:	DC authorizes Poreku to continue with construction of chapel at Zemopare after accusations by chiefs halt it. Father McCoy assures DC the project has no political significance.
8 December:	Kaleo mission officially opened.
22 December:	Catechumens and others begin to arrive to participate in Christmas at the mission.
Christmas Eve:	First formal baptismal ceremony in northwest Gold Coast. Twelve candidates, eleven of them student catechists and their wives.

1933

13 January:	Five young men from French Sudan ask to be admitted to catechist training program at Jirapa so that they can bring the Good News to their villages.
21 January:	Ten thousand catechumens gathered at Jirapa.
25 January:	Six hundred medals distributed to catechumens from French Sudan.
29 January:	Nandom naa tells Father McCoy he wants chapel at Nandom. Fears chapel Poreku is building at Zemopare will draw his people away and diminish his prestige in region.
1 February:	Nandom naa complains of Poreku to DC, who imprisons him briefly.

9 February:	Fifty specially chosen persons come to Jirapa to receive instructions on how and when to baptize those in danger of death.
11 February:	Thirty-three admitted to catechist training program.
15 February:	Twenty-five more admitted to catechist school.
18 February:	Many deaths in Northwest due to influenza and pneumonia.
22 February:	Meeting at Wessa between French colonial officials and representatives of Catholic Church in Gold Coast and French Sudan. Requested by French to discuss possibility of opening missions among Dagaabas in French colonial territory.
27 March:	Eleven of first twelve baptized Dagati Christians receive sacrament of confirmation.
15 April:	Nandom naa does not want his people to come to Jirapa to pray.
19 April:	Nandom naa and chiefs of other villages accuse Poreku before DC of fomenting disobedience and rebellion against them. Poreku imprisoned.
April-June:	Severe drought in Nandom region.
Mid-June:	Poreku released from prison. Rains return.
3 June:	Second group of Dagati catechumens to be baptized number twenty-seven adults and sixteen children.
4 June:	More than 300 catechumens receive rosary.
12 November:	Nandom mission founded.
December:	Completion of Nandom's first church.

1934

	Another group of boys sent away to school in Navrongo. Peter Dery among them.
22 February:	Death of Joseph Gbare, one of first catechists.
26 February:	Prefecture apostolic of Navrongo promoted to rank of vicariate apostolic. Msgr. Morin becomes vicar apostolic of Navrongo.
1 April:	Blessing of new church at Jirapa. Six hundred rosaries distributed to catechumens.
17 April:	Msgr. Morin ordained bishop in Montreal while on home leave.
20 May:	Pentecost Sunday. Fifty rosaries distributed.
29 June:	Feast of Sts. Peter and Paul. Four hundred rosaries distributed. Total number of rosaries distributed to date: 2,300.
8 November:	Bishop Morin returns to Navrongo from Canada via Marseilles.
4 December:	Father Leblanc takes charge of catechist training program.
Christmas Eve:	Baptism of twenty-nine adults and twenty-five children before Midnight Mass.

1935

20 April:	Baptism of eighty-five adults and thirty children.
12 July:	Jirapa mission has total of 153 baptized Christians and 5,353 under instruction leading to baptism (2,408 postulants and 2,945 catechumens proper).
25 September:	Pogpla's case begins. Kaleo naa sits in judgment.

Fall: Veronica's case, similar to that of Pogpla, becomes watershed in history of Christianity and of women's rights in Dagao.

4 October: Freedom for Christian girls to marry man of their choice finally achieved in practice.

18 November: Arrival of Father Gabriel Champagne at Jirapa.

1936

20 November: Father McCoy leaves Jirapa and Gold Coast for first time since 1925. Bound for Canada, via motherhouse of Missionaries of Africa in Algeria.

December: Baptism of Poreku, together with wife and family, at Nandom. Poreku takes baptismal name of Theodore.

1937

6 January: New stone church at Nandom, begun by Brother Basilide in August 1935, roofed in April 1936, officially blessed today by Archbishop Riberi, apostolic delegate.

Authorization received from colonial authorities to open primary school for boys at Nandom.

1938

July: Catechumens in Northwest now number 9,000

1939

14 May: Franciscan Missionaries of Mary (FMM) arrive at Jirapa with Mother Precursor in charge.

1940

Four Dagati girls request admission to the religious life. Bishop Morin sends them to Pabre (French Sudan)

where the Missionary Sisters of Our
Lady of Africa (MSOLA) agree to
train them. Father Champagne
accompanies them to Pabre.

1 July: First primary school for girls opened
by FMM at Jirapa.

1941

New brick building constructed near
FMM residence at Jirapa to house
dispensary as well as casualty, children's, and maternity wards.

1942

Holy Week: Tuesday. Cyclone inflicts heavy
damage on Jirapa church. Only sanctuary (chancel) and small part of nave
adjacent to it remain of building that
once held 2,000 people.

1944

Catechist school transferred from
Jirapa to Kaleo.

29 April: Ordination of first Dagati priest,
Father Emmanuel, at Dissin (French
Sudan).

1945

July: Father McCoy returns to Gold Coast.
Bishop Morin retains him in
Navrongo to act as treasurer of the
vicariate.

8 December: Bishop Morin and Father McCoy
bring Dagati postulants and novices
from Pabre to Navrongo to start local
Congregation of Sisters of Mary
Immaculate (SMI). MSOLA continue
to look after their religious training.

1946

February: St. Victor's, first seminary in northern Gold Coast, opened by Father J.
Alfred Richard in Navrongo.

April:	St. Victor's moved to Wiagha.
	Rome gives official approval to new Congregation of the SMI.
15 September:	First mission among Dagombas established at Tamale. Fathers McCoy, Paul Haskew, and John McNulty comprise first community.
	Ordination of first Kassena priest, Father Alexis Abatey.

1947

21 February:	Bishop Morin retires after serious illness. Later in year, Rome appoints Father Gérard Bertrand, M.Afr., to succeed him as vicar apostolic of Navrongo.

1948

May:	Father McCoy reassigned to Jirapa.
8 December:	Cornerstone laid for present church at Jirapa.

1950

18 April:	Tamale diocese established. Father Gabriel Champagne, M.Afr., appointed first resident bishop of Tamale.

1951

January:	Training centre for local Brothers of St. Joseph opened at Kaleo.
11 February:	Ordination of first Dagati priest in Gold Coast, Peter Dery.

1952

	SMI open convent in Kaleo and begin work there.
2 February:	Ko mission founded.
	Training school for midwives opened at Jirapa by Sister Cyprian (Mary Catherine Swales), FMM.

During February, Father R. Lavallée begins to organize what will later become Daffiama mission.

11 May: Missionary Sisters of Our Lady of Africa arrive in Northwest. First foundation made at Nandom.

November: Official opening of Daffiama mission.

SMI move novitiate to Daffiama.

1953

St. Victor's Major Seminary moves from Wiagha to its present location in Tamale.

10 March: Cornerstone of Jirapa Hospital laid by Mr. Burdon, chief commissioner, Tamale.

19 March: First seven Brothers of St. Joseph receive religious habit at Kaleo.

1 November: Arrival of Doctor Linn Fenimore Cooper, Jirapa Hospital's first resident doctor.

1954

January: Permission accorded to Jirapa Hospital by National Board of Nurses in Accra to begin training qualified registered nurses (QRNs) on trial basis. Sister Cyprian, FMM, in charge.

22 October: Doctor Henry Archambault ("Dr. Shambo") arrives at Jirapa. Performs first operation (for strangulated hernia).

During this year, construction of Jirapa church completed.

1955

Jirapa Hospital (St. Joseph's) opens early in year.

Late June: Chiefs of Jirapa, Tizza, and Konzo-
                kola, with their elders, come to Jirapa
                mission to pray for rain.

September: Father J. McNulty launches first
                credit union on African continent at
                Jirapa.

1956

23 April: Navrongo diocese established.
                Bishop Bertrand becomes first bishop
                of new diocese.

1957

March: First two Birofos enroll in catechet-
                ical instruction program at Jirapa.
                Others follow.

6 March: Gold Coast becomes Ghana as Great
                Britain grants political independence
                to its former colony.

1958

19 March: Anthony Yirtare of Nadoli becomes
                first Brother of St. Joseph to be
                professed in that congregation.

1959

                St. Francis Secondary School for
                Girls opens in convent of FMM in
                Jirapa.

3 November: Wa diocese established, covering civil
                districts of Wa, Lawra, and Tumu in
                northern part of Tamale diocese.
                Area: 11,547 km^2 (4,503 mi^2). Popu-
                lation: 235,000 (including 36,432
                baptized Catholics and 6,000 cate-
                chumens).

13 November: Death of Doctor Linn Cooper in
                Kanowit, Sarawak, Borneo.

1960

                Wa and Tumu parishes founded.

4 March: National Board of Nurses (Accra)
                  gives full approval for recognition of
                  Jirapa Hospital as official QRN
                  training school.

16 March: Peter P. Dery elected first bishop of
                  Wa diocese.

8 May: Episcopal ordination of Bishop-elect
                  Dery, first Dagati bishop, at hands
                  of Pope John XXIII in Rome.

1961

Ghana government begins construction of Nandom Hospital, to be
administered and staffed by MSOLA.

1963

September: St. Francis Xavier Junior Seminary
                  begins to function with twenty-eight
                  students and a staff of two: Fathers
                  Gregoire and Songliedong. While
                  awaiting completion of seminary
                  complex under construction in Wa,
                  some old mud buildings behind Jirapa
                  parish house serve as temporary
                  seminary.

                  St. Anne's Vocational Institute,
                  aimed at preparing girls as future
                  wives and mothers, opens in Nandom
                  under direction of MSOLA.

1965

September: Carpentry Workshop School started
                  by Brother Alois Bingisser, M.Afr.
                  in Wa.

                  Arrival of Brothers of the Immacu-
                  late Conception (FIC) from the
                  Netherlands to undertake training of
                  young men for religious life. The local
                  Brothers of St. Joseph merge with
                  them to form one congregation.

Nandom Hospital completed by diocese of Wa.

1966

1 December: Lawra parish officially established.

1968

September: Nandom Secondary School begun.

1969

17 July: Doctor Shambo (Henry Archambault) dies at Jirapa. Buried at entrance to hospital in which he laboured for fifteen years.

1970

30 January: Death of Father Arthur Paquet (1902-1970).

August: First general chapter of SMI convened at Daffiama. Sister Emiliana Lokore elected first superior general of Ghanaian congregation.

1971

Hamile parish begun. Parish house completed in October 1972. Modern-style church, begun in 1974 by Brother Lussier, M.Afr., completed in February 1976.

October: Pastoral and Social Institute opens in buildings of FIC Brothers in Kaleo. Father Yves Masquelier, M.Afr., named its first director. Thirteen students, all from Wa, comprise first class. The institute would move to Wa in 1972.

1972

Nandom Practical Vocational Centre, founded by FIC Brothers, opens its doors.

1974

18 November: Father Gregory Eebolawola Kpie-
                    baya elected bishop of Wa. Bishop
                    Peter P. Dery transferred to Tamale
                    diocese.

1975

15 March: Episcopal ordination of bishop-elect
                    Gregory Kpiebaya in Wa cathedral.
                    During year, MSOLA begin to hand
                    over administration and staffing of
                    Nandom Hospital to SMI.

1976

16 August: Faculty of Nursing inaugurated at
                    Jirapa Hospital.

1977

30 May: Tamale diocese promoted to rank of
                    archdiocese, with Navrongo (now
                    Navrongo/Bolgatanga) and Wa as
                    suffragan sees.

27 November: Official ceremony of enthronement of
                    Peter Dery as archbishop of Tamale.

1978

                    Inauguration of Wa Catholic Press.
November: Jubilee Year of Wa diocese begins
                    (1929-1979).

1983

8 September: Death of Brother Basilide (Willem
                    Koot) in the Netherlands (1898-1983).

1985

13 July: Joint sacerdotal celebration in Jirapa:
                    ordination of Alphonsus Bakyil, first
                    Ghanaian member of Missionaries of
                    Africa, and official celebration of
                    Father Remigius McCoy's sixtieth
                    anniversary of ordination to the
                    priesthood.

1987

1 October: Death of Father Joseph Larochelle (1904-1987) after fifty-eight years as missionary.

October: Pope John Paul II awards *Pro Ecclesia et Pontifice* (For the Church and the Pontiff) medal to four pioneers of the Church in northwest Ghana: Remigius McCoy, Joseph Larochelle, Maurice Carrier, and Thomas Tryers, all members of the Missionaries of Africa. The decoration is awarded in recognition of service to the Church and the papacy.

Appendix 1

Curriculum Vitae of Bishop Oscar Morin

Birthdate: 24 December 1878.
Minor Seminary: Ste Cunégonde (Montreal). Entered in October 1892.
Seminary of Philosophy: Sulpician Fathers. Entered in October 1898.
Tonsure: Cathedral of Montreal, 27 May 1899.
Major Seminary (Montreal): 1900-1901.
Minor Orders: Cathedral of Montreal, 1 June 1901.
Major Seminary (Quebec): 1901-1902.
Novitiate: Maison Carrée (Algeria). Entered on 27 September 1902.
Clothing ceremony (received religious habit of Missionary of Africa): Maison Carrée, 5 October 1902.
Missionary Oath: Carthage (Tunisia), 15 September 1904.
Ordained subdeacon: Carthage, 16 September 1904.
Ordained deacon: Carthage, 18 September 1904.
Ordained priest: Carthage, 28 June 1905.

Missionary itinerary:

1905

24 July:	Left Marseilles as member of twelfth caravan of Missionaries of Africa, bound for French Sudan.
14 October:	Arrived at Wagadugu.

1906

23 April: Arrived at Navaro (Navrongo) with
                       Father Chollet and Brother Eugène.
                       Father Chollet named superior.

1907

3 October: Appointed superior of Navaro
                       mission.

1915

29 May: Appointed to Wagadugu.

1916

21 July: Appointed administrator of vicariate
                       apostolic of Wagadugu (eastern part
                       only).

1920

30 November: Left for Maison Carrée.

1921

24 February: Arrived at Maison Carrée.
15 March: Left Maison Carrée for Tunis and
                       Carthage (Tunisia).
29 March: Left Tunis for Marseilles, then to
                       Canada.
23 September: Returned to Maison Carrée.
29 September: Began 30-day Ignatian retreat at
                       Maison Carrée.
9 November: Appointed regional superior of
                       Missionaries of Africa in French
                       Sudan.
12 November: Left Maison Carrée for French
                       Sudan, arriving at Wagadugu follow-
                       ing 21 January.

1923

29 October: Assumed duties as local superior of
                       Navrongo mission, replacing Father
                       Barsalou (until 3 November 1925).

1925

Before leaving to visit African troops throughout West Africa, Bishop Thévenoud (vicar apostolic of Waga-dugu) grants Father Morin all powers necessary to administer that part of his vicariate in which the Missionaries of Africa work. (At the time it consisted of two mission stations: Navrongo and Bolgatanga, the latter founded in March 1925.)

1926

2 January: Prefecture apostolic of Navrongo established.

6 February: To Rome with Bishop Thévenoud, arriving on 23 February.

4 March: Left Rome for Marseilles and Pau (France).

29 March: Arrival at Maison Carrée to attend general chapter of Missionaries of Africa.

14 April: Appointed prefect apostolic of Navrongo.

29 April: Left Algeria for Canada.

1927

29 March: Arrival at Navrongo as prefect apostolic.

April: Wiagha mission founded.

1929

30 November: Jirapa mission founded.

1932

5 December: Kaleo mission founded. Officially opened on 8 December.

1933

6 May:	To Maison Carrée, arriving on 23 May.
7 June:	Left Algeria for Rome and Canada.
December:	Nandom mission founded in early part of month.

1934

26 February:	Named vicar apostolic of Navrongo.
17 April:	Episcopal ordination in Montreal cathedral.
16 October:	Left Marseilles for Navrongo, arriving 8 November.

1946

15 September:	Tamale mission founded.

1947

21 February:	Resigned at age of sixty-seven, after having been evacuated urgently to Maison Carrée for grave reasons of health.

1952

6 April:	Died at novitiate of St. Martin (Quebec).

Appendix 2

Curriculum Vitae of Remigius Francis-Xavier McCoy

Birthdate:	1 October 1897.
Birthplace:	Mayo, Quebec (Canada). Diocese of Hull.
Father:	Michael McCoy (1850-1933).
Mother:	Sarah Lavell (1857-1924).
Siblings:	Margaret (Sr. Monica of the Sisters of Providence. Kingston, Ontario. 1874-1951).
	Walter (1876-1902).
	Joseph (1880-1964).
	Mary (1883-1975). Married Edward O'Brien (d.1933).
	Edmund (Rt. Rev. Msgr.). Calgary, Alberta. (1886-1971).
	Henry (1888-1910).
	Frederick (1890-1894).
	Rosalie (Sr. Ildefonse, Sisters of Providence. Kingston, Ontario. 1892-1977).
	Frederick #2 (1895-1976). Married Anna Kiley (1898-).

Education:

Grade School:	St. Malachy's. Mayo, Quebec. 1903-1912.

Grade Eight: St. Michael's Academy. Buck-
                      ingham, Quebec. 1912-1913.
College: St. Alexander's College (Holy Ghost
                      Fathers). Ironsides, Gatineau,
                      Quebec. 1913-1918.

                      Seminary of Philosophy. Montreal,
                      Quebec. 1918-1920. Completion of BA
                      degree in philosophy.

Missionaries of Africa:

Postulancy: Laval University Seminary. Quebec.
                      Theology I. November 1920 — June
                      1921.
Novitiate: Maison Carrée (Algeria). 27 Septem-
                      ber 1921 — September 1922.
Theology: St. Louis Scholasticate, Carthage
                      (Tunisia). Theology II, III, IV.
                      29 September 1922 — June 1925.
Solemn Missionary Oath: Carthage. 27 June 1924.
Ordained subdeacon: Carthage. 28 June 1924.
Ordained deacon: Carthage. October 1924.
Ordained priest: Carthage. 28 June 1925. (Ordaining prelate:
    Archbishop Alexis Lemaître.)
First Mass: Mayo, Quebec. 19 July 1925.

Missionary itinerary:

1925

28 June: Assigned to *missio sui juris* of
                      Navrongo, Gold Coast.
7 November: Arrived at Navrongo, via Marseilles
                      to pick up supplies.

1926

April: Opened first school in Navrongo with
                      enrollment of eighty-five boys.

1929

29 November: Left Navrongo to open first mission
                      among the Dagaabas and Sissalas of
                      northwest Gold Coast.

30 November: Arrived in Jirapa, site of first foundation in Northwest.

1936

December: To Maison Carrée for theological refresher course and 30-day Ignatian retreat.

1937

April: To Rome to negotiate with Franciscan Missionaries of Mary to obtain sisters for Jirapa.

To Canada and United States. Appointed by Bishop Birraux, superior general of Missionaries of Africa, to find U.S. diocese open to establishment of society within its borders.

1942

29 June: Took possession of house and land in Alexandria Bay, New York, in diocese of Ogdensburg.

1944

June: Acquired property in Bethesda, Maryland, for second foundation of Missionaries of Africa in United States.

1945

June: Returned to West Africa.

July: Navrongo. Appointed diocesan bursar (1945-47).

1946

14 September: Leaves for Tamale to found first mission among Dagombas.

15 September: Arrival in Tamale. Takes possession of rest house until accommodations for first missionaries among Dagombas can be built.

1948

12 May:	Re-assigned to Jirapa.
8 December:	Blesses cornerstone for new church in Jirapa.

1952

15 October:	Home leave in Ontario, Canada.

1953

1 November:	Returned to Jirapa from Canada and U.S. bringing Dr. Linn Cooper, Jirapa's first resident doctor, with him.

1958

12 May:	Home leave in Ontario, Canada. Afterwards assigned to mission promotion work in U.S.
July:	Assigned to Alexandria Bay, New York.

1959

March:	Assigned to Onchiota, New York.

1960

August:	Assigned to Chicago, Illinois. Named superior of community.

1963

August:	Assigned to Metuchen, New Jersey. Named superior of community.

1965

10 March:	Daffiama, Ghana. Appointed parish priest (1965-1967); chaplain to Sisters of Mary Immaculate (postulate and novitiate); coordinator of Jirapa and Nandom hospitals and clinics; assistant to parish priest of Daffiama (1968-1971).

1971

April:	Thornhill, Ontario. Six month appointment to Canadian province of Missionaries of Africa.

18 November: Returned to Jirapa. In semi-
                      retirement since 1980. Performs
                      occasional ministry, maintains parish
                      accounts; and, in accord with Dagati
                      custom and instructions from Bishop
                      Kpiebaya in 1980, "gives advice".

Appendix 3

First Catechumens in NW Gold Coast

On the feast of Christmas 1930, the first group of catechumens in northwest Gold Coast received the medal of the Blessed Virgin Mary signifying their adherence to the Ngwinsore.

Name*	Village
(John) Kyefondeme	Jirapa
(Alexis) Yelesigra	Jirapa
(Felix) Dosogla	Jirapa
(Francis) Bagile	Jirapa
(Luka) Bobata	Jirapa
(Theodore) Poreku	Zemopare
(Mauricio) Naatee	Zemopare
(Remi) Kabiri	Kokolugu
(Joseph) Anglieremwin	Jirapa
(Elias) Ninang	Jirapa
Nimbare (headman of Tampoe)	Tampoe
(Paulo) Nora	Jirapa
(Joseph) Gbare	Tizza
(Yacobi) Kpiende	Tizza

o

---

* If eventually baptized, the baptismal name is placed first (in parentheses).

Appendix 4

First Baptismal Class in NW Gold Coast (1932)

On the feast of Christmas 1932, the first class of catechumens to complete the catechetical program was baptized before the Midnight Mass. The ceremony took place on the second-storey verandah of the mission house in Jirapa*. In the case of Dominic Gbang, who had already been baptized at an earlier date (in danger of death), the ceremony was merely completed.

Name	Village
Peter Dery	Zemopare
John Kyefondeme	Jirapa
Joseph Gbare	Tizza
James Nyangwane	Sabuli
Teresa (wife of James Nyangwane)	Sabuli
Remi Kabiri	Kokolugu
Anna (wife of Remi Kabiri)	Kokolugu
Yacobi Kpiende	Tizza
Michael Kpienbare	Sabuli
Paulo Nora	Jirapa
Oscar Gokyi	Jirapa
Dominic Gbang	Jirapa

* Now the residence of the Franciscan Missionaries of Mary.

Appendix 5

Second Baptismal Class in NW Gold Coast (1933)

The second class of catechumens to be baptized in Jirapa, on 3 June 1933, consisted almost entirely of student catechists and/or their wives. Some of the husbands had been baptized the previous Christmas Eve.

Name	Village
Bernadette Dubome (wife of John Kyefondeme)	Jirapa
Maria Welle (wife of Joseph Gbare)	Tizza
Helena Sangireme (wife of Yacobi Kpiende)	Tizza
Yoakim Zuena	Lambusie
Monica Bura (wife of Yoakim Zuena)	Lambusie
Matthew Tankpa	Sigri
Edita Mwinsaga (wife of Matthew Tankpa)	Sigri
Luka Bobata	Jirapa
Agatha Nengeme (wife of Luka Bobata)	Jirapa
Thomas Tuuri	Jirapa
Flora Nabuma (wife of Thomas Tuuri)	Jirapa
Philip Galenyoni	Jirapa
Joanna Poayele (wife of Philip Galenyoni)	Jirapa
Pio Nama	Jirapa
Antonio Dabuoh	Lyssa

Lucia Bagber (wife of Antonio Dabuoh)... Lyssa
Stephen Puspel .... Gyeffiri (Sigri)
Catherina Mwinbon (wife of Stephen
    Puspel) .... Gyeffiri (Sigri)
George Aabaare .... Touri
Felicitas Dieyala (wife of George
    Aabaare) .... Touri
Fabian Quabag............................... Gbare
Perpetua Bonkanyure (wife of Fabian
    Quabag) .... Gbare
Andrew Dakyie............................... Nadoli
Angela Poasang (wife of Andrew Dakyie) Nadoli
Cyprian Kanveng............................ Duong
Rosa Ranburo (wife of Cyprian
    Kanveng).................................. Duong

Appendix 6

First Contact with Christianity and Early Impressions
by Father Alfred Bayo

It must have been in the middle of the year 1930 that I made my first contact with Christianity.

John Kyefondeme, one of the first catechists, came to Kalesegra, his mother's village, to inform us about the coming of the "men of God" to Jirapa. The matter, he said, was too important for us to sit quietly as if unconcerned. People from all sides were flocking there and we should not be the only people left out, he said.

On the catechist's word, about thirty of us (of all ages) left for Jirapa the following Saturday evening. It was about ten miles from Kalesegra. Arriving late, we had to wait until the next morning to catch a glimpse of the men of God and their ways.

Our curiosity was rewarded. At the catechism place, a short man in a long gown emerged from a doorway. There was an excited murmur and everyone rose, to the disappointment of us smaller ones because our view was blocked. With some effort, we manged at last to get a satisfactory viewing spot. Quite a while later, a taller figure, dressed in the same way as the shorter man, appeared. The same murmur and movement of curiosity took place,

---

Father Bayo is priest of the Wa diocese.

and all eyes were directed toward the figure. I had now been able to see two men of God and to hear their message. We were so fascinated that we gave our names as catechumens and went back every Sunday thereafter to pray.

The short man was Father Arthur Paquet, and the tall man was Father Remigius McCoy, the superior. Later on we met Brother Basilide Koot.

My early impressions of John Kyefondeme were that he looked so good and kind. I had never noticed anyone looking like that before. His words sounded so true and convincing that they made a lasting impression in the heart. We loved to listen to him for hours....

As for the missionaries, they looked so innocent, so kind and delicate in their constitutions. Their speech was so soul-stirring and captivating, it was very hard to part with their presence. The feeling one had was like that of Simon Peter and the others on Mount Tabor: it was good to be with them always. The general impression my companions and I had of them was that they were just sent straight down from heaven to give us the message, and that there was no question of their having had parents.

Everything about God was so completely new that it went straight to the heart. It is true that we knew the name of God and of His existence, but we had never heard anything so consoling as the life of Jesus Christ, the mystery of the Holy Trinity, and the life of the world to come. No wonder we could never become tired of hearing that. On the contrary, the constant hearing of it served as sweet music to the heart.

The message worked in my mind when the time of question-and-answer catechism came up. Up to then I had never in my life concentrated on anything worthwhile. The catechism taught me orderly thinking.

Among the reasons for perseverance in the faith were the personal goodness of the missionaries and their love for the people. Both were expressed in their faces and in their behaviour toward people, that is, their kindly manner and polite way of talking with them. It was also manifested in their devoted service to the people, especially in their care of the sick. They were tolerant with everyone, wearing a constant smile on their faces.

Other reasons for perseverance were the convictions produced by the doctrine or message itself: the Fatherhood of God and His goodness to all people without exception; the Incarnation of Jesus Christ and the universal dimensions of His saving death; the destiny of all persons for eternal life with God.

One very serious infantile question bothered my mind at that time, however. How could they (the missionaries) call a person's name just from a book without even looking up at him? What part of the person did they see there in the book? Was it possibly his soul that was seen there? I remained in the dark on this for years, with my great curiosity to know the answers to these questions going unsatisfied.*

Toward the end of 1934, probably in October, I was tested for the rosary.# Father Rochon, who did the testing, asked me if I wanted to go to school. I answered very joyfully in the affirmative, but added sadly that I was the firstborn of my parents and that I had two younger brothers and a sister, all too young to be of any help to them, and for that reason I feared I might not be allowed to go to school. Father Rochon asked the catechist John

---

* Father Bayo here refers to the early practice of name-giving to catechumens about to be baptized. Father Chantereau in particular had the habit of assigning names straight from the pages of the Roman Martyrology, especially when confronted with hundreds to be baptized at the same time. Later the practice was discontinued and the catechumens were allowed to pick their own baptismal names from approved lists. In the traditional life of the Dagaabas, a name was not lightly chosen. It identified the person bearing it in a special way since it nearly always referred to some event that touched or marked the baby's birth in some way. For instance, the name Wienaa (meaning bush farm or field) might indicate that the child so named had been born, probably unexpectedly, in a field outside the village where the mother had gone to work on the family farm. Similarly, Dery (born again) was the name given to a male child who succeeded a deceased brother. In this second child, the first was "reborn", in other words. (Its equivalent would be Renato in Italian or René in French.) The young Bayo assumed that people like Father Chantereau were able to do the same thing in an impersonal way just by looking in a book. He wondered what special powers enabled them to find the proper name for each of the hundreds of catechumens presenting themselves. — Ed.

Marking the end of the pre-catechumenate stage and the beginning of the catechumenate proper, with two more years of instruction remaining before being admitted to baptism.

Kyefondeme, my father's cousin, to contact my father on that issue. My father had no objection to my going to school. He even added that the missionaries could take me anywhere they judged best for my education because they too had left their parents and come to help us. That was a big sacrifice on my father's part, though I only came to appreciate it later.

In 1935, in the early part of the year, a group of us from Nandom, Kaleo, and Jirapa, came together in Jirapa to depart for school in Bolgatanga. Each of us had been carefully selected and interviewed by his parish priest. In my case, Father McCoy had called me to the mission one evening so that we could have a talk. While pacing up and down between the missionaries' house and the old mud church, the two of us alone, he asked me the same question Father Rochon had asked me: Do you want to go to school? I repeated the same answer I had given before. How happy I was when he told me that my father had no objection to my education. It was from Father McCoy that I learned of the results of the interview John Kyefondeme had had with my father.

To cut a very long story short, twenty-two of us, all boys, left for Bolgatanga one early morning, arriving at Navrongo by noon. Here I must mention that some other boys had been sent to Navrongo Primary School a year or two before us. We were glad to meet them there for the very first time. They included Peter Dery (later archbishop of Tamale) and Lawrence Kyemaalo (later monsignor), as well as some others who were even senior to them, such as Matthias Banoeyeni and others.

After a short break we were told, to our surprise, to get back on the lorry again. An hour later we arrived at Bolgatanga and were informed that we had reached our destination, that this was to be our learning ground for many years to come. We were very kindly received by our first local manager, Father Kenelm Haskew (from England). Our parish priest, Father Rosaire Robert (from Canada), was the vicar general of the vicariate under Bishop Oscar Morin. The other father, who was really like a mother to us, was Father Camille Lafrance (from Canada). We were so happy there and so eager to learn, that the time went quickly. We made such rapid progress that we were able to do the work of six years in five.

Out of the original group sent to Navrongo, two became priests: Archbishop Dery and Monsignor Kyemaalo. Of the original group sent to Bolgatanga, three of us became priests: Hippolyte Putiere, Evarist Kuuwulong, and myself. For this, many thanks must go to Father J. Alfred Richard (of the United States).

The mystery of our selection for the priesthood — why some were chosen and some were not — is best known to God alone. We were all given the same opportunities, all constantly fed the same rich spiritual food by the same kind and zealous priests. Quite a number of us got as far as the minor seminary and some even as far as the major seminary before dropping out for one reason or another. The reason why some went on through to the priesthood and others did not can never be answered satisfactorily by anyone in this world. We shall all know why in the world to come when we see with the vision of God Himself.

It is not in a short contribution like this that one can do justice to all the priests, teachers, and people who contributed to one's vocation. There are so many I have not mentioned here for lack of space and so many I have forgotten or have never even known but who will be revealed one day by God and rewarded accordingly. But surely He chose our beloved old Father McCoy to be the first to plant the tree of faith in Him among the Dagaabas.

Appendix 7

Some Personal Reminiscences on the Coming of Christianity to the Northwest

by Father Evarist Kuuwulong

I was one of the fortunate boys Father McCoy sent to school. I was born in Ullo, a village twenty-four miles from Jirapa by road and eighteen miles by footpath through the bush. When my father died, I was still very young (one or two years old) so I did not really know him. His brother took care of me. I must have been about eight years old when Father McCoy paid his first visit to our village.

After Father McCoy and his companions arrived in Jirapa, people from all the surrounding villages began going to see them for the purpose of joining the new religion they had brought to the area. People from Ullo also went, among them some of my own cousins. Like many other visitors to Jirapa, they registered for instruction to become Christians.

They were anxious to learn what was being taught at Jirapa but it was not easy to go there with any frequency. One day when they returned from the mission, they told my uncle (who was then chief of the village) that all the villages around were sending delegates to welcome the missionaries and that unless he did too,

---

Father Evarist Kuuwulong is a priest of the Wa diocese.

they would never come to our village to teach us the new religion. My uncle the chief agreed at once without hesitation. He sent some of my cousins to Father McCoy, the superior, with a big white sheep as a token of welcome.* He also gave them a message for him. "When you see him, tell him that my son is sick, and that I am begging him to send me some medicine for him or to come himself and see what he can do to help him." I was the sick boy. At the time the delegation was being sent, I had a very painfully swollen shoulder.

When the envoys returned from Jirapa, they told the chief that Father McCoy promised to visit him in Ullo on a fixed date in about a week's time. They also told him that the father wanted him to send me to Jirapa for treatment. When I heard that my sickness had been reported to him, and that he was now aware that I needed help, I was very happy even though I knew there was no means of transport to take me to Jirapa.

The day on which Father McCoy was to pay his first visit to Ullo came. Many people were at the *barakyi* (the government rest house) from early morning waiting for him to arrive. Among those waiting, I think I was the most anxious to see him. I made sure to stand very close to my uncle the chief, hoping thereby to get a good close-up view of the priest.

As we stood there waiting, some people who had already seen Father McCoy were describing how he spoke Dagaare. Before long we heard his *popo* (motorcycle), and soon he was on the spot, greeting the people. After the greetings, he made the sign of the cross.

"*Saa — ne — Bie — ne — Voorong Song — yuori enge. Amina.*" He said it very slowly and loudly for everyone to hear. Then he spoke with the people for a while and promised to send a catechist to them every Sunday. His visit took about twenty minutes. When he was about to leave, he said: "I have to go now or else I will be caught in the rain." As the people did not see any sign of rain, they laughed and told him not to worry about that; there was no chance of rain that day. But a little while after he left, it rained on Ullo. (It was the beginning of the rainy season.)

---

* The Jirapa mission diary records this as taking place on 30 July 1932.

Following Father McCoy's visit, catechists began coming to Ullo to give instructions every Sunday. There were too many people for just one catechist to teach, so three or four of them would come together.

During the class one day, the catechist of my group was teaching on the Sacraments and telling us about the priesthood of the missionaries. He told us that we should not think that there was a country or countries where everybody was a priest and that they all came from there. He said: "If any boy goes to school and is baptized, he can become a priest if he wants to." Then he pointed his finger at me and said: "Look at that boy sitting there. If he studies and is baptized, he too can become a priest someday if he wants to." My heart jumped, and I said within myself: I will try to become a priest. And from that day onwards, though I did not know how to pray yet, I used to say:

"N saa Naamwin, e kam pke sakuur, a lie faara." (My Father God, make me go to school and become a priest.)

When I was alone, I would repeat this over and over, just above a whisper, always making sure that nobody overheard me. I was afraid of my people, thinking that they would not let me go. Meanwhile, I was interested in learning the catechism. I did not find it difficult to memorize formulas.

One day, when Father Leblanc was in our village on trek, he asked my uncle for two school boys and a catechist. That is, he wanted the chief to make available two boys to be sent off to school and a young man to be trained as catechist. My uncle called all the boys and young men from his household. His was a very big compound, with about three hundred persons living in it. Some thirty boys and young men came at the chief's bidding, myself among them. I thought that certainly my chance to go to school had now come. But when we lined up so that the priest could look us over and choose the ones he wanted, I found myself at the end of the line. He started at the beginning, and before he had reached me he had already found the two boys and the young man he wanted. I went away from the crowd and wept.

Still I continued to say: *"N saa Naamwin, e kam pke sakuur, a lie faara."*

The two boys went to the catechist school in Jirapa. One got sick and came home. The other one ran away to Kumasi. The young man who was sent to become a catechist also left.

Sometime afterwards, Father Leblanc was in Ullo again, on his monthly trek. Whenever he was on trek in the region, he slept at Ullo. This time we were five or six boys who went to speak with him at his hut in the evening. He had brought the newly printed catechism book with him, the contents of which we had already learned by heart. He showed it to us and said: "If any of you can answer all the questions in this book correctly, I will give you a rosary." Then he started asking questions. After asking a few boys, he was on me. I answered his questions until I was tired, but he kept on testing me. Finally, he shut the book and fixed his eyes on me for a long time. Then he said: "You have answered all the questions in the book correctly." I jumped up with my hands outstretched to receive the promised rosary. I did not get it, but I got a much bigger reward instead.

The next time Father Leblanc came to our village, I was the first person he spoke to. He said to me: "Father McCoy wants you to come to Jirapa to study. Do you want to go to school or not?" I answered him with a very broad smile. Then he asked: "Will you uncle agree to let you go to school?" I told him I did not know. He went to the house and talked to my uncle about me, telling him that Father McCoy was asking for me to go to school. My uncle called me and asked whether I wanted to go or not, and I told him that I did. He then told Father Leblanc that he could take me to Father McCoy.

A week later, I found myself in Jirapa attending school for the first time (1935). After a few weeks there, I was sent with other boys to Bolgatanga school. We were nine boys whom Father McCoy sent to Bolgatanga that time. Of those, three became priests: Alfred Bayo, Hippolyte Putiere, and myself.

Appendix 8

My First Year in Saint Paul's Primary, Nandom (1937)
by Father Irenaeus B. Songliedong*

Late one afternoon, shortly after Easter 1937, a group of young men and boys arrived at the catechist's house in Bo. After drinking water and exchanging the usual greetings, the leader produced a loincloth and a shirt sent by the parish priest, Father J.B. Durand, for Irené, the son of the catechist, who was to proceed to Nandom school with the group. I was seven years old.

The catechist did not doubt for a minute. The matter was simple. "Father wants Irené to go to school, he is going to school." It was not all that simple for the mother. She had to go home to Eremon to consult the family. When she returned, however, I had already gone to Nandom.

My father entrusted me to a fairly grown-up boy from Eremon, Victor Tang, giving him some shillings and some groundnuts for me, and adding a blanket to the stock already sent by the parish priest. I was instructed not to run back home or send for anything. If he thought I needed anything, he would send it on his own initiative.

We walked and walked wondering if we would ever reach Nandom. Finally we saw towers piercing the skies. We rejoiced

---

Father Irenaeus Songliedong is vicar general of the Wa diocese.

but soon realized there were still miles to go as we were on the Zemopare hills. We finally reached it.

The school comprised some small round huts (the dormitories), a large one (the dining hall), and a long rectangular building of mud with a grass roof (the classrooms). The enrollment of seventy ranged from young men of marriageable age to boys of six or seven. Within a few days we were sorted out into three classes. The staff consisted of Father Eugène Coutu, Mr. Paul Tiewiir and Mr. Denis Puntana. We learned the alphabet by tracing the letters in the sand with our fingers.

Several things stand out in my memory. For instance, the first realization that our dialects differed and the teasing that followed, sometimes degenerating into little fights. All the young ones got homesick after the novelty had worn off and there were no letters to receive or to write. Food was sometimes a great problem, the bigger boys leaving very little to the small ones. Hygiene was extremely primitive, the water was bad, and many of us harvested a good crop of guinea worms and ulcers.

But there was also the joy of finally being able to read and write, and the privilege of travelling places, even if not far. Those made us the envy of the village boys and were worthy compensations for the hardships we put up with.

---

* Irenaeus B. Songliedong, "My First Year in Saint Paul's Primary, Nandom (1937)." In *That They May Have Life: An Account of the Activities of the Church in Northwest Ghana 1929-1979*. Wa (Ghana), August 1979, p. 73.

Appendix 9

Jirapa Mission/Parish Staff 1929-1979*

1929-1930

Remigius F. McCoy, *Hull, Canada* — Arthur Paquet, 1902-1970, *Quebec, Canada* — Brother Basilide Koot, 1898-1983, *Utrecht, the Netherlands*.

1931-1932

R.F. McCoy — A. Paquet (fell ill in mid-July 1931; away for a year) — Eugène Coutu, 1901-1973, *Joliette, Canada* (temporary; from Wiagha, July-Nov. 1931) — Joseph Larochelle, 1904-1987, *Quebec, Canada* (arrived Nov. 1931 via England) — Bro. Basilide — Bro. Evarist Kingseller, 1904-1944, *Westminster, England* (arrived Nov. 1931).

1932-1933

R.F. McCoy — A. Paquet (appointed to Kaleo, Nov. 1932) — J. Larochelle — Robert Lavallée, 1904-1977, *Ste-Anne-de-la-Pocatière, Canada* — Stanislas LeBlanc, (1905-1988), *St-Hyacinthe, Canada* — Bro. Basilide (to Kaleo) — Bro. Evarist.

---

* Information in italics indicates diocese and country of origin.

APPENDIX 9

1933-1934

R.F. McCoy — J. Larochelle (to Nandom, Nov. 1933) — R. Lavallée — S. LeBlanc — Ubald Rochon, 1907-1980, *Joliette, Canada* (arrived from Canada, Nov. 1933) — Bro. Evarist (fell ill; sent to motherhouse in Algiers).

1934-1935

R.F. McCoy — S. LeBlanc — R. Lavallée (to Kaleo, Nov. 1934) — U. Rochon — Jean-Baptiste Durand, 1898-1970, *Sherbrooke, Canada* (from Kaleo for catechist training school, Nov. 1934).

1935-1936

R.F. McCoy — S. LeBlanc — U. Rochon — J.-B. Durand — Gabriel Champagne, 1908-1976, *St-Hyacinthe, Canada* (from Canada, Nov. 1935).

1936-1937

R.F. McCoy (leaves for motherhouse and Canada on 20 Nov. 1936) — J.-B. Durand (appointed superior of mission, 20 Nov. 1936) — S. LeBlanc — U. Rochon — G. Champagne.

1937-1938

J.-B. Durand — G. Champagne — E. Coutu (from Nandom, Oct. 1937) — S. LeBlanc (to Nandom, Sept. 1937) — Bro. Armand (left, Sept. 1937) — A. Paquet.

1938-1939

J.-B. Durand (to motherhouse and Canada, Nov. 1938) — G. Champagne (appointed superior from Nov. 1938) — A. Paquet — R. Lavallée — Gérard Dallaire, 1912-1941, *Chicoutimi, Canada* (from Canada, Nov. 1938). — Bro. Basilide.

1939-1940

G. Champagne — A. Paquet — R. Lavallée — Bro. Basilide (till Jan. 1940) — Bro. Ludovic (Jan Bonenkamp), 1901-1984, *Utrecht, the Netherlands* (from Navrongo).

1940-1941

G. Champagne — A. Paquet — R. Lavallée — G. Dallaire — Bro. Ludovic.

1941

G. Champagne — R. Lavallée — G. Dallaire (died, 24 Aug. 1941) — E. Coutu (from Kaleo, Aug. 1941) — Joseph-Edouard De Serres, 1914-1972, *Trois Rivières, Canada* (from Canada, Nov. 1941) — A. Paquet (to Canada, 22 Aug. 1941).

1942

G. Champagne — E. Coutu — J.-E. De Serres — R. Lavallée.

1943

G. Champagne — E. Coutu (to Wiagha in Dec.) — R. Lavallée —J.-E. De Serres — Francis Briody, *Motherwell, Scotland* (from Scotland in Nov.).

1944

G. Champagne — R. Lavallée (to Canada) — J.-E. De Serres — F. Briody — A. Paquet (from Canada in Aug.).

1945

G. Champagne (to Canada) — A. Paquet (superior of Jirapa from Nov.) — F. Briody.

1946

A. Paquet — J.-E. De Serres — F. Briody — Gérard Vachon, *Manchester, USA* (arrived in March).

1947

A. Paquet (to Nandom in May) — J.-E. De Serres — E. Coutu (from Kaleo, 1 July) — F. Briody.

1948

R.F. McCoy (from Tamale, 10 May) — E. Coutu — J.-E. De Serres — J.-B. Durand (from Kaleo in June) — Bro. Basilide (from Nandom).

1949

R.F. McCoy — J.-B. Durand (to Canada, 8 Dec.) — E. Coutu (to Canada) — A. Paquet — Eudore Arsenault, 1912-1976, *Valleyfield, Canada* (to motherhouse, then England and Canada, 8 Dec.) — Bro. Basilide — G. Vachon (from Tamale) — Jacobus Haring, 1922-1974, *Rotterdam, the Netherlands* (from the Netherlands, 21 March).

1950

R.F. McCoy — A. Paquet — G. Vachon (appointed general manager of schools for Tamale diocese) — J. Haring — Bro. Basilide.

1951

R.F. McCoy — G. Vachon (to USA in April) — E. Coutu (from Kaleo, 14 Aug.; appointed bursar) — J. Haring.

1952

R.F. McCoy (to Canada, 27 Sept.) — John McNulty, *Motherwell, Scotland* (from Tamale in Jan.; appointed superior in Sept.) — E. Coutu — J. Haring — Lawrence Kyemaalo, *Wa, Ghana* (from Ko, 20 Nov.) — A. Paquet (to Canada, 25 April) — Bro. Basilide (to the Netherlands, 19 Aug.).

1953

J. McNulty (to Scotland in Oct.) — R.F. McCoy (from Canada, 1 Nov.; reappointed superior) — E. Coutu — J. Haring — L. Kyemaalo — Bro. Lorenzo Carignan, *Nicolet, Canada* (from Nandom, 19 Jan.; to St. Victor's Seminary, Tamale, 17 May) — Bro. Basilide (from the Netherlands, 9 April) — Bro. Normand (Emile Soucy), *Ste-Anne-de-la-Pocatière, Canada* (from Navrongo, 23 May).

1954

R.F. McCoy — E. Coutu — L. Kyemaalo — Bro. Basilide (to Ko, to build church) — Bro. Normand — Bro. Aidan (John Ryan), 1904-1977, *Birmingham, England* — Bro. Suso (Ludwig Wille), *Rottenburg, Germany* (from Germany via Great Britain, 24 Dec.).

1955

R.F. McCoy — E. Coutu (to Kaleo as superior, 14 Feb.) — J. Haring — L. Kyemaalo — Bro. Aidan (to Tamale, 26 April) — J. McNulty (from Scotland, 13 Feb.).

1956-1957

R.F. McCoy — J. McNulty (to Yendi, 27 Dec. 1957) — J. Haring (to the Netherlands, May 1956) — L. Kyemaalo (in charge of schools in diocese) — Michel Graëff, *Grenoble, France* (appointed bursar) — Bro. Suso (to Brothers of St. Joseph training centre, Kaleo, 3 Feb. 1957) — Bro. Germain Lussier, *Sherbrooke, Canada* (to novitiate of SMI, Daffiama, Feb. 1957) — Jacques Nefkens, *'s-Hertogenbosch, the Netherlands* (arrived 23 Dec. 1957).

1958

R.F. McCoy (to Canada, 29 Dec.) — M. Graëff (superior and bursar from 29 Dec.) — L. Kyemaalo (to Kaleo, 13 Feb.) — J. Nefkens (credit union and schools) — Eugene Lallemand, 1911-1985, *Manchester, USA* (from Damongo, 11 Feb.; appointed to hospital) — J. Larochelle (from Nandom, 2 May) — Bro. Normand (arrived 15 July; to Tamale, 29 Dec.).

1959

M. Graëff (till 9 Oct.) — L. Kyemaalo (from Kaleo, 25 Oct.; appointed superior) — E. Lallemand (to Damongo, 4 Feb.) — J. Nefkens — Bro. Normand (appointed diocesan lorry driver; to Daffiama, 13 June) — Herbert Herrity, *Glasgow, Scotland* — A. Paquet (from Canada, 16 Oct.).

1960

L. Kyemaalo (appointed parish priest of Jirapa) — A. Paquet (appointed superior of community; chaplain of hospital and religious) — H. Herrity (appointed bursar; to Scotland, 26 Nov.) — J. Nefkens (to Ko, 4 Oct.; manager of diocesan schools) — Thomas Rathe, *Middlesbrough, England* (arrived 10 Oct.) — J. McNulty (arrived 16 Oct.) — Bro. Basilide (arrived 12 Nov.).

1961

L. Kyemaalo (parish priest and schools manager) — A. Paquet (superior of community, hospital sisters' chaplain) — J. McNulty (till 20 Oct.) — T. Rathe (appointed bursar) — Bro. Basilide (to Kaleo, 22 June).

1962

A. Paquet — L. Kyemaalo — E. Coutu (appointed bursar) — T. Rathe (manager of schools and credit union) — Bro. Basilide (arrived 5 Oct.) — Bro. Konrad Grunwald, *Paderborn, Germany* (arrived 4 March).

1963

A. Paquet — L. Kyemaalo — T. Rathe (bursar and credit union) — Irenaeus Songliedong, *Wa, Ghana* — Bro. Basilide — Bro. Konrad (to Daffiama, 11 Feb.) — E. Coutu (to Canada, 17 April).

1964

A. Paquet — L. Kyemaalo — T. Rathe — Günter Mester, 1934-1988, *Paderborn, Germany* — I. Songliedong (to Wa, 9 Jan.) — Bro. Basilide (to Kaleo, 15 Jan.) — J. Alfred Richard, *Providence, USA* — Josef Rohrmayer, *Regensburg, Germany* — Bro. Aloysius (Jacques Blekemolen), 1920-1985, *Haarlem, the Netherlands* (for language study under J.A. Richard) — John Wade, *Leeds, England.*

1965

A. Paquet (to Canada in May) — L. Kyemaalo — T. Rathe (to England) — G. Mester (to Germany) — Gerard Smulders, *'s-Hertogenbosch, the Netherlands* (arrived 5 May) — Marcelin Lévesque, *Ste-Anne-de-la-Pocatière, Canada* (temporary; arrived in Nov.).

1966-1967

L. Kyemaalo — G. Smulders (to Wa in May) — J. Wade — Guido Krämer, *Rottenburg, Germany* — Emilio Asie, *Wa, Ghana* — A. Paquet (from Canada in May 1966) — Bro. Basilide — Evarist Kuuwulong, *Wa, Ghana.*

1968

L. Kyemaalo — Alfred Bayo, *Wa, Ghana* — E. Asie — A. Paquet — Charles Timoney, *Waterford, Ireland.*

1969

L. Kyemaalo — A. Bayo — M. Lévesque — A. Paquet (to Canada) — C. Timoney — Bro. Suso — Bro. Konrad — E. Asie (to Ko).

1970

L. Kyemaalo — A. Bayo (to Kaleo in May) — M. Lévesque (to Canada in May; return to Jirapa in Nov.) — C. Timoney — Kizito Malinee, *Wa, Ghana* — Bro. Konrad (to Germany in May) — Bro. Aloysius (arrived in Nov.).

1971

L. Kyemaalo (to Nandom in April) — M. Lévesque (to Daffiama in April) — Bro. Suso (to Germany in Jan.) — K. Malinee — C. Timoney — Bro. Konrad — G. Mester (returned from Germany in Nov.) — Bro. Aloysius (to Wa in April) — J. Rohrmayer (appointed parish priest in April) — André Schaminée, *'s-Hertogenbosch, the Netherlands* (arrived in June) — R.F. McCoy (arrived 18 Nov. from Canada).

1972

J. Rohrmayer (to Germany in July) — K. Malinee — C. Timoney (to Ireland in April) — R.F. McCoy — Augustine Dery, *Wa, Ghana* (newly ordained, arrived in July) — G. Mester (to language school, 31 Dec.) — Leo Dabuoh, *Wa, Ghana* (newly ordained, arrived in Dec.) — Bro. Francis.

1973

R.F. McCoy (parish priest; to Canada, 20 March) — K. Malinee (local manager of schools) — A. Dery (chaplain for secondary school and nurses) — L. Dabuoh (to Kaleo temporarily) — Bro. Konrad — J.A. Richard (arrived 10 Jan.; to USA, 30 June) — G. Mester (arrived 18 May).

1974

Gervase Sentu, *Wa, Ghana* (arrived 2 March; appointed parish priest) — R.F. McCoy — J.A. Richard — G. Mester — K. Malinee — A. Dery — Bro. Konrad.

1975

Gervase Sentu — R.F. McCoy — G. Mester — Yvon Yangyuoro, *Wa, Ghana* (secondary school and parish) — L. Dabuoh — Bro. Vincent Davies, *Liverpool, England.*

1976

Gervase Sentu (until Feb.) — Y. Yangyuoro — L. Dabuoh — G. Mester — R.F. McCoy — Bro. Vincent — E. Kuuwulong (arrived 11 Feb. to take over as parish priest).

1977

E. Kuuwulong — L. Dabuoh — Hans Schering, *Munster, Germany* — R.F. McCoy — Bro. Vincent — Gerard Murphy, *Dromore, Ireland* (White Father seminarian; chaplain duties at secondary school).

1978

E. Kuuwulong — L. Dabuoh — H. Schering — R.F. McCoy — Bro. Vincent — G. Murphy.

1979

E. Kuuwulong — R.F. McCoy (bursar) — M. Graëff (hospital and secondary school chaplain) — John Bosco Buarayiri, *Wa, Ghana* — Bro. Vincent (house bursar) — G. Murphy (religious instruction at secondary school; 30 June, return to Ireland and then London to complete theological studies) — Robert Illidge, *Sydney, Australia* (from Bole) — Stephen Kantubog, *Wa, Ghana* — Anthony Tucker (student working at hospital).

Appendix 10

Interview with Robert Bongvlaa, Catechist*

Robert Bongvlaa was born in Ko in 1906. He became a catechist in 1933 and retired in 1975.

Robert, could you tell us something about your family background?

I was born in Ko. I came from a very big family... my father had three wives and fourteen children. Out of these fourteen, only five became Christians because the others died when very young.

Traditional worship was the religion practised before the arrival of the missionaries. What do you have to tell us about this?

Worship always had an important part in our life. In our traditional worship we believed that through the ancestors we were worshipping a God who was all powerful. This God was so great that we could not reach Him directly. Each family had a different way of worshipping. In our family we carved the persons of our ancestors, others took a supporting beam from the roof and worshipped it. The sacrifices we offered were to God and not to our ancestors, but we believed that He could bless us only through them. We wanted God to give us a long life, peace, a good harvest, and healthy children.

How often did you sacrifice?

The number of sacrifices depended on what happened during the year, but usually we sacrificed for four main reasons: We offered a) sacrifices of oblation, b) sacrifices for good crops, c) sacrifices for God's blessing of children, d) sacrifices of thanksgiving for no death in the family.

I will just say a word about the first type of sacrifice since the other three types need no explanation.

We offered the sacrifice of oblation only when one of our relatives died because he had done some evil deeds. Usually the soothsayer was consulted when a person died. If the soothsayer said that it was a natural death, then no sacrifice was offered; but if he declared that the man had died because of some evil deeds, such as stealing, poisoning, etc., then a sacrifice was offered as an oblation. We believed that if God was not offered a sacrifice, another relative would die. So this was done as a purification to protect the family.

How did you hear about the arrival of the missionaries?

When the missionaries arrived in Jirapa, I was working in Obuasi. My eldest brother sent me a message saying that I should come home because some white men had arrived and were talking about a new God. A month later, Poreku, Archbishop Dery's father, called me home. After hearing all about their kindness, curing of the sick, and the many miracles these white men were performing, I became interested. Just then Poreku was asked by Father McCoy to select a few people and send them for instruction. I was chosen and sent for instruction.

How long was the period of instruction before being baptized or becoming a catechist?

The length of the instruction was four years. During these four years an initiation ceremony was performed and a medal was given. Then two years later a rosary was given and this indicated the regular beginning of the catechumenate. At the end of the third year, there was a very strict test. Then an intensive course of two months was organized before the exam was taken to be baptized.

The period of training for the catechists was three years. Due to lack of catechists, our group was prepared for baptism and trained as catechists in two years time. We had a period of instruction and went off to impart what we had learned. During the training I was sent to Nandom and Dano to instruct and baptize. The people then came back to Jirapa for further instruction.

Where did the instruction take place and how was it organized?

The instruction and training of the first catechists and Christian catechumens took place in Jirapa. We had huts to live in and were allowed to go home from time to time to get some food.

I was sent to Nandom in 1934, right after my baptism. The people came from different villages and each village had four huts. It was possible for them to stay at the mission only for a certain period of time.

At the beginning, the Sissalas went to Nandom in the hundreds for instruction. Because of their big numbers, a centre was organized for them in Lambusie. Catechism classes were given every day, after which the people returned to their homes.

What was expected of the catechumens?

In those days, to become a Christian was a very serious affair. One of the first conditions was regular attendance. Good behaviour was counted as a must. If two catechumens quarrelled seriously, they would be sent home and weren't accepted back before they had shown real sorrow for their evil deeds. Once you became a catechumen, the juju had to be left aside. A catechumen was expected to be a bond of unity among all brothers and sisters, and he couldn't have more than one wife.

Did the moral code which existed among the Dagaabas clash with the new Christian teaching?

Our moral code was a good one, even though people lived and acted in fear of the evil spirits and other punishments. The one big clash was that of marriage. As soon as the person became a catechumen, most of our customs had to be renounced, and traditions regarding marriage had to be adapted if not given up.

According to our customs, if a man happened to marry a child-
less wife [i.e., a sterile woman], he was allowed to have a lover
and beget children. Or if a couple had no children, the wife was
allowed to get another husband with the permission of the family
and of her husband. But these ways were not accepted by Christianity. Another custom which was very common among the
Dagaabas was the inheriting of your brother's wife. If your brother
died, the wife and children belonged to the eldest brother. He
was obliged to look after the children and to keep the woman as
his wife. Christianity did not accept this concept. So, for those
who believed, there was a real radical change in their lives. Many
could not make it.

*Are there any special reasons why Christianity flourished so
quickly at the beginning?*

One can never tell for sure because God calls people in different
ways and for different reasons. Certainly God had His own way
of attracting us to Himself. It was His grace given freely to us.

At the time the missionaries arrived, our people were passing
through a very difficult time. There was a lot of human misery.
The groups were poor due to lack of rain, the children were dying
in great numbers and, on top of this, the chiefs and the district
commissioner were imposing forced labour on everybody. When
the missionaries arrived and the people heard about the miracles
that were performed in Jirapa, they became very interested in
these white people and their new God. People were also attracted
by the kindness and love shown to them, especially when compared
with the colonials and the chiefs. They believed and hoped that
the white men of God would not make them suffer and would free
them from their slavery and misery.

I think that these were some reasons why people embraced
the new religion. Nevertheless, it was a fact that many drew back
when they realized that despite the religion of the white men,
children were still dying, the rain didn't always come, and the
DC's forced labour was still on.

Where did you work in your career as a catechist?

As soon as I finished training, I was appointed to Nandom
where I stayed for nineteen years. Then I was sent to Fielmon

for a year, after which I was appointed to Ko parish. In the area covered by Ko, I spent one year in Guo, three years in Tom, and fourteen years in Topare.

To be able to spread the Word of God to your brothers and sisters, it must have cost you a lot of sacrifices and hard work. Could you tell us some of the difficulties encountered?

Yes, indeed, there were many difficulties that we had to face every day in those early times. At that time, transport did not exist and therefore we had to walk wherever we wanted to go. At the very beginning, catechist Anthony and I used to walk from Jirapa to Dissin and Dano and back. On the way we had to stop, rest, and cook the little food we managed to get.

Snakes, scorpions, and wild animals were an everyday scene on our travels. I still remember one evening when one of our catechumens in Nandom had a very sick child and I accompanied him to Lawra dispensary. When we reached the Kamba River, we saw two lions in front of us. There was nothing to do but stop and wait until they went off into the bush. We said some rosaries while sitting nervously waiting for the animals to give us way.

I have seen many serious cases of poisonous snake bites. We all thought that the person would soon fall and die, but after having given him a mixture of charcoal and milk, we prayed over the sick person and he was healed right away. It was God's love and protection for us in those days because we believed in His great power and trusted in Him for everything.

In the villages to which I went to preach the Word of God, I usually had good response from the people. The only hardship I encountered was at the hands of the chiefs. They gave me a lot of trouble. Enough to say that I was taken to court more than once. The cause of this trouble was the fear that with this new religion, they would lose their wives. In fact the chiefs were very keen on what the missionaries were doing, but they didn't want their own household to know about it.

Having been a catechist these last fifty years, how do you see the future of the Church?

As for the future of the Church, I can't say much because everything is in the hands of God. But I hope and pray with all my heart that our young people and the generations to come will not give up the faith which the Almighty Father in His great love has given us. In letting us know Him, He has given us a great treasure which should be passed on to our children's children until the end of time.

---

* Robert Bongvlaa, "Interview with Robert Bongvlaa, Catechist." In *That They May Have Life: An Account of the Activities of the Church in Northwest Ghana 1929-1979*. Wa (Ghana), August 1979, pp. 65-69.

Appendix 11

The Woman in Traditional Dagati Society
by
Rt. Rev. Gregory E. Kpiebaya, Bishop of Wa*

In traditional Dagati society, a woman is considered to be only a grown-up child. She doesn't have equal rights with the man in many respects. This mentality has given rise to all sorts of adverse customs and practices against the woman. For instance, in marriage the woman is considered to be the property of the husband and his clan, but the man is by no means her property. Even the children she begets are not hers, legally speaking. Being property or a "person owned", she is expected to give unconditional obedience and submission to her husband, like the dog to its master, but the husband is in no way bound to obey or submit to her. She helps the husband in his principal occupation, that is, farming; but she still has all the household chores to perform: fetching water and firewood, sweeping the house, bathing the children, drawing water for the men to bathe, and preparing the family meal. These menial tasks are considered to be strictly "women's work", and custom forbids a man to do them.

This attitude of treating the wife as property and as a hired hand is strengthened by payment of the bride-price for a wife, though originally the dowry was a pledge that both families were concerned to ensure the stability of the marriage. In point of fact, the bride-price, though a necessary legal requirement for marriage, does not constitute the essence of Dagati marriage. Strictly speaking, what is essential is that both the boy and the girl accept responsibility toward each other and toward their respective families. Also, the capacity to bear children is a serious consideration to be reckoned with. That is why there can be a breakdown in marriage, possibly leading to divorce, if one of these essential elements mentioned above is not there, even though the dowry might have been paid.

The inferior position of the wife also legitimizes the practice of the man taking multiple wives or indulging in conjugal infidelity. A man has exclusive sexual rights over his wife, but not the wife over her husband. Custom also demands that a husband should not love his wife more than his blood relatives. It is wrong, therefore, for a husband to side with his wife against, say, an unjust and malicious blood brother. Paradoxically, the wife is always a stranger in her husband's house since, most of the time, she is of a different blood and does not belong there by any blood ties.

These are some of the adverse ideas about the wife among the Dagaabas which, I think, still need to be purified....

---

* Rt. Rev. Gregory E. Kpiebaya, "Living the Christian Faith Today." In *That They May Have Life: An Account of the Activities of the Church in Northwest Ghana 1929-1979*. Wa (Ghana), August 1979, pp. 22-23.

Appendix 12

Doctors Who Served at Jirapa and/or Nandom Hospitals*

Name	Country	Period	Field
Linn Fenimore Cooper	USA	1953-54 1955-56	Int.Med.
Henry Archambault	USA	1954-69	Surgeon
Barbara Chapper	USA	1956-57	M.D. Ped.
Doctor Allegri	Italy	1958-60	Surgeon
A. Cumberbatch	England	1958-59	G.P.
Antonio Matias	Philippines	1964-66	Surgeon
J.A. Pollice	USA	1963	G.P.
Rossi C. Villaruel	Philippines	1966-68	G.P.
Edna Villaruel	Philippines	1966-68	G.P.
D.G. Empleo	Philippines	1966	G.P.
E. Baloing	Philippines	1966	G.P.
P.G. Girardi	Italy	1967	
Marlene Long	USA	1967-72	G.P.
John Oosternink[1]	Netherlands	1968-69	G.P.
Jean B. Kelly	USA	1969-72	Ob-Gyn

---

* This list is regrettably incomplete. The author apologizes to those who have been overlooked (inadvertently) in compiling it.

Joseph Kelly	USA	1969-72	Dentist
C.M.H. Hageraats	Netherlands	1970-72	G.P.
K. Sabilo	Poland/USA	1970-71	
Ron Puley	Canada	1970-71	Res.Int.Med.
Thomas Numan	Ireland/ Canada	1972-73	G.P.
Dermid Bingham	Canada	1972-73	Surgeon
Elizabeth Glitz	West Germany	1972	G.P.
Graham Stratford	Canada	1972	G.P.
Harm Kwikkel	Netherlands	1973-75	G.P.
Roy Laine	Canada	1974-76	Surgeon
Dyllis Noble	England	1974-76	G.P.
Howard Lee	England	1974	G.P.
Craig Carris	USA	1974	
Francis Scola	USA	1974	Radiologist
Patricia Scola	USA	1974	Ob-Gyn
Will Chamberlane	USA	1975	G.P.
Peter Poore	England	1975	Surgeon
Mary Anne Williamson, FMM	USA	1975-83	Surgeon
T. Ocampo	Philippines/ Canada	1976-78	G.P.
James T. Murphy	USA	1976-78	E.N.T.
Kofi Ametam	Ghana	1976-77	G.P.
Leonard Kaledzi	Ghana	1976-77	G.P.
Doctor Ackiebo[2]	Ghana (V.R.)		G.P.
Eugene Posnock	USA	1977-78	Pediatrics
Thomas Green	USA	1977-78	Surgeon
J.W. Mold	USA	1977	G.P.
Rosina Gepi-Attee	Ghana	1978-80	G.P.
Samuel Gepi-Attee	Ghana	1978-80	G.P.
Edward N. Gyader	Ghana	1978-82	Surgeon

Rob Nevin (CUSO)[3]	Canada	1978	G.P.
Rene Asselbergs	Netherlands	1980-82	G.P.
Marie Therese Chambers, FMM	Scotland	1981-	
Pauline Wadden		1981-82	
Francis Miller	USA	1982	Res.Surgery
Francis Banka	Ghana	1983-	Rural Health
Francis Rosario	Ghana		G.P.

---

[1] Dr. Oosternink was on loan for six months from the Presbyterian mission hospital in Bawku.

[2] Doctor Ackiebo contracted hepatitis in 1977(?) while working at Jirapa Hospital. Because there was no one to replace him there at the time, he refused to leave his post to take a much-needed rest, but continued his work until extreme weakness finally forced him to give it up. While being evacuated by ambulance to the South, he died, just forty miles from his destination.

[3] CUSO (Canadian University Students Overseas). The organization recruits university graduates for overseas service and sends them on assignment.

Notes

Chapter One

[1] Throughout this book, "Missionaries of Africa" and "White Fathers" will be used interchangeably to indicate the missionary institute founded by Cardinal Lavigerie in Algiers, Algeria, in 1868. A brief explanation of these titles may be found on the copyright page at the front of the book.

[2] One war (1899-1900) was led by a Lieutenant Babatu, and another (1901) by a Lieutenant Samouri. Both soldiers had been trained by the French in what is now Mali, and had gone on the rampage in neighbouring countries, forcing the conquered to swell the ranks of their armies and taking the women as slaves. They had raided and devastated all of northwest Gold Coast.

[3] Bolgatanga, the second mission station, was opened in January 1925.

Chapter Two

[1] See Chapter One, footnote 2.

[2] One of these, the mainly Muslim Wala group, is closely related to the Dagaabas.

Chapter Three

[1] Indirect rule: British colonial policy of governing through "native authorities". In this system, which was less costly than direct rule, the colonial power made use of traditional rulers (chiefs, emirs, etc.) in the subject country, permitting them to exercise on its behalf and under its more or less strict surveillance certain limited customary powers — executive, judicial, and legislative. Where such traditional authorities did not exist, the British simply created them and imposed them on the people.

[2] Moré is the language of the Mossis, an important ethnic group across the northern border with the French Sudan. Many in the group, including

the chief, would be familiar with the language because of its similarity to their own, Dagaare, and their frequent contacts with the Mossis with whom they traded regularly.

[3] Rest houses were simple buildings put up by the British administration at strategic points in the country-side. They functioned as official shelters for the DCs and other government personnel when they travelled about the towns and villages. When the DC was in residence in one of them, the British flag flew from the flagstaff in front of it. Anyone with a petition, complaint, or case to be judged could force an audience with him if that person could manage to slip past the caretaker, get inside the grounds, and cling tenaciously to the flagstaff.

[4] *Mwinpuorobo:* "one who prays" (i.e., a practicing member of an organized religion). *Mwinbapuorobo:* "one who does not pray" (i.e., one who is not a practicing member of an organized religion). The Dagaabas preferred the latter term to the inaccurate "pagan" or "infidel" introduced by English-speakers.

Chapter Four

[1] With the outbreak of the First World War in 1914, massive recruitment of African soldiers took place everywhere but Ethiopia and the small Spanish territories, which remained neutral. These troops served in Europe, the Middle East, and in the compaigns in the four German colonies of Togo, Cameroon, South West Africa (Namibia), and German East Africa (Tanzania). Countless more men, women, and even children were drafted as carriers and labourers for the African campaigns.

[2] *Tendaama* (plural form of *tendaana*): literally, "those who have custody of the land". The people of the Northwest do not buy land as Europeans or Americans do. They merely use it. The land belongs to the spirits and cannot be bought or sold. Their way of acquiring it goes back to the first settler in the area. When he arrived, he staked out a considerable expanse of territory, much more than he needed or could farm. When successive settlers followed him, they each went to the first, the tendaana, and asked him to give them a piece of his land, which he did. Though small gifts, such as a chicken or some cloth, might pass between them out of courtesy and gratitude to the tendaana who was apportioning the land under his care, no payment as such was made or expected. If it was later found that the petitioner was not making use of the land he had received, the tendaana might reclaim it for himself or give it to another. This system continues to be honoured in the Northwest. The office of tendaana also includes cultic duties. As the "priest of the Earth", he must make sacrifices to the powerful Earth spirit.

[3] *Muriyi:* "Snooper", especially one who has a habit of appearing unexpectedly, as if from nowhere.

[4] "Jirapa" is a British deformation of *gyirba*, the term used by the Dagaabas at that time to describe the area of useless grass, brambles, stones, and thorny plants. Literally, *gyirba* means "a low place where the *gyira* grows".

[5] Paying the wages of our workers presented unusual problems in the early days of the mission. To do so, it was necessary to have money shipped down from Navrongo literally by the truckful! Father Melançon, in a letter to some American friends in 1931, wrote: "I have been travelling so much lately that I had no time to write. I transported provisions, sheet-iron, flint, wood for the brick-kiln, and a heap of other things, *even three tons of money for Father McCoy at Jirapa*. These three tons equalled exactly 1,600,000!" He went on to explain that he was not speaking of dollars but of shells. At that time, the preferred exchange medium among the people of West Africa was the cowrie shell from the India Ocean. The British recognized the cowrie as legal tender within the territories they administered, setting a value for it against their own currency of between 1,200 and 1,500 cowries to the pound sterling. Since an ordinary labourer then received about three shillings a week and a mason twice that, a truckful of money did not go very far. Furthermore, the ordeal of counting out a week's payroll left one nearly shell-shocked, if I may be forgiven the pun. It had not occurred to me what this might entail until I sat down to do it for the first time late one Saturday afternoon. By the time I had paid the first three men in line, labouriously counting out some fourteen thousand cowries in the process, darkness was falling, making it impossible to continue. I was obliged to ask the rest to return for their pay on Monday, which they readily agreed to do.

Chapter Five

[1] A section of Jirapa town located on what was then the road to Lawra.

[2] Father Paquet would sterilize the surgical instruments in his room. Whenever he did this, the children would gather to watch in rapt fascination, convinced he was cooking up a batch of money!

[3] Sobita is Bismuth and Sodium tartrate (BP), a water soluble compound used extensively in the 1930s and 1940s to treat yaws in Africa and the Pacific Islands. Soluble Bismuth salts were also used in the treatment of venereal syphilis.

[4] Emetine was the first preparation used for treatment of amoebiasis. Because of its highly irritant and potentially cardio-toxic properties, it had to be administered by intra-muscular injection. Emetine and Dehydro Emetine, though still available, are rarely used today.

Chapter Six

[1] To "carry the mat", permission had to be sought from the chief. Strictly speaking, he could not give it since the British administration forbade the practice.

[2] Much the same procedure was followed across the border in the French Sudan, except that there the mat was replaced by the corpse of the "murdered" person borne on the shoulders of four men. The chief, rather than the witch doctor, conducted the investigation, and no reed was employed. The results, however, were the same: death for an innocent outcast of village society.

Chapter Seven

[1] On 6 January 1931, an incident occurred which helped to dampen the chief's interest in becoming a Christian. There was an outbreak of chicken pox in his compound and he did not report it. When I discovered it, I informed the government medical officer in Lawra who came to inspect immediately. The chief was furious with me, especially because the medical officer obliged him to build an isolation camp for the infected. As the people left the chapel after Mass a few days later, he stood outside requisitioning workers from among them to build the camp. We intervened to stop the strong-arm tactics of his men and to advise him politely that mission property was not to be used for such purposes. After that, relations between us were cool for some time. Though they improved again later, from that moment on the chief no longer attended Mass or showed any interest in becoming a Christian.

[2] Ngmankurinaa was also known as Ngmenzie. (Note: In transcribing spoken Dagaare, the initial "ng" is often dropped, producing "Mankurinaa" or "Menzie". The correct pronunciation, however, preserves this nasal sound. Part of the problem arises from the fact that Dagaare has no standardized orthography as yet, thus giving rise to a variety of spellings for the same word.)

[3] *Kolle* (plural of *kolaa*): "spirits of the rivers or lakes".

[4] To be precise, Poreku and his companions were only "postulants" at this early stage of their Christian instruction. The term "catechumen" was reserved by the White Fathers for those preparing for baptism, that is, those in the last two years of the mandatory four-year instruction program in vigour in all White Father missions at the time. For the sake of convenience, "catechumen" is used here and throughout the text to refer to anyone enrolled in the instruction program, no matter at what stage he or she may be. Likewise, "catechumenate" refers to the whole of the four-year program.

[5] A few years later (1933), a permanent mission was established there, staffed by Fathers Joseph Larochelle and Eugene Coutu (both Canadians), and Father J. Alfred Richard (USA). Nandom area is now about seventy per cent Catholic.

[6] "My father Poreku was baptized at Nandom in 1936, just before Christmas, together with my mother and the whole family. He took the name Theodore. I was baptized before them, on Christmas Eve of 1932, before the Midnight Mass. My father's baptism was delayed for two years due to his polygamous situation at the time." (Archbishop Peter P. Dery, in a letter to Father Rene Dionne dated 2 November 1987.)

[7] Five shillings at that time was equivalent to about $1.25 in United States currency. Quite a respectable sum.

[8] I owe the facts of Maria's story to Father J. Alfred Richard, since I was absent from the Gold Coast at the time it took place.

Chapter Eight

[1] The catechumenate consisted of three stages leading finally to baptism. Stage I lasted two years. It was a kind of postulancy divided into a three-month introduction to God, Creation, Jesus Christ, and Prayer (after which the candidates received a medal of the Blessed Virgin Mary, marking them as belonging to "those who pray", i.e., the Christians) and twenty-one months of instruction on the Commandments. This first stage ended with an examination and the reception of the rosary.

The catechumenate proper began with Stage II, lasting one year. It consisted of a review of the first two years, Bible History, and the study of the Church and the Sacraments, ending with another examination.

Stage III was a continuation of the previous stage, lasting one year as well and ending with the examination leading to admission of the catechumen to baptism. The latter part of this stage was devoted especially to the immediate preparation for reception of the sacrament.

Instructions and examinations were only part of the catechumenate, however. All through the four-year period, candidates were expected to show by their way of life that they were capable of living as Christians and that they fully intended to do so. The conditions for reception of the rosary were especially strict. Aside from having to pass a thorough examination, the catechumens had to prove their good intentions by renouncing once and for all the making of sacrifices to spirits and, in the case of polygamists, their extra wives. They had to decide which wife to keep and, if she agreed to remain with her husband, send the rest back to their families. The chosen wife should be a catechumen too, if at all possible, and be baptized with her husband when the time came. The decision to become a catechumen, of course, had to be the wife's own, freely taken.

[2] Ten shillings equalled about two U.S. dollars in 1931.

[3] This original classroom building, now covered by a corrugated metal roof, serves today as the parish hall.

[4] When bicycles became available in 1933, the area of the catechists' apostolate expanded to include Nandom, Kokolugu, Fiang, Norong, and even part of the French Sudan. The bicycles (Royal Enfields) were shipped from England unassembled in lots of thirty. We assembled them ourselves and sold them to the catechists at cost price: £3.10s (about $15 in U.S. currency then).

Chapter Nine

[1] In 1952, Daffiama became a parish in its own right, with resident priests and a burgeoning Christian population that today numbers about ten thousand baptized Catholics. The village has given four priests to the service of the Church in Ghana and many sisters as well. It is also the site of the headquarters of the Sisters of the Immaculate Conception, a Ghanaian congregation founded in 1955.

Chapter Ten

[1] "France, eldest daughter of the Church!"

[2] Dano and Dissin were the first of many missions to be opened among the Dagaabas in that part of the French Sudan which later became Upper Volta (now Burkina Faso). The Church developed very rapidly among them, as it was doing in the Gold Coast, with a corresponding growth in vocations to the lay apostolate (mostly catechists), priesthood, and religious life. In 1968 the region became the diocese of Diebugu, with Jean-Baptiste Somé, another local priest, as its first bishop.

[3] This incident was treated by Father Alfred Bayo in an article entitled "He Shot His Way to Catechism" (*White Fathers Missions*, September 1948, pp. 1-2). I owe the facts to him since I was not in the area when the event took place.

[4] We did meet with the chief and his elders to discuss the matter a month later. See p. 101.

[5] The catechist's promise, in translation from the Dagaare original, reads as follows:

In the name of the Father, and of the Son, and of the Holy Spirit. Amen.

I, _____, stand here now in God's presence and affirm to Father Superior here present that I want to give myself to God as a catechist in order to help to make Him known and loved.

I promise to work under the direction of the Father in charge, who indicates God's will to me in this.

I promise to do my best to lead an exemplary Christian life.

I promise to try to help others to follow God's path through my prayers, my instructions, and my example of Christian living.

I make this promise freely and with full knowledge of what I am doing. Conscious of the fact that I cannot keep it by my own strength alone, I ask the Blessed Virgin Mary and all the angels and my patron saint to help me to always be a faithful co-worker of Our Lord and Saviour Jesus Christ.

I now place myself in God's hands, wherein lies my only hope of reward. This is what I have in my heart and mind.

Signed:

A photograph of an authentic text of the promise in Dagaare, used in a ceremony of commission, may be found among the illustrations following p. 108.

[6] Monsignor Morin became Bishop Morin in 1934 when the Holy See raised the prefecture apostolic of Navrongo to a vicariate apostolic. His episcopal appointment, dated 26 February 1934, reached him in Canada where he had gone to seek badly-needed funds for the prefecture. On 17 April, he was ordained bishop in the Montreal cathedral.

[7] The first Dagati priest on either side of the British-French border was Father Emmanuel, ordained in Dissin (French Sudan) for the vicariate of Bobo-Dioulasso on 29 April 1944.

[8] The small boy Bayo eventually became Father Alfred Bayo. See Appendix 6, p. 279.

[9] See "Interview with Robert Bongvlaa, Catechist," in Appendix 10, p. 299.

Chapter Eleven

[1] When the grinding stones became worn and useless, they were enclosed in the base of a small fetish altar of dried mud built at the door of the house. Offerings were made on it to the kontoma or household spirits.

[2] *Pogpla:* "White woman", referring to the light color of her skin.

[3] According to local tradition, when the dowry for the girl had been paid by the prospective groom's family to the head of the girl's family, she automatically became a member of her future husband's clan and had to go to live in his house immediately, even before the formal marriage ceremony took place. If she died after the dowry had been paid, she would be buried in his burial ground even if the two had not yet come together.

[4] The Eremon catechist at that time was the father of a young son named Irenaeus, the future Father Irenaeus Songliedong of Wa diocese.

[5] At this writing, one of their daughters, Blandina, is regional education officer in Wa. James, a son, is regional planning officer in the same town.

[6] Jirapa mission at that time covered some two thousand square miles (5,200 square kilometres).

[7] Dagati tradition insists that once the dowry has been paid, all children born of the woman for whom it is paid belong to the extended family of the husband.

Chapter Twelve

[1] Thérèse Belzile from Amqui, Matapédia, on the Gaspé Peninsula of Canada's Quebec Province.

[2] Sister Cyprian (Mary Catherine Swales) was a Scots RN and midwife; Sister Clementine (Gertrude Lapointe), a Canadian RN; and Sister John (Gladys Hayford), an English RN.

Sisters Antimond (Fleurette Brochu) and Evremond (Imelda Drapeau), while not RNs, occupied themselves with a variety of tasks which freed others for more specialized work. In the process, both became fluent in Dagaare. Sister Antimond was in charge of the local help employed by the sisters around the convent: a gardener and several girls who worked under her in the laundry and in the convent itself. She also taught sewing in a school for young adult women. During her later years in Ghana, she taught catechism in Tamale. Sister Evremond worked in the dispensary at Jirapa and assisted in the clinics set up by the sisters at regular intervals in the surrounding villages. When an "orphanage" was begun privately to care for new-born infants whose mothers had died in childbirth, she was placed in charge. (The infants were cared for during the critical first two years of life, after which they were turned over to the father and/ or his family.) An excellent cook, she left a special mark on the Northwest by accepting to train local cooks, including those employed in mission stations. She and Sister Antimond arrived in Jirapa in 1941 and returned to Canada, for reasons of health, in 1980.

Sister Emilia (Géraldine Bastien) arrived in 1943. Though not an RN either, she was especially gifted with the sick and devoted all her considerable energies to working among them in the dispensary. She returned to Canada in 1963.

I am grateful to Sister Hermine Audet, FMM, for correcting my memory on some of the above information and that concerning Sister Clementine further on in the book. She herself served in Jirapa for twenty-two years, arriving as an RN at Jirapa Hospital in 1958 and returning to Canada in 1980. From 1964 until her departure sixteen years later, she was teacher and resident nurse at Saint Francis Secondary School, a boarding school for girls opened by the FMM in 1959. She was perhaps better-known there by her religious name: Sister Paule-Alix.

[3] This well continues to supply the hospital. In the thirty-five years since its inauguration, it has never run dry.

[4] For lack of funds, none of these projects was realized, although later a metal reservoir was constructed on the hospital grounds.

[5] Eventually the mission was able to obtain civil service status for all the employees so that government now pays their salaries. The diocese continues to recruit personnel for the hospital, however.

[6] "I do not have words to express my admiration for the sisters," Doctor Cooper wrote in 1955. "Their dedication, devotion, and skill have enabled them to overcome, year in and year out, almost insurmountable difficulties. Indefatigable, cheerful, kind, and patient, they have carried on, sustained by their faith." He went on to cite an "extreme example" of this in the record of one trying month at Jirapa. "During that period, one sister took care of a sick colleague, treated the dispensary and hospital patients, and delivered eighty-four babies, all but two of whom chose to come at night. And this woman had been at Jirapa, without leave, for ten years." (The "sick colleague" was himself, then the sole doctor at Jirapa.) "Although I worked only at Jirapa, there are doubtless scores of other outstations throughout the world where nursing sisters, unseen and unsung, are doing a doctor's work. Yet few persons are familiar with their heroic achievements, for their story has never been adequately told. It was an inspiring and heart-warming experience to be privileged to work with such a group." (Linn F. Cooper, M.D., "Saving Lives, Saving Souls", *White Fathers Missions*, Washington, D.C., June 1955, pp. 8-9.)

[7] The term "leaver", as used here and elsewhere in the book lends support to those who say that Britain and the United States are two countries separated by the same language. In the U.S., the term when applied to formal education suggests a person who has terminated his or her schooling before completion of the normal program set down. In Britain, however, the opposite meaning applies, namely, someone who has completed the years of compulsory schooling determined by law. "Graduate" would be the preferred term in the U.S.

[8] On 4 March 1960, the National Board of Nurses gave full approval for the recognition of Jirapa Hospital as an official qualified registered nurse (QRN) training school. The faculty of nursing was inaugurated on 16 August 1976, at which time the first step toward autonomy was taken. This was granted during the 1978-79 fiscal year, with Sister Cyprian as principal tutor and Mr. Charles Kunko as secretary and tutor. Today all staff members are Ghanaians, headed by Mr. Kunko and Sister Matilda Dery, SMI. Since its beginning, the school has graduated over two hundred midwives, nearly as many QRNs, and some three hundred State enrolled nurses (SENs). The QRN program was finally discontinued. Some years later, a State registered nurse (SRN) training school was opened which has put Jirapa Hospital on a par with the best hospitals anywhere in the world in regard to nurses training.

[9] A grant was later obtained from the government of the Netherlands to build the nursing school. With other smaller grants, two needed wards, a laboratory, bungalows, and senior staff quarters were built and additions made to the administration block. Doctors Cooper and Archambault paid for the construction of tuberculosis wards themselves.

[10] Sister Clementine (Gertrude Lapointe, niece of Father Gérard Lapointe, M.Afr.) also served as superior of novices at Jirapa and later at Tumu when the FMM novitiate moved there. Eventually named provincial superior, her jurisdiction extended to the FMM working in Ghana, Upper Volta, Niger, Liberia, Senegal, Togo, and (during her second mandate), Congo-Brazzaville. Today, after more than forty years, she is still at work in Africa, now stationed in Monrovia, Liberia.

In 1974, Sister Aline Giroux (FMM/Canada) took over as administrator of the hospital. A person very highly qualified for the job, she was able to set up the administration according to the new guidelines issued by Doctor Adibo, then regional medical officer in Bolgatanga. Today the administrator is a Ghanaian layman, Mr. Damiano Dong. Doctor Marie Therese Chambers (FMM/Scotland) is superintendent of the hospital.

[11] See p. 193 (Chapter Thirteen).

They were not always wrong, however. On at least two occasions, volunteer doctors did marry while in service at Jirapa Hospital. One of these was Doctor Ron Puley, a cardiac specialist now practising in the Waterloo/Kitchener area of Ontario, Canada. After arriving at Jirapa in 1970, he proposed by post to Sandra Brown, a nurse he had known while in residency at Toronto General Hospital, telling her that if she really wanted to marry him, she would come to Ghana and do it. She did. They were married in Saint Joseph's Catholic Church in Jirapa in November of that year. The Reverend Steadman, Methodist minister from Wa, presided, and Father McCoy gave the bride away.

The second occasion was almost identical to the first. This time it was Doctor Jan Harm Kwikkel, from the Netherlands, who proposed by post to his fiancée, Geilsa, in late 1973. See too accepted, and the Kwikkels were married in Saint Joseph's Church soon after that. Again the Reverend Steadman officiated while Father McCoy had the honor of giving the bride away. — Ed.

[12] His memory was still green ten years later when the diocese of Wa celebrated the fiftieth anniversary of the evangelization of northwest Ghana. One of the features of the week-long celebration was a special jubilee film compiled and produced by Brother Bernard Cyr, M.Afr., head of the diocesan media office, tracing the history of Christianity in the region from the arrival of the Missionaries of Africa in 1929 until the present. When Doctor Archambault's picture appeared on the screen, there as a spontaneous burst of loud and prolonged applause which drowned out the commentary and made it superfluous. The people had not forgotten, nor have they to this day.

[13] Sister Colomban (Constance Gemme from Worcester, Massachusetts) is an RN and midwife. At the time of the transfer of responsibility for Nandom Hospital to the Sisters of Mary Immaculate, she was hospital matron there. She is now stationed in Tamale.

[14] Doctor Dermid Bingham, an English surgeon, was yet another of those — recognized professionals in their fields — who, despite the prestige they enjoyed at home, heeded the call to interrupt their cosy medical practice and put their skills to the test where they were more urgently needed. Doctor Bingham was not unacquainted with Africa. He had served in Egypt as head surgeon of the British North African Forces, with headquarters in Cairo, during the Second World War. Sometime afterwards, he went to Canada to teach surgery at Queens University Medical School in Kingston, Ontario, where he became head of the surgery department. We had a talk during my six-month stay in Canada in 1971. The result was that the following year, he and his wife, Catalon, a member of the famous Cadbury family of England, arrived in Jirapa. Mrs. Bingham worked in the hospital archives while her husband dealt daily with the usual heavy load of surgical operations. Despite the demands made on his skills, he always remained calm, never raised his voice or became excited in the operating room, was never less than courteous in his dealings with staff and patients alike. The nurses especially loved him for it and he was very popular with them. But Doctor Bingham was more than a doctor and a surgeon. This simple, down-to-earth man was able to do anything, even manual work, with ease. Whenever the electricity failed — and it did so regularly — he would fix it. Once I helped him to rig-up an air-conditioning system for the operating room. He was one of those rare multi-talented individuals who, while not advertising his knowledge, always seemed to rise to the occasion when something went

wrong or needed repair. His practical nature and experience were evident too in his use of drugs for his patients. At a time when pharmaceutical companies in Europe and North America had begun to vie with one another in bringing out the latest in sophisticated drugs each year, Doctor Bingham studied them and found that with some forty basic and relatively inexpensive drugs, he could obtain the same results and manage the hospital quite well.

Chapter Thirteen

[1] This was actually the second attempt by the Missionaries of Africa to establish themselves in the United States. An earlier effort had met with a favourable response from the bishop of Cleveland, Ohio; and on 17 August 1929, Mass was offered for the first time in the society's new centre in that city. But the Cleveland community experienced many trials, not the least of them being financial ones. Following a visit by the superior general, Father Paul Voillard, in 1934, it was decided to close the house. Now a new superior general had been elected, Bishop Joseph Birraux, and he was interested in making a fresh start in the United States.

[2] This was not yet the Congregation of the Sisters of Mary Immaculate which was to be founded the following year (1945) in Navrongo. These four sisters belonged to the Congregation of the Black Sisters of the Immaculate Conception, founded at Pabre, near Wagadugu, by the Missionary Sisters of Our Lady of Africa.

[3] Sister Gabriel de l'Annnonciation (Yolande Branchaud from Canada), Sister Edmond Campion (Beatrice Dines from England), and Sister Christoph (Catharina Wolff from the Netherlands).

[4] Sister Louise Myriam (Louise Carrier from France), Sister Theresa of the Child Jesus (Shirley Bourbeau from the United States), and Sister Jean de la Lande (Laurette Drouin from Canada).

[5] The Ghana educational system comprises six years of primary school followed by four years of middle school. Secondary education begins after the first two years of middle school, if one passes the required examination. Failure to do so bars one effectively from advancing to secondary schooling in the system. In that case, one continues in middle school for the remaining two years.

[6] Tamale became a diocese on 18 April 1950, followed by Navrongo on 23 April 1956, and Wa on 3 November 1959. On 30 May 1977, Tamale was raised to the rank of archdiocese, with Navrongo (now Navrongo-Bolgatanga) and Wa as suffragan sees.

[7] "Your father superior is a good man, all right", or, "Your 'boss' isn't the least bit afraid of work. His father and mother conceived him well."

Peter Dery Poriku [sic], "As I Remember Him," *White Fathers Missions*, Washington, D.C., August-September 1958, pp. 4-10.

[8] In 1955, Father Carrier was replaced as superior at the centre by Father Gérard Lapointe; as instructor in carpentry, by Brother Suso

(Ludwig Wille); as instructor in masonry, by Brother Konrad Grunwald; and as instructor in mechanics, by Brother Aloysius (Jacques Blekemolen).

[9] The official Latin title of the congregation is: *Fratres Immaculatae Conceptionis Beatissimae Virginis Mariae Matris Dei*. In Ghana, the congregation is known popularly as "the FIC brothers", from the initials of the first three words of their title.

[10] "The Jirapa Credit Union, the pioneer society, flourished very well from the beginning, a success which was generally attributed to the careful instruction over several months that members and officers of the society received before the society actually began collecting savings." (From *A History of the Ghana Cooperative Credit Union Association*, outlining the first ten years of the Ghana National Credit Union Association, 1968-1978.)

[11] See James 2:14-17.

Chapter Fifteen

[1] Rt. Rev. Gregory E. Kpiebaya, "Living the Christian Faith Today." In *That They May Have Life: An Account of the Activities of the Church in Northwest Ghana 1929-1979*. Wa (Ghana), August 1979, p. 19.

[2] I refer here to what one might call the *professional* missionary, a member of a missionary institute whose charism is essentially that of "going forth" to plant the seed of faith in areas where it has never before been scattered or where it has not yet taken firm root. Every Christian is called to be a *domestic* missionary, of course, and to cultivate a missionary consciousness, no matter what other charism or principal vocation one has.

[3] Rt. Rev. Gregory E. Kpiebaya, "Africanization of the Church, what does it mean?" In *Petit Écho*, no 674 (1979/9), pp. 496-497.

Epilogue

[1] *Bundaa* is but one name used to designate the small lizards that abound in the area.

Glossary

Bride-price. Dowry

Dagaaba(s). (1) Plural form of Dagao. Ethnic group inhabiting area of NW Ghana and SW Burkina Faso. (2) May also be used as an adjective: Of or pertaining to the Dagaabas (as in: *the Dagaaba population*).

Dagaare. (1) Language spoken by the Dagaabas. (2) May also be used as an adjective: Of or pertaining to the Dagaabas (as in: *In Dagaare society, communal responsibility already existed in the extended family system*).

Dagao. (1) Singular form of Dagaaba. A member of the Dagati (Dagaaba) ethnic group: *The average Dagao is honest and industrious*. (2) The land or territory inhabited by the Dagaabas as a people: *The first missionaries to arrive in Dagao did so in 1929*.

Dagati. The most common form of the adjective: Of or pertaining to the Dagaabas (as in: *The average Dagati woman is used to hard work*, or, *They arrived in Dagati territory on 29 November 1929*.

Dagbane. Language of the Dagombas.

Dagombas. Ethnic group inhabiting the Tamale region of northern Ghana.

Ditina. A go-between in the matter of arranging marriages in the Dagati culture. The ditina represents the prospective groom's family in negotiations with a girl's family to secure her hand in marriage.

Ggiel stones. Granite stones used by the Dagati women to grind millet. When worn and no longer useful for that purpose, they were enclosed in the base of a small fetish altar constructed of mud at the door of the family dwelling.

Kassem. Language of the Kassenas.

Kassenas. Ethnic group inhabiting the Navrongo area of northern Ghana.

Kolaa. Spirit inhabiting a river or lake.

Kolle. Plural form of kolaa.

Kontoma. (1) Benevolent spirits believed to protect the home and its inhabitants from the influence of evil spirits. (2) Also, the figure carved by a kontoma priest to be enshrined in the home and to which sacrifices were offered regularly by the inhabitants.

Malam. Local Muslim leader.

Mwinbapuorobo. Literally: one who does not pray (i.e., one who is not a practicing member of an organized religion).

Mwinpuorobo. Literally: one who prays (i.e., a practicing member of an organized religion).

Naa. Chief.

Ngwinsore. The Way of God. A term used by the people of NW Ghana to refer to the Christian religion in the early days of the mission there.

Nim tree. A species of acacia.

Peter's Pence. An annual collection taken up among Catholics throughout the world for the support of the Holy See and its works.

Pito. A mild local beer brewed by Dagati women from millet grain.

Prefect apostolic. A priest with broad jurisdiction over a district known as a prefecture apostolic. Though normally without episcopal ordination, he enjoys the ordinary powers of a bishop, except that he cannot confer the sacrament of holy orders.

Prefecture apostolic. An ecclesiastical territory, usually in a mission area, where the hierarchy has not been established. It is headed by a prefect apostolic.

Rest house. A simple building constructed under the British administration at strategic points in the countryside, to be used as official shelter for the district commissioners and other government personnel when travelling about the towns and villages.

Sitana. Satan.

Suobo. An evil spirit bent on devouring the souls of its enemies, and thus killing them, while they slept. The Dagaabas believed it did this through the agency of a person whom it possessed for that purpose.

Tendaama. Literally: those who have custody of the land. Plural form of tendaana.

Tendaana. Traditional Dagati office of some power and prestige having to do with the custody, distribution, and use of land. The tendaana is a kind of custodian of the land, which he allots freely to anyone who requests a plot or an area to farm. He does not own the land, which belongs to the spirits and cannot be bought or sold. He is consulted on important occasions, especially in connection with the election of a chief. The office of tendaana also includes cultic duties. As "priest of the Earth", he must make sacrifices to the powerful Earth spirit.

Tengaama. Spirits of the land or earth.

Tengaane. Shrine of the spirits of the land or earth.

Vicar apostolic. Usually a titular bishop who has jurisdiction over a mission territory called a vicariate apostolic.

Vicariate apostolic. The territory administered in the name of the Holy See by a vicar apostolic. It is equivalent to a diocese but is usually in an area where the ordinary hierarchy has not yet been established. The vicariate is divided into missions rather than parishes.

Index

91-92, 101, 129, 133-38, 159-60, 167, 170, 250, 251, 302, 312 n.3 (Chap. 3). *See also* Ardron; Armstrong; Functionaries
Divorce, 162-63
Doctors, 55-56, 60, 92, 169, 172-73, 190-91, 307-9. *See also* Archambault, Henry; Bingham; Chambers; Chapper, Barbara; Cheverton; Cooper; Kwikkel; Puley
Dong, Damiano, 319 n.10
Dongyire, Charles, 214
Dosogla, Felix, 72, 74, 273
Dowry, 69, 154, 160-61, 317 nn.3,7 (Chap. 11)
Drapeau, Imelda (Sister Evremond, FMM), 169, 317 n.2 (Chap. 12)
Drought, 80-82, 100, 107-24, 125, 251
Drouin, Laurette (Sister Jean de la Lande, MSOLA), 199, 321 n.4
Dubome, Bernadette, 277
Durand, Jean-Baptiste (M.Afr.) *See* Missionaries of Africa
Durrieu, Louis (M.Afr.), 126
Dysentery, 58

Ecology, 235
Education, 40, 145, 147
 adult, 145
 for marriage, 161-62
 middle, 321 n.5
 primary, 40, 145, 147-48, 164, 321 n.5
 secondary, 164, 204, 257, 259, 321 n.5
 of women, 40, 147, 164-65
 See also Schools; Seminaries; Literacy
Educational system (Ghana), 321 n.5
Elizabeth (laywoman), 189
Emmanuel, Rev., 254, 317 n.7 (Chap. 10)
Emetine solution, 58, 59, 313 n.4
Equality of sexes, 149-65
Eremon village, 70, 157, 289
Esquerre, Msgr. Césaire (M.Afr.), 126, 127
Eucharist, 102-3, 143. *See also* Blessed Sacrament
Eugène (Gall), Brother (M.Afr.), 30, 264
Evangelization, 200, 239, 248
Evil, 221, 235, 300

Faith, 175-76, 215-16, 230, 231, 232, 233, 234-35, 241, 280
Family, extended, 36, 143

Fauna, 43, 303
Fetishes, 129, 133, 221-22, 247-48. *See also* Kontoma; Religion, traditional
Fetishists, 113, 206. *See also* Ngmankurinaa; Witch doctors
FIC. *See* Brothers of the Immaculate Conception
Fixation abcess treatment, 59
FMM. *See* Franciscan Missionaries of Mary
Forced labour. *See* Labour, requisitioned
Frambesia. *See* Yaws
Francis of Assisi, Saint, 216
Franciscan Missionaries of Mary, 147, 164, 168-69, 171-72, 174, 177, 180, 182, 193-94, 253, 257, 275, 318 n.6
 Antimond (Fleurette Brochu), 169, 317 n.2 (Chap. 12)
 Blane, 168
 Caltry, Mother (Thérèse Belzile), 168, 174, 182, 183, 242, 317 n.1 (Chap. 12)
 Cannice, 168
 Chambers, Marie Therese, 237, 309, 319 n.10
 Clementine (Gertrude Lapointe), 169, 183, 317 n.2 (Chap. 12), 319 n.10
 Conrad, 168
 Cyprian (Mary Catherine Swales), 169, 177-78, 255, 256, 317 n.2 (Chap. 12), 319 n.8 (Chap. 12)
 Emilia (Géraldine Bastien), 169, 318 n.2
 Evremond (Imelda Drapeau), 169, 317 n.2
 Giroux, Aline, 319 n.10
 John (Gladys Hayford), 169, 180, 183, 317 n.2 (Chap. 12)
 Marguerite, Mother, 172
 Mary of the Passion, Mother, 172
 Paule-Alix (Hermine Audet), 318 n.2 (Chap. 12)
 Precursor, Mother, 168, 253
 Sabina, 217, 218
 Williamson, Mary Anne, 308
 Wynnin, 168
Free will, 175-76
Freedom
 of choice, 229
 of choice in marriage, 112, 116, 123, 154-61, 253
 of individual, 235

Tebano, 83-84
Technical training, 204-5
Tendaana (custodian of land), 48, 95, 134, 312 n.2 (Chap. 4)
Tenga, George, 208-9
Tengaama (spirits), 63, 77
Tenganabang, 145
Tengane earth (fetish), 222
Teresa (wife of James Nyangwane), 140, 275
Theatre (plays), 213
Thévenoud, Joanny. See Bishops
Thomas, Governor, 101-2, 133-36, 149, 242
Tiewiir, Paul, 290
Tissup (chief of Birofo), 224-27
Tizza, 75, 103, 122, 273, 277
Tradition
Dagati, 36-37, 82, 305-6, 317 nn.3,7.
See also Customs general, 136
Trypanosomiasis, 59-60
Tsetse fly, 60
Tumu, 44, 91-92, 319 n.10
Tuuri, Thomas, 277

Ullo, 248, 285-86
Universities
California (Berkeley), 224-26
Louvain (Belgium), 203
St. Francis Xavier (Antigonish), 203, 210
Urbanism, 231
Uriko, Alfred, 146

Veronica, 157-61, 253, 317 n.5
Vicariate apostolic
Bobo-Dioulasso, 317 n.7 (Chap. 10)
Navrongo, 252, 254, 255, 266, 316 n.6
Sudan, 29, 32
Wagadugu, 265
Voillard, Paul (M.Afr.), 321 n.1
Vocations, religious, 146, 194, 195, 199, 203, 225, 238-39, 283
Vows, religious, 194

Wa, 28, 30, 70, 136, 144, 169, 170, 204, 258, 259, 260
Wa Catholic Press, 260
Wagadugu (Ouagadougou)
town and mission, 126, 192, 194
region of, 31, 32
Wages, 206, 313 n.5
Walas (people), 230, 311 n.2 (Chap. 2)
Wars
of Babatu and Samouri, 30, 35, 47,

125, 243, 311 n.2 (Chap. 1)
World War I, 31, 312 n.1
World War II, 195-97, 205
Washington Post, 176
Water, 170-71. See also Drought
Water and Sewage Corporation of Kumasi, 170-71, 194
Welle, Maria, 277
Wells, 170, 171, 318 n.3
Wessa (Ouessa), 125, 126, 247
White Fathers, 31, 32, 33, 40, 55, 126, 183, 192, 209, 237, 311 n.1 (Chap. 1). See also Missionaries of Africa
White Sisters, 189. See also Missionary Sisters of Our Lady of Africa
Whittal, Colonel, 34, 40, 44-45, 48
Wiagha, 28, 33, 201, 265
Wille, Ludwig (Brother Suso, M.Afr.), 295, 297, 321 n.8
Witch doctors, 56, 64-65, 77-78, 88, 100, 103, 110, 112, 133, 203, 206, 313 n.2 (Chap. 6). See also Ngmankurinaa; Soothsayer
Witches, 65-69, 245. See also documents in photo section
Witness of faith, 233-35
Wolff, Catharina (Sister Christoph, MSOLA), 199
Women, 40, 65-66, 67, 69, 82-83, 84-89, 99, 112, 116, 149-65, 168, 213, 226-27, 258, 275-76, 302, 305-6, 315 n.1 (Chap. 8), 317 nn.3,7 (Chap. 11). See also FMM; MSOLA; Religious; SMI
Worship, traditional, 299-300. See also Sacrifices
Wotare, Mr., 67

Yangyuoro, Rev. Yvon, 298
Yaws, 56, 57, 189, 313 n.3
Yelesigra, Alexis, 18, 72, 273
Yelkyere, 145
Yelpoe I (chief of Jirapa), 122, 170
Yennaa, Raphael, 146
Yirtare, Anthony, 202

Zabog, 47
Zabpo, 247
Zage, Maurice, 146
Zambogo (raiders), 125. See also Babatu, Lieutenant
Zemopare, 70, 76, 78, 79, 202-3, 290
Zuarungu, 91-92
Zuena, Yoakim, 277

Great Things Happen

Type: Times Roman 10 pt
Paper: 55 lb. Hi-Bulk
Photo stock: Rolland ST-101 paper 120M
Cover: Cornwall 10 pt, film laminated
Composed, printed, and bound by Imprimerie Gagné Ltée,
Louiseville, Québec